ON THE DEVELOPMENT OF CHINA'S INFORMATION TECHNOLOGY INDUSTRY

ON THE DEVELOPMENT OF CHINA'S INFORMATION TECHNOLOGY INDUSTRY

JIANG ZEMIN

Professor, Shanghai Jiao Tong University
Former President, People's Republic of China

AMSTERDAM • BOSTON • HEIDELBERG • LONDON • NEW YORK • OXFORD
PARIS • SAN DIEGO • SAN FRANCISCO • SINGAPORE • SYDNEY • TOKYO
Academic Press is an imprint of Elsevier

Editorial Director, Asia Pacific, Elsevier Science & Technology Books: *Denise E.M. Penrose*
Vice President, Elsevier Science & Technology Books, Asia-Pacific: *Sanjiv Pandya*
Managing Director, Elsevier Science & Technology China: *Zhang Yuguo*
Managing Director, Elsevier Science & Technology Books, China: *Ying Zhongfeng*

Academic Press is an imprint of Elsevier.
30 Corporate Drive, Suite 400, Burlington, MA 01803, USA
525 B Street, Suite 1900, San Diego, CA 92101-4495, USA
Radarweg 29, PO Box 211, 1000 AE Amsterdam, The Netherlands
Linacre House, Jordan Hill, Oxford OX2 8DP, UK
32 Jamestown Road, London NW1 7BY, UK

Library of Congress Cataloging-in-Publication Data
A catalog record for this book is available from the Library of Congress

British Library Cataloguing in Publication Data
A catalogue record for this book is available from the British Library

Chinese edition ISBN: 978-7-313-05610-8
English translation ISBN: 978-0-12-381369-5

For information on all Academic Press publications
visit our website at elsevierdirect.com

Printed and Bound in China
10 11 12 13 10 9 8 7 6 5 4 3 2 1

Working together to grow
libraries in developing countries

www.elsevier.com | www.bookaid.org | www.sabre.org

ELSEVIER   **BOOK AID** International   **Sabre Foundation**

Translated by: The Central Translation Bureau, Beijing

*Translators: Jia Yuling, Alan A. Johnston, Liu Liang, Richard A. O'Connell, Sun Xianhui, Tong Dongjie,
Tong Xiaohua, Wang Lili, and Zhu Yanhui*

CONTENTS

A native of Yangzhou, Jiangsu Province, China, Jiang Zemin was born on August 17, 1926.

Starting in 1943, he took part in student movements led by underground organizations of the Communist Party of China (CPC), and eventually joined the CPC in April 1946. He graduated from the Electrical Engineering Department of Shanghai Jiao Tong University in 1947.

After the liberation of Shanghai, he served successively as deputy engineer, chief of the works section and concurrently as head of the power workshop, Party branch secretary, and first deputy director of the Shanghai Yimin No. 1 Foodstuff Factory; first deputy director of the Shanghai Soap Factory; and chief of the electrical appliances section of the Shanghai No. 2 Design Sub-bureau of the First Ministry of Machine-Building Industry.

In 1955, he was a trainee at the Stalin Automobile Works in Moscow, USSR.

After his return to China in 1956, Jiang Zemin served successively as deputy chief of the power section, deputy chief power engineer, and director of the power plant of the First Automotive Works in Changchun.

After 1962, he served successively as deputy director of the Shanghai Electrical Appliances Research Institute, director, acting Party committee secretary, and Party committee secretary of the Wuhan Thermo-Engineering Machinery Institute, and deputy director-general and director-general of the Foreign Affairs Bureau of the First Ministry of Machine-Building Industry.

After 1980, he served as vice chairman and concurrently as secretary general of the State Administration Commission on Import and Export Affairs and the State Administration Commission on Foreign Investment, and was a member of the leading Party groups of these two commissions.

After 1982, he served as first vice minister of the Ministry of Electronics Industry and deputy secretary of its leading Party group, and later as its minister and secretary of its leading Party group.

After 1985, he served as mayor of Shanghai and as deputy secretary, and later as secretary of the Shanghai Municipal Party Committee.

In September 1982, he was elected a member of the CPC Central Committee at the Twelfth CPC National Congress.

In November 1987, he was elected a member of the Political Bureau of the CPC Central Committee at the First Plenary Session of the Thirteenth CPC Central Committee.

In June 1989, he was elected a member of the Standing Committee of the Political Bureau and general secretary of the CPC Central Committee at the Fourth Plenary Session of the Thirteenth CPC Central Committee.

In November 1989, he assumed the position of chairman of the CPC Central Military Commission at the Fifth Plenary Session of the Thirteenth CPC Central Committee.

In March 1990, he was elected chairman of the Central Military Commission of the People's Republic of China at the Third Session of the Seventh National People's Congress.

In October 1992, he was elected a member of the Political Bureau and its Standing Committee and general secretary of the CPC Central Committee, and was appointed chairman of the CPC Central Military Commission at the First Plenary Session of the Fourteenth CPC Central Committee.

In March 1993, Jiang Zemin was elected president of the People's Republic of China and chairman of its Central Military Commission at the First Session of the Eighth National People's Congress.

In September 1997, he was reelected a member of the Political Bureau and its Standing Committee and general secretary of the CPC Central Committee, and was appointed chairman of the CPC Central Military Commission at the First Plenary Session of the Fifteenth CPC Central Committee.

In March 1998, he was reelected president of the People's Republic of China and chairman of its Central Military Commission at the First Session of the Ninth National People's Congress.

In November 2002, he was appointed chairman of the CPC Central Military Commission at the First Plenary Session of the Sixteenth CPC Central Committee.

In March 2003, he was reelected chairman of the Central Military Commission of the People's Republic of China at the First Session of the Tenth National People's Congress.

In September 2004, the Fourth Plenary Session of the Sixteenth CPC Central Committee accepted his resignation as chairman of the CPC Central Military Commission.

In March 2005, the Third Session of the Tenth National People's Congress agreed to accept Jiang Zemin's resignation as chairman of the Central Military Commission of the People's Republic of China.

EDITORS' NOTE TO THE ORIGINAL CHINESE EDITION

Since the beginning of the 1980s, Jiang Zemin has closely followed development trends in the information technology (IT) industry and the development course of informationization in the world. He has also conducted thorough research on issues surrounding the development of the IT industry and informationization in China, and articulated a series of important ideas concerning developing the IT industry and promoting informationization in the country.

This book comprises 27 articles, reports, speeches, and essays concerning the IT industry and informationization written by Jiang Zemin between August 1983 and November 2008, plus two appendices. Thirteen of these were written between 1983 and 1985 when Jiang Zemin held the position of Minister of Electronics Industry of the People's Republic of China; one was written in 1989 when he was both a member of the Political Bureau of the Central Committee of the Communist Party of China (CPC) and secretary of the CPC Shanghai Municipal Committee; ten were written between 1989 and 2002 when he was general secretary of the CPC Central Committee, president of the People's Republic of China, and chairman of the Central Military Commission; and three were written after 2004. In "Development of Our Country's IT Industry in the New Period," dated 2008, Jiang Zemin reviews China's experience in developing its IT industry.

The author has reviewed and approved all the materials appearing in this book.

Party Literature Research Center of the CPC Central
Committee and Shanghai Jiao Tong University
April 2009

PREFACE*

November 8, 2008

Energy resources and information technology (IT) are two strategic industries that affect China's future development, and are also two fields that I have long taken an interest in. To understand the reason for my lasting interest in energy resources and IT, we need to begin with my youth. I majored in electrical engineering at university. I had a deep interest in energy resources and electronics, and acquired a certain understanding of them. Later, as director of the power plant at Changchun First Automotive Works and Minister of Electronics Industry, I conducted research on cutting-edge issues in these fields.

In 1989, at the age of 63, I was considering to become a professor at my alma mater, Shanghai Jiao Tong University, after retiring from my position as secretary of the CPC Shanghai Municipal Committee. To become a professor one needs accreditations; so, I wrote two articles, one on energy conservation and the other on microelectronics. They were later published in the *Journal of Shanghai Jiao Tong University*, and I successfully defended them at a meeting of the university's Academic Committee, whereupon the university appointed me as a professor. Thereafter, I began working at the CPC Central Committee. In 2007, the university invited me to write an article. As I thought that now that I had really retired, I should complete my unfinished research. Considering the great changes that have taken place in the energy resources and electronics industries in nearly 20 years of development since then, I delved deeper into the research I had done for those two articles, summarized the past, explored the future, and offered recommendations. As a result, "Reflections on Energy Issues in China" came out in March 2008, and "Development of Our Country's IT Industry in the New Period" was also published recently.

The IT industry is the strategic high ground for international competition, and it has been developing rapidly since the mid-20th century. In the

---

*Speech at a meeting with the participants in a seminar on the article "Development of Our Country's IT Industry in the New Period."

early 1980s, when I was Minister of Electronics Industry, I deeply felt the momentum of this development, and perceived that the discrepancy between China's level and the world's advanced level was so great that we had to do our utmost to catch up. At that time, I proposed the policy of "building a foundation, raising our level, improving quality, pursuing profits, octupling the gross output value, and getting 10 years ahead of the rest of the national economy."[1] In 1984, I published "Revitalize the Electronics Industry and Promote the Four Modernizations"— modernization of agriculture, industry, national defense, and science and technology—in the journal *Red Flag*, in which I argued that the electronics industry has a leading position in modernization. After beginning work at the Central Committee, I continued to pay close attention to the development of the electronics and IT industries, and frequently listened to reports from various sources concerning them. After the Gulf War broke out in 1991, I proposed that in preparing for future military struggles, we had to focus on winning local wars fought under modern technological conditions, especially high-tech conditions, and urged that informationized weapons and equipment should become a vital element in our army's fighting capabilities. At that time, the Central Committee made a number of policy decisions and arrangements to promote the development of the IT industry. Against the background of reform and opening up, and with the concerted efforts of the entire sector, the IT industry entered a period of rapid development, and is now in excellent condition. I believe that our country now has a foundation, a market, the technology, and qualified people, and that the coming period will be a time of great achievement for this industry. It is important for us to seize this strategic opportunity, clarify our thinking on development, and focus on the industry's priorities. As long as we work tirelessly and intensify our efforts, we can certainly transform our country into a leader in the IT industry.

---

[1]This is a summary of the electronics industry's development tasks for the foreseeable future made at a national working meeting of heads of departments and bureaus of the electronics industry. "Octuple the gross output value and get 10 years ahead of the rest of the national economy" means by 2000, the 1980 gross output value of China's electronics industry should be octupled and major products and production technologies should reach the level advanced industrialized countries will have reached around 1990, with certain technologies reaching the world's advanced level prevailing at that time. The latter objective is 10 years more ambitious than the objective the government set for the national economy as a whole of reaching the level those countries reached around 1980.

In "Development of Our Country's IT Industry in the New Period," I review the experience in developing the IT industry since the introduction of reform and opening up, and summarize the cutting-edge issues in the industry, and thus this article addresses both the field of science and technology and the science of policy making. I spent more than half a year writing it, during which time I asked a number of comrades to survey a vast quantity of material for me and I discussed it with experts on more than ten occasions. I changed its structure and content many times in order to make it cohesive, scientific, standard, and able to withstand the test of time. I tried to express myself in as simple language as possible in the hope that this would induce more people to pay attention to, reflect on, and study our country's IT industry, and work together to explore avenues for its successful development. I am convinced that the publication of this article will play a positive role in developing our country's IT industry. All of you present here today hold positions of responsibility in the IT industry. I would therefore like to share with you comrades my hopes and desires. Naturally, some of these issues remain open for further discussion.

First, we need to value the role and position of the IT industry. IT evolves quickly. It is very versatile and highly pervasive, and it will become one of the most important areas of future scientific and technological innovation. I do not exaggerate in saying that any industry will make tremendous progress if it incorporates IT; no other technology can compare with IT in this regard. In the course of more than half a century of development, the IT industry has experienced ups and downs, but it has never stopped innovating, which is a manifestation of its tremendous vitality. The IT industry has become a multiplier of economic growth, a transformer of development patterns, and a propeller for industrial upgrading. Furthermore, the IT industry epitomizes a country's international competitiveness, national defense capability, and overall national strength. Therefore, we should be fully aware of the role and position of the IT industry in economic and social development. We not only need to understand this but also reflect this understanding in our work and strive to make the industry strong and large in order to provide strong support for economic and social development.

Second, we need to grasp the development trends in the IT industry. Since the beginning of this century, IT has been updating and upgrading more rapidly than ever before, engendering major new breakthroughs.

The trend toward clustering and integration in the industry is becoming increasingly evident, competition in intellectual property and standards is becoming increasingly intense, and ubiquitous network environments are emerging. There can be no doubt that informationization is the general trend of development in our time and that the IT industry will become an ever more important engine driving economic growth and scientific and technological innovation. We should keep updating our knowledge, conduct in-depth investigations and studies, and strive to grasp the trends and tendencies in informationization. As long as we have a good idea of what the future holds in store, our study of plans and policies for informationization will have the right orientation and we will formulate correct policies. Of course, this study and research will also help our cadres learn more about science, improve their scientific literacy, master scientific methods, foster a scientific spirit, and become better equipped to make scientific policy decisions.

Third, we need to identify the key links in the development of the IT industry. To accelerate the development of the industry, we must clearly define development strategies and priorities. In "Development of Our Country's IT Industry in the New Period," I summarize the current conditions of the IT industry in terms of scale, capacity for innovation, development of enterprises, IT application, and structures and institutions.[2] On the basis of a review of experiences and an analysis of problems in the development of the IT industry, I expound the principles of independent controllable development, open and compatible technologies, integrated and comprehensive applications, military and civilian interaction, and a

---

[2]The passage in "Development of Our Country's IT Industry in the New Period" reads, "Our country's IT industry has already grown to a considerable size, but it still has serious structural weaknesses that make it very difficult for the industry to strengthen or expand further. Although it has great capacity for innovation in some areas, it will long be subject to pressure from developed countries' overall competitive superiority, and the mechanisms for funding innovation and turning research results into practical applications still need to be improved. Enterprises are now market players, but they still lack the ability to face stiff competition and participate in the international division of labor, and it will take a long time for them to cultivate overall competitive advantages. Some successes have already been achieved in IT application; however, informationization is uneven and there is an urgent need to deepen the integration of informationization with industrialization. The state has been very successful in its efforts to support and guide the IT industry, though structural and institutional obstacles hindering the industry's development remain and reform and opening up are in dire need of new breakthroughs."

market-driven approach for skipping development stages. This means that we must be able to exercise independent control of IT relating to national security; be self-reliant and endeavor to develop core technologies that we cannot acquire by purchase or trade; persevere in further opening to the outside world, pay attention to conforming with international standards, and constantly improve our country's position in the division of labor within the global industry; establish industrial bases that benefit from concentration, promote interconnection and convergence of different disciplines, and encourage integrated innovation; integrate military and civilian applications, combine military with civilian production, develop mechanisms that prompt them to stimulate each other, and achieve bidirectional transformation and balanced development; give full play to the basic role of the market in allocating resources, strengthen government guidance, and stimulate the vitality of all types of market entities; and develop ambition and acumen for innovation and confidence in success, aim for advanced technology, and strive to skip stages in the process of developing the IT industry. We must then use informationization to drive industrialization and use industrialization to promote informationization, thus creating a path for developing the IT industry with Chinese characteristics. The information industry is extensive and includes many categories; thus it is impossible to develop all areas at the same time. Therefore, we must focus on key projects and set others aside. The development of core basic industries such as microelectronics, computers, software, and key components and their materials must be given priority, as well as industries in which China enjoys an international competitive advantage such as broadband mobile communications, next-generation networks, and information services. We need to concentrate our strength on tackling key problems in these areas and strive to make major breakthroughs.

Fourth, we need to provide more policy support for the IT industry. The US, Japan, European countries, and other developed economies have launched national strategies for developing their IT industries, and have introduced many policies for developing core technologies, dominating information resources, controlling the Internet, and formulating international standards. Our country has long been successful in its efforts to support and guide IT industry development, though there still remain structural and institutional obstacles hindering development, and policy support for the IT industry's development is still relatively weak. We should give high priority to policies on the IT industry in our system of economic policies, including launching major state projects; promoting the integration of telecommunications, computer, and radio/cable TV networks; encouraging domestic production; and implementing effective fiscal and taxation policies, investment and financing policies, and human resources policies. We need to provide effective guidance, formulate market rules, remove departmental and regional barriers, and improve laws and regulations in order to create a favorable policy environment for developing the IT industry.

Fifth, we need to pay close attention to informationizing our national defense equipment. Local wars fought since the 1990s clearly indicate that the form of war in human society has shifted from mechanization to informationization and that profound changes have taken place in battle patterns, battle theories, and force structures. We must adapt to world trends and make informationization the core of the revolution in military affairs with Chinese characteristics. Comrades from the army and the fields of national defense-related electronic science and technology must take a broad view and use foresight in promoting the revolution in military affairs with Chinese characteristics, utilize electronic IT to boost and elevate the systematic capability of our weapons and equipment to confront an enemy, and quicken the pace of army informationization.

While writing "Development of Our Country's IT Industry in the New Period," a number of organizations provided me with a wealth of materials and information, and the comrades who helped with the writing gave me a great deal of concrete assistance. I wish to express my thanks here to all of them once again.

PART *One*

Development of Our Country's IT Industry in the New Period*

October 28, 2008

In today's world, the rapid development of new- and high-technology industries, as exemplified by the IT industry, is promoting global industrial restructuring, optimization and upgrading, and bringing about profound changes in human lifestyles and production patterns. Since the beginning of the 21st century, IT has been changing with each passing day, and its popularization and application have an increasingly significant impact on economic, political, social, cultural, and military development. The IT industry of a country or region has become an important yardstick of its overall strength, international competitiveness, and degree of modernization. How to fully grasp the current development trends in IT, and determine the development philosophy and policy orientation for the future of our country's IT industry is a critical issue that requires our earnest study and consideration.

I. POSITION AND ROLE OF THE IT INDUSTRY

In the mid-18th century, the First Industrial Revolution, epitomized by the steam engine, ushered in the age of mechanized industry in human society. From the late 19th to the mid-20th century, the Second Industrial Revolution, epitomized by electrical machines, thrust humankind into the electrical age. In the second half of the 20th century, the Third Industrial Revolution, epitomized by computers and the Internet, swept the globe, causing the production pattern in human society to change from a dominance of industrialization to a combination of both informationization and industrialization. As a result, labor productivity has risen sharply, and the productive forces and human civilization have reached an unprecedented level. The world has entered the information age (see Fig. 1).

---

*Originally published in the *Journal of Shanghai Jiao Tong University*, No. 10, 2008.

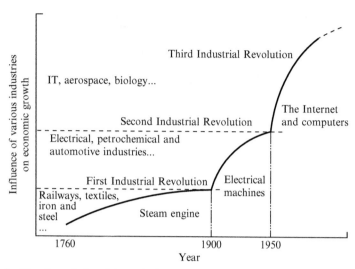

Figure 1   The three industrial revolutions.

A. IT is the frontier of scientific and technological innovation

IT is one of the most rapidly evolving, widely used, and pervasive high technologies in the world today. The level of a country's IT is a prominent indication of its capacity for innovation. The history of the development of science and technology reveals that it formerly took a long time to turn scientific discoveries and technological innovations into industrial applications. Today, by contrast, innovation in contemporary IT is more dynamic. New technologies are emerging in a steady stream in the fields of computers, microelectronics, software, communications, and the Internet. In particular, the key technologies, processes, and performance of integrated circuits are upgraded more rapidly (see Table 1).[1] In 1965, Gordon E. Moore predicted exponential growth in the density of integrated circuits [1]. On average, from 1960 to 1975, the number of transistors on an integrated circuit doubled annually. From 1970 to 2004, the number of transistors on dynamic memory doubled almost every 18 months and the number of microprocessors doubled approximately every 24 months. From 1971 to 2006, the cost of a single

---

[1]Research Report on IT Development Trends by the Ministry of Information Industry of the People's Republic of China, 2007.

Table 1 Generational transitions in integrated circuit technology development

Components and their performance	First generation 1975–1985	Second generation 1985–1995	Third generation 1995–2005
Characteristic dimension (μm) (each generation has decreased by about 1/3)	≥1	1–0.35	0.35–0.09
Wafer diameter (cm) [Wafer diameter (inch)]	10.16–15.24 (4–6)	15.24–20.32 (6–8)	20.32–30.48 (8–12)
Mainstream DRAM Bit (Mb)	≥1	4–16	64–256
Number of transistors in a CPU	10^4–10^5	10^6–10^7	10^8–10^9
Wavelength of light source used for lithography (nm)	436	365	248

transistor in a CPU dropped tenfold approximately every 7 years, and the price/performance ratio of integrated circuits rose significantly (see Fig. 2).[2]

The invention, creation, and widespread application of IT effectively spurs the integration of hardware manufacturing with software development, goods production with service management, and the real with the virtual economy, thus providing a powerful impetus for economic and social development. Having pervaded every discipline and field, IT powerfully stimulates the development of physical sciences, life sciences, new energy, new materials, aviation, aeronautics, and other engineering technologies. It boosts interconnection and integration between different disciplines and enormously improves our ability to understand, protect, adapt to, and change nature. Widespread use of the Internet in particular significantly speeds up the accumulation and dissemination of knowledge and creates the conditions for comprehensive breakthroughs in science and technology.

---

[2]Research Report on IT Development Trends by the Ministry of Information Industry of the People's Republic of China, 2007.

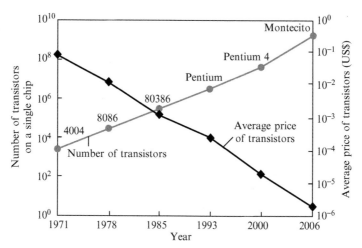

Figure 2   Density of transistors on a CPU compared to price per transistor.

B. IT is already a leading industry in the national economy

IT is a typical general-purpose technology (GPT) [2].[3] Compared to specialist technologies, the use of IT in combination with traditional technologies can produce greater collaborative results that give an impetus to every field of the national economy. IT revolutionizes the production patterns and organizational forms of traditional, agricultural and service industries, constantly creates new areas for economic growth and new derivative industrial sectors, and effectively improves the quality and benefits of economic growth. The IT industry is characterized by a rapid growth rate, fast technological advances, high profits, and close association with other industries, which are basic features a leading industry should have. The IT industry has become an important engine driving economic growth in the new period (see Table 2).[4]

Since the middle of the last century, the growth of the world's IT industry has clearly accelerated, with an annual average growth rate higher

---

[3]Normally, a general-purpose technology should meet the following conditions: great potential for technological improvement, multiple uses, applicability in most economic fields, and mutual complementarity with other technologies.
[4]DigiWorld 2007, p. 24.

Table 2 Contribution of sectors of the IT industry to global GDP growth in 2007

Sector	Contribution to global GDP growth (%)
Communications services	2.7
Communications equipment	0.6
Software and computer services	1.7
Computer hardware	0.8
TV	0.7
Consumer electronics	0.7
Total	7.2

than that of the petroleum; mining; chemical engineering; food, beverage and tobacco; and transport industries.[5] As the scale of the IT industry and its proportion of the economy constantly grow, the industry plays an increasingly important role in every country's economic development. In 1978, the value added of the global IT industry accounted for 1.5% of global GDP. This figure rose to 3.4% in 2000 and 4.3% in 2006. From the 1970s to the beginning of the 21st century, the proportion of the value added of the US IT industry in the US GDP almost doubled. Since the beginning of the 1990s, this proportion has also increased significantly in the EU, Japan, and the Republic of Korea (ROK) (see Fig. 3) [3].

C. IT is a major force promoting sustainable development

In modern society, the factors contributing to economic growth have expanded from capital, land and labor to include technology, knowledge and information. Information is a production factor available for limitless use, and it can produce incremental benefits, expand sources of growth and promote sustained economic growth [4]. The development and use of information enables technology, knowledge, and other new production factors to fully play their role in economic development, and make an ever-increasing contribution to it. In developed countries, the

---

[5]IC Insights, ST.

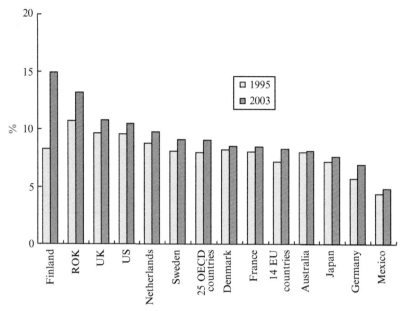

Figure 3 IT industry as a percentage of GDP in some OECD countries, and OECD and European Union averages.

contribution of technological advances based on information use generally accounts for about 70% of economic growth [5, 6].

According to statistics, the energy consumption per unit of value added of the IT industry is significantly lower than the average for all industries. For example, the energy consumption per unit of value added of our country's electronics industry is 7.7% of the average for all industries (see Table 3).[6] Rapid growth of the IT industry thus benefits resource conservation and environmental protection. Using IT to upgrade conventional industries may achieve precise control of time, space, quantity, and quality during the course of production; reduce resource consumption, space occupancy and pollutant discharge; and increase productivity. By taking advantage of IT tools such as modern logistics networks, e-commerce, and enterprise resource planning (ERP), enterprises can effectively reduce inventories, decrease consumption and improve efficiency, which in turn leads to full utilization of all kinds of resources. Wide use of geographical IT such as aerial surveying, remote sensing and global positioning in the geological, oceanic,

---

[6]National Bureau of Statistics of the People's Republic of China.

Table 3 Energy consumption per unit of value added in different industries in China in 2007

Industry	Energy consumption per 10,000 yuan of value added [ton of coal equivalent (TCE)]
All industries	1.9594
Electric power	7.3673
Metallurgy	4.2155
Building materials	3.8234
Chemicals	3.3967
Coal	2.7113
Petroleum and petrochemicals	1.5968
Nonferrous metals	1.5067
Textiles	0.9186
Light industry	0.7425
Pharmaceuticals	0.6274
Machinery	0.2995
Electronics	0.1502

hydrological, and meteorological fields significantly improves our ability to monitor and predict ecological changes, adapt to and protect the natural environment, and respond to and deal with major incidents. Therefore, the IT industry and the development of IT applications have become an indispensable element of the harmonious relationship between man and nature.

D. IT has profoundly changed humankind's production patterns and lifestyles

Every major technological revolution has had a profound impact on humankind's production patterns and lifestyles. The use of IT enables people to break their past reliance on conventional means of transportation and communication, and expands their scope of development and contacts. Advances in IT optimize humankind's production patterns by making it possible for workers, tools and objects of labor to be integrally combined even when spatially separated. Revolutionary changes in labor tools and the application of intelligent equipment in the production process greatly improve conventional mechanized and automated production, thus further liberating people from heavy manual labor and allowing them to engage in more complex mental work. Rigid production patterns are being transformed into flexible ones, and uniform centralized large-scale production is changing into production of modular constituents on a more limited scale. As a result, the ability of enterprises to adapt to changes in the marketplace has improved significantly.

IT development raises people's living standards. Online shopping, remote medical services, video on demand, videophone, and e-mail all enrich people's lives, make them more convenient, expand the scope of social contacts and information exchanges, and increase free time. Most important of all, due to breakthroughs achieved in super-large capacity storage, information searching and other technologies, the ability to obtain, transmit and utilize knowledge has risen to an unprecedented level. E-learning and distance education have changed traditional ways of learning, enriched course content, improved learning efficiency and promoted lifelong learning; this has sped up the accumulation of human capital and created a better climate for all-round personal development (see Table 4).

E. IT is the core driving force of the new revolution in military affairs

The new revolution now taking place in military affairs has swept the globe, and encompasses all military sectors. Rapidly developing new and high technologies, exemplified by IT, provide technical conditions for the new revolution in military affairs. At the core of this revolution is a shift in the form of war in human society from mechanization to informationization. The role of information combat has become more conspicuous in both actual engagements and deterrence. Discrete electronic warfare equipment units are linking up via networks. The connection between information systems and weapons is becoming ever more integrated. New methods of information operations are maturing. Information warfare will become an

Table 4 Statistics for global Internet users,[7] mobile phone users,[8] e-mail accounts, e-services[9] and e-commerce[10]

	Year						
	2001	2002	2003	2004	2005	2006	2007
Number of Internet users (in millions)	491	618	717	854	1021	1096	1320
Number of mobile phone users (in millions)	964	1167	1412	1758	2162	2659	3300
Number of e-mail accounts (in millions)	670	800	950	1080	1300	1520	1990
Export of e-services (in trillions of US dollars)	1.5057	1.624	1.8654	2.1924	2.2627	N/A	N/A
Revenue from e-commerce in the US (in trillions of US dollars)	1.08	1.51	1.706	2.051	2.579	2.937	N/A

important, highly controllable form of warfare with a high effect-to-cost ratio. With the support of IT equipment, the ability to acquire and process information, the accuracy of weapons and the transparency of battlefields have reached unprecedented heights, and features of warfare such as the surprise factor, three-dimensionality, maneuverability, speed and deep-strike ability have become very prominent. Whoever has high-tech superiority has better battle effectiveness and initiative on the battlefield. Informationized weapons and equipment have become an important part of the combat capabilities of an army. Profound changes have taken place in battle

[7]Internet World Stats and the Internet Telecommunications Union.

[8]Internet Telecommunications Union.

[9]UN Commodity Trade Statistics Database.

[10]US Census Bureau.

patterns, battle theories and force structures. Many countries in the world are adjusting their military strategies to adapt to the requirements of the new international situation and military conflicts. Winning an informationized war has become the main objective of the new revolution in military affairs in the world today.

F. The IT industry has become the strategic high ground in international competition

The IT industry provides vital support for informationization and economic development, as well as a strong foundation for national defense modernization, and has become the focus of global economic, political, cultural, social, and particularly scientific and technological, as well as military competition. International competition in the IT industry is becoming increasingly complex, and competitive pressure in the field is intensifying. The US, Japan, European countries, and other developed countries have adopted national strategies for developing their IT industries. Some major developed countries have already established control over core technologies and online information resources, and their advantage in IT and information resources enables them to expand their influence on developing countries. Every military power in the world is strongly emphasizing the development of military IT and IT equipment. Multinational companies seek to strengthen their position in global competition by controlling core technologies and important standards. Many developing countries are adopting strategies to catch up with or even surpass developed countries and actively improving their investment environments, absorbing foreign advanced technologies, promoting industrial transformation and upgrading, and spurring accelerated development of their IT industries. At present, competition in overall national strength, which centers on the control of IT and information resources, revolves around a country's IT capabilities.

II. GLOBAL DEVELOPMENT TRENDS IN THE IT INDUSTRY

Materials, energy and information are the three main elements of the objective world. In the mid and late stages of industrialization, IT became an advanced intelligence tool, information resources became important strategic resources, and IT innovation became the main orientation of the development of advanced productive forces. From the 1990s onward, the development of IT has been oriented toward high performance, wide scope and multiple usage and the orientation toward digitization, integration, and making products more intelligent and network based has continued. The ability to process large quantities of complex information has improved remarkably, allowing resources to be utilized and allocated with much greater efficiency. New materials and processes are being widely utilized, constantly easing bottlenecks restraining industrial development. The division of labor in the industry has deepened and new management methods are gradually increasing. Competition in intellectual property and standards has intensified, changing the nature of competition between enterprises. Ubiquitous network environments, digitized production and services, and informationized weapons and equipment have increasingly become the frontiers for the application of cutting-edge technologies, and new development trends are emerging as the IT industry faces the future.

A. IT engenders major new breakthroughs

In the world today, IT has never slackened its fast pace of development and is ever on the brink of a new cycle of major technological breakthroughs. With the constant upgrading of semiconductor and optoelectronic materials and advances in techniques, equipment and processes, integrated circuits have entered the nano age. In the near future, chip integration levels and processing capabilities of CPUs and similar equipment will continue to increase exponentially,[11] and wafers will become larger with ever-increasing integration and ever-decreasing characteristic dimensions (see Fig. 4).[12] System on chip (SoC) will become the future development trend with much lower energy consumption and costs.

Network technology is developing faster toward broadband and wireless and becoming more intelligent. Mobile and fixed communications

---

[11]The 2007 International Technology Roadmap for Semiconductors issued by the International Roadmap Committee predicts that, compared to 2007, the characteristic dimensions in 2022 will be reduced by 80.8%, the integration level will increase by a factor of 31 and the clock frequency will be 2.05 times faster.

[12]2007 International Technology Roadmap for Semiconductors, http://www.itrs.net/.

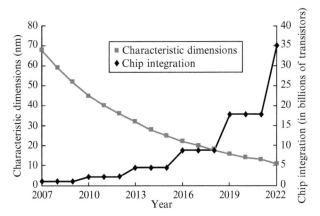

Figure 4   Characteristic dimensions and chip integration.

are becoming integrated through the spread of broadband to mobile communications and the mobilizing of fixed communications. Many kinds of access technologies are emerging, and the applications for radio frequency identification (RFID)[13] technology are spreading by the day. Use of optical communications technology featuring super-large capacity storage, ultra-high speed and extra-long distance is accelerating, as is the adoption of Internet protocol (IP) based communications networks (see Fig. 5). There is a clear tendency toward the integration of telecommunications, computer, and radio/cable TV networks, their combination will form a powerful multichannel and multimedia information platform, and information networks will incorporate all sorts of terminals.

High-performance computing is becoming more computation and data intensive, driving the improvement of both capability and capacity computing, which will gradually meet the requirements for doing large-scale scientific and engineering computations and solving complex problems. High-performance computers and servers are taking the path of multicore CPUs[14] and multistage parallel structure, reaching the speed of a trillion operations per second or faster, and shifting their emphasis from the single-minded pursuit of faster computing speed to comprehensive information processing performance. At present, the emerging

---

[13]Radio frequency identification technology is also known as electronic labeling.

[14]A multicore CPU, short for multicore central processing unit, is a microprocessing unit integrating two or more cores in order to improve computing capability.

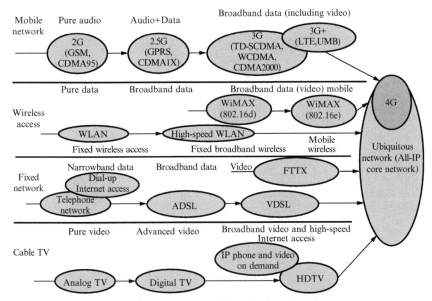

Figure 5   The trend in information network technology development.

"cloud computing" can create a virtual computer using online resources to provide users with the computing resources they need. In addition, new breakthroughs are expected in quantum computing, photonic computing, biological computing and artificial intelligence technology. Computing technology and computer architecture are undergoing thorough changes.

Software systems are quickly developing toward being network based, intelligent, and highly reliable. The tendency toward open source codes is intensifying, and operating systems, databases and middleware are being integrated into a uniform system software platform. In the open and dynamic environment of Internet applications, software as a service (SaaS) has become a major direction in software development.

B. Growth of the IT industry is becoming sustained and steady

In the 1990s, the global IT industry experienced extraordinary growth, before returning to reasonable levels when the dot-com bubble burst at the turn of the century. In recent years, the growth of the IT industry

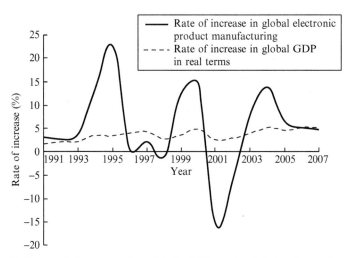

Figure 6 Rate of increase in global GDP and global electronic product manufacturing.

has become steadier, with longer cycles and smaller amplitudes (see Fig. 6).[15] For some time in the future, the rapid development of new products and services in the IT industry will engender a large number of new needs. The speed at which IT is being applied and spread is increasing, expanding the market for the industry's development. The information network infrastructure is shifting to the next-generation network, expanding the prospects for information services and applications. Many countries in the world are giving their IT industries more support and gradually improving their IT policies and regulations. These factors will help improve the climate for developing the IT industry and promote its sustained and steady growth.

Of course, IT industry development could be affected by uncertainty in the world economic situation in the short term, but it is unlikely to fluctuate radically in the long term. It is anticipated that upgrading and updating IT products will accelerate and the demand for information services will steadily expand (see Fig. 7).[16] This will have an ever-greater impact on and contribute even more to global economic growth.

---

[15]Data on electronic manufacturing worldwide are from the *Yearbook of World Electronics Data* for the relevant years, and data on world GDP are cited from the IMF Data Mapper.

[16]World Information Technology and Services Alliance Public Policy Report, 2007 (figures for 2008 and 2009 are estimates).

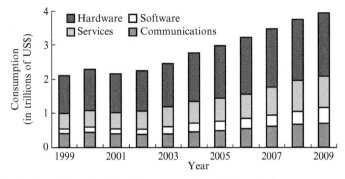

Figure 7   Projected trend of global consumption of IT products.

C. Industrial clustering and integration are becoming increasingly evident

Under the influence of global economic restructuring, the IT industry is transforming at a faster pace and forming a number of highly concentrated industrial bases which guide the direction of the global IT industry's development. The effects of clustering are closely associated with the short life cycle of IT products and detailed division of labor in the industry. IT product users make very high time, quality, cost, and service (TQCS) demands, which objectively necessitates a considerable geographical concentration of related enterprises. Each enterprise that forms a link in the division of labor needs to focus on its own production processes as well as collaborate closely with other enterprises and industries from the production chain in the same or nearby localities. Industrial clustering helps reduce production and transaction costs and results in improved economies of scale and overall collaborative capability. From a development perspective, the effects of geographical clustering will influence the layout of the world IT industry for a long time to come.

The integration of the IT industry will further increase as IT advances and new IT products and services constantly replace old ones. This integration will mainly be manifested in the functional integration of terminal products, that is, integration of personal computing, communications, and consumer electronics; in the integration of services on an operating platform, i.e., the integration of communications, content, and computing services; and in the integration of telecommunications, computer, and radio/cable TV networks. Application services based on IT and the Internet are in the ascendancy and will inevitably promote the expansion of traditional service industries, boost the development of modern service industries and significantly raise service efficiency. Furthermore, IT is rapidly permeating other industries, transforming and upgrading traditional industries, creating new technological fields, management styles and industrial forms, and having an ever greater impact on the entire national economy.

D. Intellectual property and standards are increasingly at the center of competition

Patents, intellectual property and standards are all important institutional safeguards for encouraging innovation and critical factors for the development and success of enterprises. According to data issued by the World Intellectual Property Organization, the number of patent applications in the semiconductor field in 2006 was 67.1% higher than in 2002 (see Table 5).[17] In order to obtain IT intellectual property, different countries and enterprises have increased investment in R&D, and adopted and implemented intellectual property strategies. Consequently, the number of patent applications has become a critical indicator of a country's

Table 5   Patent Cooperation Treaty (PCT) patent applications in the field of IT

| Field | Year of public release | | | | | Annual growth rate from 2002 to 2006 (%) |
	2002	2003	2004	2005	2006	
Audio-video	5391	6057	6075	6718	7322	35.8
Telecommunications	11,167	10,821	10,441	11,674	13,478	20.7
Computers	11,096	9916	9535	11,026	13,428	21.0
Semiconductors	3612	4051	4109	4727	6034	67.1
Total	31,266	30,845	30,160	34,145	40,262	28.8

---

[17]WIPO Patent Report 2007.

Table 6   Comparison of IT PCT patent applications in China, the US, Japan and the EU

	Year						
	2000	2001	2002	2003	2004	2005	2006
US	17,246	15,721	14,395	14,953	14,525	14,077	16,427
EU	11,927	12,508	12,082	12,207	12,016	12,845	12,549
Japan	4525	4994	5934	7288	8658	11,031	11,250
China	221	303	478	723	1078	1075	1853

competitiveness and development level in the IT industry (see Table 6).[18] Some large multinational companies buy up small enterprises that own patented technologies while expanding their own patents to maintain their competitive edge. Some have even formed intellectual property and patent exchange alliances with a view to leading the development trend in their industry.

Using technical standards to maximize the benefits of intellectual property has become a typical means of competition in the IT industry. Internationally, the formulation of technical standards should be open and universal and facilitate the dissemination and sharing of intellectual property. However, some IPR holders transform their sole ownership of intellectual property into exclusive standards in order to gain greater profits and long-term benefits. More and more enterprises realize they gain a competitive edge only by acquiring IT intellectual property or standards. This has become an important aspect of competition, cooperation and development in the IT industry and will remain so for a considerable period of time.

E. Information networks are ubiquitous

In the 21st century, driven by fast-developing new technologies such as wireless access, RFID, network applications, and man-machine interaction, the ubiquitous network—an entirely new network that can achieve

---

[18]Data for 2000 to 2004 are cited from OECD Work on Patents, and those for 2005 to 2006 are provided by the Electronic Intellectual Property Center of the Ministry of Information Industry of the People's Republic of China.

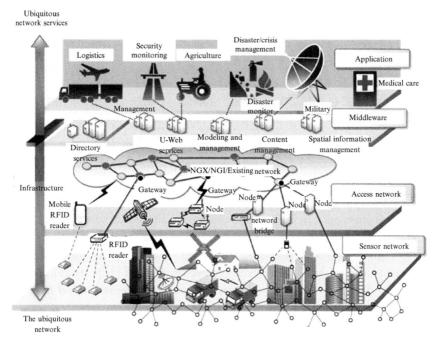

Figure 8 The ubiquitous network.

person-to-person, person-to-object, and object-to-object communication anytime and anywhere (see Fig. 8)—and ubiquitous computing are becoming a reality and gradually coming into use. Person-to-object and object-to-object communications are regarded as outstanding characteristics of the ubiquitous network. The rapid development of wireless, broadband, and Internet technologies constantly raises the use of the ubiquitous network to a higher level. The integration of different networks, access and applied technologies will create a seamless information link between production, transportation, exchange and consumption of goods. The widespread application of networks has caused a change in the traditional organizational decision-making process from a hierarchical to a flat structure, a change in the organizational structure from a vertical chain to a horizontal network, a change in the organizational pattern from departmentalization to integrated collaboration, a change in organizational behavior from low efficiency to fast response, and a change in decision making mechanisms from highly centralized to closer-to-site decision making.

The ubiquitous network has fortified the application services of existing networks and spawned a slew of new service fields. It can satisfy people's increased demands for public and commercial services, medical care, education, entertainment, environmental control and domestic work, substantially improve the quality of life and open up a broader realm for digitalized life. Moreover, it enables people to effectively prevent, warn against and cope with natural disasters and unexpected incidents, improving their ability to respond to and deal with emergencies. The ubiquitous network promotes a high degree of integration between hardware and software, systems and terminals, and content and applications, significantly joining together and extending the original industrial value chain, forming more value-added applications and giving powerful impetus to IT industry development. One might prophesize that the ubiquitous network will become a general infrastructure, just like power grids and pipelines, merged into people's daily lives and work, and become a key platform for economic, political, cultural, and various other social activities.

While regarding the positive function of IT and the IT industry, we should be aware of problems their development brings, such as issues of scientific and technological ethics, the digital divide, information security and Internet governance. We should exploit the merits and avoid the disadvantages so that IT and the IT industry can benefit humanity more effectively.

III. CHARACTERISTICS OF OUR COUNTRY'S IT INDUSTRY'S DEVELOPMENT

Since reform and opening up, the scale of our country's IT industry has expanded rapidly. Particularly in the past two decades or more, IT has made enormous advances, the industrial structure has constantly been optimized, and the industry has taken a path characterized by government guidance, market orientation and open development. This progress has greatly promoted economic and social development and begun to satisfy the people's ever-increasing demands for IT products and services (see Fig. 9).[19]

---

[19]Ministry of Information Industry of the People's Republic of China.

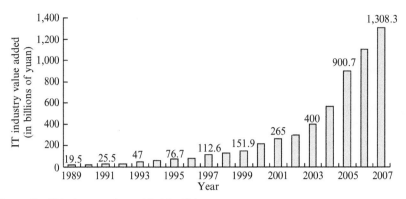

Figure 9   IT industry value added in China.

A. National strategic decision making guides IT industry development

Our country attaches great importance to developing the IT industry, emphasizes research into the nature and direction of development in the global IT industry, and fully understands the laws of its development. Proceeding on the basis of the needs of national economic development, our country lost no time in formulating development strategies and plans, defining the course of and objectives for development, and launching incentive policies and measures. This work has played an important role in guiding and promoting sound development of the IT industry.

In 1983, the government decided to speed up development of the electronics industry and set a target to octuple the industry's gross output value between 1980 and 2000 and increase its share of the country's gross industrial and agricultural output value from 1.4% to about 3%. In 1984, the government gave a clearer statement of its development policy, which is to "build a foundation, raise our level, improve quality, pursue profits, octuple the gross output value, and get 10 years ahead of the rest of the national economy."[20]

---

[20]This is a summary of the electronics industry's development tasks for the foreseeable future made at a national working meeting of heads of departments and bureaus of the electronics industry. "Octuple the gross output value and get 10 years ahead of the rest of the national economy" means by 2000, the 1980 gross output value of China's electronics industry should be octupled and major products and production technologies should reach the level advanced industrialized countries will have reached around 1990, with certain technologies reaching the advanced world level prevailing at that time. The latter objective is 10 years more ambitious than the objective the government set for the national economy as a whole of reaching the level those countries reached around 1980.

In due course the government designated consumer electronics as a development priority, and implemented a project to produce color TV sets entirely domestically. By 1990, the output value of consumer electronics accounted for more than 50% of the electronics industry's gross output value. Moreover, the government adopted effective measures to support the growth of basic and big-ticket products such as integrated circuits, computers and program controlled telephone exchanges, and by 1990 the electronics industry's gross output value was almost eight times that of 1980.

In the 1990s, the government designated the electronics industry as a pillar industry of the national economy and set forth the strategic thinking of promoting informationization of the national economy. It put industrial policies into effect to promote the development of mobile communications, software and integrated circuits and inaugurated special projects such as the project to produce digital program controlled telephone exchanges domestically and the "908" and "909" integrated circuit projects. Driven by market demand, the microelectronics, computer, communications, software and information services sectors all developed and industrial restructuring constantly accelerated. By 2000, the proportion of the output value of big-ticket products having high technological levels and high value added approached 40%. Practice demonstrates that the government's strategic decisions have effectively stimulated industrial development. By 2000, the electronics industry had reached a scale much greater than planned in 1984 and had become an important pillar of the national economy.

At the beginning of the 21st century, the government set a development strategy of using informationization to drive industrialization, and using industrialization to promote informationization, thereby following a new path of industrialization. Further, the government stressed that it was giving high priority to developing the IT industry and widely applying IT in economic and social fields. At present, our country ranks number one in output of electronic and IT products (see Table 7),[21] with an average annual growth rate from 2001 to 2007 of nearly 30%,[22] and the output of many IT products ranking number one in the world.[23]

---

[21] *The Yearbook of World Electronics Data 2007.*

[22] Ministry of Information Industry of the People's Republic of China.

[23] China's output of tens of complete products including mobile telephones, notebook computers, color TV sets, digital program controlled telephone exchanges and digital cameras, as well as components and materials such as color kinescopes, capacitors, resistors, micromotors, loudspeakers, magnetic materials, printed circuit boards and network cables ranks first in the world.

Table 7   The world's ten leading electronic and information product manufacturing countries and regions by output value in 2007

Country/Region	Output value (in billions of US$)	Annual growth rate (%)
China	359.427	19.00
US	283.355	2.11
Japan	187.562	0.62
Republic of Korea	112.10	5.24
Germany	74.433	1.94
Malaysia	58.609	6.28
Singapore	54.226	2.28
Taiwan, China	47.212	7.34
Mexico	45.421	13.75
UK	34.682	0.05

B. Market-oriented reform is creating a new micro development mechanism

The electronics industry was one of the first sectors in our country to undergo market-oriented reform. From the early years of the People's Republic to the mid-1980s, most of the country's electronics enterprises operated under the planned economy. In 1986, the electronics industry took the lead in reform of the planned management system. Departmental and regional barriers came down; government administration was separated from enterprise management; enterprises of the central government were decentralized; and enterprises were given more decision-making power over their operations. These measures greatly increased the vitality of enterprises. In 1992, the government set the reform objective of creating a socialist market economy. Afterwards, market-oriented reform of the electronics industry picked up speed and management of the industry gradually shifted from the government to the industry itself. As the result of the introduction of a shareholding system, establishment of a modern corporate structure and improvements in the development environment, state-owned, private, foreign-funded and other enterprises under various forms of ownership flourished in competition, and a number of large domestic enterprises with good comprehensive strength and small and medium-sized enterprises with special advantages rapidly sprung up. In 2007, the revenue of the leading enterprise among the top 100 IT enterprises in China exceeded 140 billion yuan, 160 times more than the revenue of the leading enterprise in 1987, and sales revenues for each of the top three enterprises exceeded 100 billion yuan.[24]

The rise to prominence of enterprises and the gradual maturity of the market system have led to an effective micro development mechanism, guided the optimal allocation of industrial resources, promoted elimination, merger and reorganization of underperforming enterprises, and increased industrial concentration. Of the 57 color TV manufacturers previously subsumed under government planning, none attained reasonable economies of scale. At present, the combined sales revenue of the top five color TV manufacturers accounts for 70% of the total sales revenue of color TV sets in the country. Both our country's output and exports of color TV sets rank first in the world. Chinese enterprises specializing in manufacturing communications equipment, personal computers, electronic terminals and peripherals are rapidly coming of age, and their share in international markets is increasing steadily. As the result of the invigoration of the microeconomy, a number of strong enterprises came to prominence, attracted a wealth of capital and talent, and promoted clustering in the industry. This clustering is apparent in the Pearl River Delta, the Yangtze River Delta and the Bohai Rim region, and these areas account for more than 80% of the country's total in benchmark areas such as industrial value added, sales revenue, profits and number of employees [7]. Furthermore, a new batch of industrial clusters are now taking shape.

C. Opening up promotes an outward orientation

The electronics industry was one of the first sectors in our country to use foreign capital. Opening up effectively promoted the adaptation of our country's electronics industry to the international division of labor in the industry. By the end of 2007, the accumulated utilization of foreign capital

---

[24]Ministry of Information Industry of the People's Republic of China.

by the IT industry exceeded $160 billion, and all multinational IT firms listed in the Fortune 500 had invested in China [7].

The IT industry is a capital-, technology-, and knowledge-intensive industry, so accelerating our opening up was a necessary choice to offset the domestic shortage of funds and improve technological capabilities. Opening up in the IT industry started with the introduction of advanced technologies; processing trade in the form of processing imported materials, assembling imported parts and producing products according to supplied samples; and compensation trade. As a result of foreign businesses increasing their investment in China every year and our IT industry becoming better able to play a complementary role, our country has become the largest IT industry base in the world. Our export of IT products continues to increase rapidly (see Fig. 10).[25] The share of IT exports in total industrial sales increased from 23% in 1989 to nearly 60% in 2007.

Following China's accession to the WTO, our IT enterprises have been globalizing at a faster rate. The ability of major communications equipment manufacturers, PC manufacturers, and telecommunications service providers to run their businesses and manage their capital on a multinational scale has improved conspicuously. A number of small and

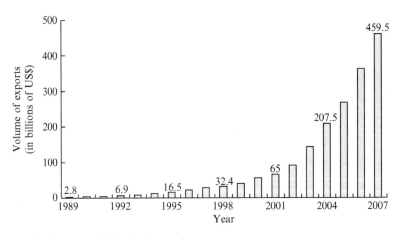

Figure 10   Volume of China's IT product exports.

---

[25] *Ibid.*

medium-sized enterprises that are highly dynamic and full of growth potential have achieved notable success in opening up financing channels, innovating business models and developing new forms of business. China's IT industry has become an important part of the global IT industry.

D. Technological progress is reaching new heights

For a long time, our country primarily pursued the strategy of following in others' footsteps due to limitations in economic strength and technological levels. In order to catch up with the world advanced level, the government placed great emphasis on importing, assimilating, absorbing and innovating advanced IT. Investment in scientific and technological innovation increased every year, and the range of entities receiving investment was extended from research institutes to include innovative enterprises. As a result, the innovative and technological capability of IT enterprises has grown steadily. After years of effort, considerable breakthroughs have been made in fields such as communications, integrated circuit design, high-performance computing, and application software. China's technology in digital program controlled telephone exchanges, mobile communications, digital trunked communications, and optical communications is now among the best in the world. Specifically, TD-SCDMA,[26] for which our country holds the core IPR, has become one of the international standards for third-generation mobile communications. Our terascale large computer systems and domestically produced high-performance computers and servers are among the best in the world. General-purpose CPUs and other middle- and upper-end chips have undergone successful R&D and gone into production. China is able to design integrated circuits of less than 90 nm with an integration exceeding 30 million gates, greatly narrowing the gap with foreign advanced technologies. Our country has successfully developed digital TV terrestrial transmission technology[27]

---

[26]TD-SCDMA stands for time division-synchronous code division multiple access. It was proposed by China and has become an interfacing technology standard officially issued by the International Telecommunications Union for third-generation mobile communications.

[27]Digital TV terrestrial transmission technology sends digital TV programs from the transmitter to the user's receiver terrestrially.

and digital audio–video coding and decoding technology,[28] which support the development of the digital TV industry. Domestically produced middleware, financial and enterprise management software, and anti-virus software are already very competitive with foreign products.

E. Integration of military and civilian applications promotes development of the IT industry

In the early days of the People's Republic, the electronics industry focused on military applications and developed a large quantity of communications, computer, radar, surveillance, and electronic warfare equipment for military use. As a result of large-scale development from the first to the fifth Five-Year Plan periods, the electronics industry was comprised of a fairly complete mix of sectors, and reached a considerable scale and a certain level of technological sophistication. After reform and opening up, our country's electronics industry accelerated its orientation toward civilian applications. Some enterprises began to produce TV sets, video tape recorders, hi-fi equipment and other consumer electronics. The focus gradually shifted from military to civilian applications, thus forming the necessary technical and material foundation for the all-round development of our country's IT industry.

In the 1990s, in line with the trend of the world's new revolution in military affairs, the government made a series of timely and strategically important decisions concerning the modernization of national defense and the army, which presented new opportunities for the development of the IT industry, especially the military electronics industry. By carrying out major special projects, military electronics enterprises have completed R&D on an array of urgently needed, key IT equipment, achieved breakthroughs in some critical technologies, and formed an R&D system for military IT equipment. More and more military technology such as components and software are being put to civilian use, and some civilian IT enterprises have begun to undertake military IT research and production tasks, thus promoting the development of both military and civilian IT research and production.

---

[28]Digital audio–video coding and decoding technology is technology that codes digital audio–video signals and reduces their rate to meet the requirements for storage and transmission using existing technology.

F. Integration of production and application creates more room for development

The IT industry is a strategic and pillar industry of our national economy, and it constantly contributes to improving the quality and benefits of economic development and meeting the people's ever-increasing material and cultural needs. In addition, wide use of IT also stimulates booming industrial growth. Over the past 10 plus years, huge demand in the communications market has spurred rapid development of IT infrastructure and communications equipment manufacturing and facilitated breakthroughs in the wireless, landline, exchanges, and transmission fields. Our IT network infrastructure has skipped development stages and its performance has been comprehensively upgraded, with the size of the network and the number of telephone and Internet users ranking first in the world (see Fig. 11).[29] Our country's informationization, together with the IT-based upgrading of traditional industries, has opened up vast new areas for the development of the IT industry. Golden Card, Golden Customs, Golden Tax, and other golden projects centering on the application of IT in banking and taxation have been successively launched, and a raft

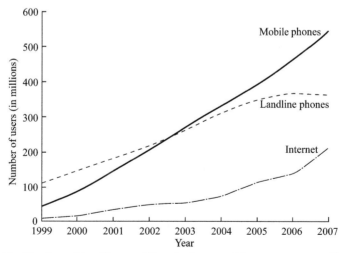

Figure 11   Number of landline, mobile telephone and Internet users in China from 1999 to 2007.

---

[29]Ministry of Information Industry of the People's Republic of China.

of important e-government systems have come into use in government agencies. All of these are direct examples of the wide application of IT. In 1993, the Golden Card Project was implemented. After more than 10 years of effort, 1.6 billion UnionPay cards were issued nationwide, and the number of intelligent IC cards issued reached 4 billion by the end of 2007. E-commerce and e-government provide a vast market for domestically produced network exchanges and core routers. The need for complex computations in geology, natural resource exploitation and meteorology has stimulated domestic R&D on high-performance computers, while the upgrading of the petrochemical, metallurgical, equipment manufacturing, and electric power industries has promoted the integration and application of automatic controls, computer simulation, and artificial intelligence.

Although our country's IT industry has developed rapidly, it still has a long way to go to catch up with the advanced world level and continues to have difficulties and problems in its course of development. The main problems are as follows.

1. Other countries dominate core technology. Foreign firms control an overwhelming majority of IPR and technical standards in upper-end chips, core software, critical components, and special equipment. Our country relies on imports for some core technologies, products and equipment and this restrains the independent development of the IT industry.

2. The industrial structure is in dire need of optimization. Within the international division of labor in the industry, most Chinese IT enterprises occupy the lower rungs on the industrial ladder and the lower links in the value chain. A large portion of their work involves processing and assembly, which has low profit margins. Furthermore, Chinese IT enterprises have weak independent development capacity, and we lack a group of large internationally competitive enterprises.

3. The level of IT application remains low. In every sector of the national economy, most IT applications are in their infancy. The lack of an overall strategy to employ IT in order to increase competitiveness, particularly the failure of certain sectors and departments to more fully use IT applications in process reengineering, market response and decision-making analysis, restricts the overall upgrading

of IT applications. Users are generally inclined to import foreign equipment and services, focus more on hardware than software and on development rather than maintenance, and fail to combine application with production. The domestic market has yet to exert a powerful pull on domestic industrial development. Moreover, domestic industrial technology has difficulty meeting the needs of domestic applications.

4. The industrial system and mechanisms need to be improved. The venture capital system is not fully established, and enterprises have not yet accumulated substantial capital; enterprises, universities and research institutes remain unlinked; the mechanism for applying the fruits of innovation in industry is deficient; the technological innovation system for enterprises needs to be improved; the institutional obstacles of industrial monopolies, departmental and regional barriers, and self-sufficiency restrain the positive interaction between networks, industries and applications; government agencies need to further improve their ability to provide macro guidance, market oversight and public services for the industry's development; and long-range, comprehensive strategic research is still weak.

IV. DEVELOPMENT STRATEGY FOR THE IT INDUSTRY IN THE NEW PERIOD

At present and for some time to come, our country will have strategic opportunities to accomplish a great deal. Accelerating development of the IT industry is the inevitable choice for modernization, an objective requirement for taking a new path of industrialization with Chinese characteristics, and a prerequisite for making the country prosperous and the army strong. Our country's IT industry has already grown to a considerable size, but it still has serious structural weaknesses that make it very difficult for the industry to strengthen or expand further. Although it has great capacity for innovation in some areas, it will long be subject to pressure from developed countries' overall competitive superiority, and the mechanisms for funding innovation and turning research results into practical applications still need to be improved. Enterprises are now market players, but they still lack the ability to face stiff competition and participate in the international division of labor, and it will take a long time for them to cultivate overall competitive advantages. Some successes have already been achieved in IT application; however, informationization is uneven and there is an urgent need to deepen the integration of informationization with industrialization. The state has been very successful in its efforts to support and guide the IT industry, though structural and institutional obstacles hindering the industry's development remain and reform and opening up are in dire need of new breakthroughs. As we face the future, we need to stay grounded in China's realities while adopting a global perspective, be farsighted in our research and planning, make overall plans and arrangements, clarify the position of the industry, formulate and adopt new development strategies, make full use of the role of the IT industry as an multiplier of economic growth, a transformer of development patterns and a propeller for industrial upgrading, and lose no time in making new strides in the IT industry. This is the strategic basis for the development of China's IT industry in the new period.

A. The strategic line of thought

In order to turn China into a powerful country with a strong IT industry by 2020, in accordance with the requirements of building a moderately prosperous society in all respects and taking a new path of industrialization with Chinese characteristics, we must adhere to the principles of independent controllable development, open and compatible technologies, integrated and comprehensive applications, military and civilian interaction, and a market-driven approach for skipping development stages. We must transform the emphasis of the IT industry from volume and growth rates to innovation and profits, and give full play to the dynamic function the IT industry plays in strategic economic restructuring and all-round economic and social development. We must use informationization to drive industrialization and use industrialization to promote informationization, thus setting the IT industry on a path of development with Chinese characteristics.

1. Aim for advanced technology and master proprietary IPR

Mastering proprietary IPR through independent innovation and standing in the front ranks of IT are choices we must make if we are to take the path of developing the IT industry with Chinese characteristics. We must be able to exercise independent control of IT relating to national security, and we must be self-reliant and endeavor to develop core technologies that we cannot acquire by purchase or trade. There is considerable room for innovation in IT, and we therefore need to choose advanced research areas in which important breakthroughs can be made or that can lead to technological transformation to receive priority support, and strive to achieve original innovation in those areas. We need to seize opportunities for IT to permeate and integrate with other areas, encourage interdisciplinary development and vigorously promote integrated innovation. We also need to make use of the fact that IT is highly internationalized by steadfastly studying and drawing upon advanced results from around the world, gathering together results of all kinds from a wide variety of sources, and making greater efforts to absorb and assimilate them and use them as the basis for further innovation. Through the partnership of enterprises, universities, research institutes and users, we need to create a complete innovation chain that stretches from R&D all the way to production and application, and strive to make breakthroughs in key areas of IT. Enterprises need to assume a role in innovation and improve their capacity for R&D in order to increase IPR and the IT industry's core competitiveness.

2. Make the most of the strengths of the domestic market and use application to drive industrial development

China is a large country with a huge market, and this gives it a unique advantage that we need to fully exploit in taking the path of developing the IT industry with Chinese characteristics. At present, our country is maintaining steady and rapid economic growth; its industrialization, informationization, urbanization, marketization, and internationalization are all deepening; and the consumption pattern is in the process of being transformed and upgraded. We need to promote informationization of the national economy and society; speed up IT-based upgrading of the existing machine manufacturing, metallurgy, transportation, light, and textile industries; promote development of modern services industries, such as finance, business, and trade, logistics and e-commerce; start up e-governance; and raise the level of informationization in education, research, health and other social programs. We need to provide widespread information services, popularize the use of computers and networks, and open up the market among the rural population and low-income groups. These measures can help create a broader market and greater demand for IT products. To develop the IT industry, we must seize market opportunities, have a solid grasp of market trends and tap the market's potential. We must also constantly improve product and service quality, integrity, and after-sales service quality; develop large enterprise groups that are competitive and have brand name products; and win consumer trust. In addition, we need to strengthen market supervision and services, encourage and standardize market competition, and minimize government intervention in order to create a favorable market environment for the IT industry's development.

3. Seek development through opening up in order to elevate our country's position in the international division of labor in the industry

Opening up has been a successful experience in China's rapid development and a policy that China should adhere to for a long time as it goes down the path of developing the IT industry with Chinese characteristics. To adapt to the accelerated flow of production factors and the relocation of industries that have been brought about by globalization, we should actively seize the initiative to become integrated into the international division of labor in the industry, strive to occupy an upper rung in the vertical division of labor, expand market share in the horizontal division of labor, fully participate in the international division of labor and cooperation in areas of production, services and research, and achieve mutual benefits. At the same time, we should strengthen our strategic cooperation with large multinational companies that have global influence, attract more of the world's leading high-end information product manufacturers and information service providers to do business in China, encourage foreign companies to come to China and build global or regional R&D and operation centers, and promote domestic development and integration of R&D, production and services. We need to actively solicit IT outsourcing (ITO) and business process outsourcing (BPO) work and improve the mix of imported and exported IT products. We need to change the pattern of trade development, expand the service trade market, seek out a new model for international investment and technological cooperation, participate in work on international technology and industry alliances, and elevate our "go global" capability.

4. Focus on linking the government and the market, and exploit our ability to concentrate resources to accomplish large undertakings

Integrating government guidance with market mechanisms is an inherent requirement for taking the path of developing the IT industry with Chinese characteristics. As the socialist market economy improves, we need the market to play its basic role in allocating resources more effectively in order to develop the IT industry. We need to allow the market to solve the problems it is capable of handling and urge economic entities under different forms of ownership to make the most of their ability to compete in the market, mutually stimulate each other and develop together. On the other hand, the IT industry cannot be left to develop in the absence of government support and guidance. The country should formulate scientific development plans and corresponding policies and measures in accordance with the characteristics of different development stages, areas and locations and the degree of market maturity, in order to remedy market failure and compensate for its flaws. To eliminate bottlenecks constraining development of the IT industry, we also need to carry out major projects and special scientific and technological programs to promote military and civilian interaction and bidirectional transformation. We must give expression to the will of the government, give priority to using the results of innovation, and stimulate domestic industrial development. We need to continue to deepen reform to solve structural and institutional problems that constrain the development of the IT industry.

B. Strategic priorities

The IT industry encompasses an extensive area and many categories. We cannot speed up development of all areas at once; therefore, we need to stress important areas and do some things while setting others aside. We should focus on developing key basic industries such as microelectronics, computers, software, key components, and the materials they use as well as industries in which our country is most internationally competitive, such as broadband mobile communications, next-generation networks, and information services. Though these industries have great market prospects, fast technological progress and cross-industry synergy, we face intense international competition and are likely to fall behind if we do not make continuous progress. We need to control the high ground of industrial development and safeguard the lifeblood of the country's industries as our starting point, and concentrate all available resources on making major breakthroughs in key areas.

1. Microelectronics

Microelectronics is the foundation of the IT industry. Microelectronic technology is advancing rapidly, and there is huge market demand and an enormous amount of investment. There is a relative degree of international monopoly on some key techniques and equipment, which is a significant factor in the technology embargos imposed by certain countries. As the characteristic dimensions of microelectronic technology are reduced to nanometer scale, major revolutions in new materials, new structures, processing techniques, interconnection techniques and design techniques will inevitably occur. Industry insiders generally believe that the key to integrated circuit technology is development beyond the 90 nm point, and revolutionary changes are expected to occur when the 45/32 nm point is reached (see Fig. 12). Therefore, it is important to draw up farsighted plans for original innovative R&D work for futuristic technologies and focus on design technologies, key processing techniques, specialized equipment and key materials in order to establish a complete

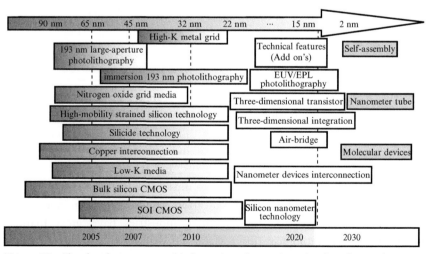

Figure 12   The development trend in key microelectronic technology beyond 90 nm.

system of independent innovation. We also need to emphasize nurturing a group of IC design and manufacturing enterprises that are internationally competitive, improving the overall technological level of the microelectronics industry and building a microelectronics industry base that occupies an important place in the world.

a. High-end design technologies   IC design plays a vital role in the development of the microelectronics industry. However, it is also at present a weak link hindering development. SoC is an important direction of integrated circuit development. With high performance, low cost, and small size, SoC represents a new development opportunity in the field of integrated circuits. Therefore, we ought to strengthen design research on system architecture, algorithms, and coordination of software and hardware (see Fig. 13); make breakthroughs in design, verification and testing technologies for high-end embedded chips, radio-frequency circuits and digital and analog mixed circuits; develop advanced and appropriate design-aided tools; try to find a way to develop high-speed terahertz integrated circuits; and develop SoCs with proprietary IPR in areas with huge market demand such as mobile communications, digital TV, smart cards, network terminals, and information security, so that independently designed mainstream products can reach world advanced levels.

b. Key manufacturing equipment and measuring instruments   Manufacturing equipment and measuring instruments are decisive factors that determine the development level of the microelectronics industry, and our country urgently needs to make breakthroughs in these areas. Photolithography machines, etching machines and ion implanters are key equipment for manufacturing chips, and we need to achieve mass production and wide application on the basis of prototype development. It is extremely important for us to develop next-generation lithography (NGL),[30] which will enable our country to develop nanometer ICs from a more advanced starting point. EUV lithography technology, which is currently under development, makes it possible to reduce the linewidth by adjusting the wavelength of light and multiple-lens reflection (see

---

[30]NGL is an area currently undergoing exploratory research. It principally concerns EUVL, EPL, XRL and EBDW equipment, with EUVL and EPL equipment generally considered the most promising research areas.

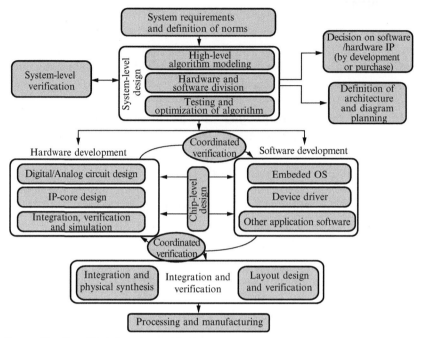

Figure 13   Simplified flowchart of SoC.

Fig. 14). In addition, since equipment is the physical realization of tech-nology, we need to pay close attention to the trend toward embedding manufacturing technologies and techniques in equipment, and put great effort into developing automatic manufacturing equipment such as state-of-the-art high-density packaging equipment, as well as key processing modules, measuring instruments and auxiliary tools.

Electronic measuring instruments are essential for testing the per-formance and quality of all electronic materials, products, equipment and systems. We must accelerate development of measuring instruments such as SoC measurement systems, and those used in parameter measurement in new monitors, R&D on and trial production of digital audio and video products, online measurement of chip components and consistency tests of mobile communications terminals. In addition, electronic measuring instruments and meters are being extensively applied in different sectors of the national economy, and this is also an indispensable condition for promoting the spread of IT. High-performance and general-purpose measuring instruments and meters provide an important basis for

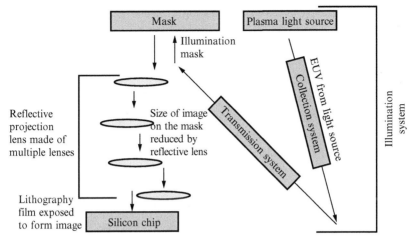

Figure 14   Schematic diagram of EUV lithography.

ensuring high-level IT applications and system performance and security and therefore warrant our close attention.

c. New materials   Breakthroughs in integrated circuit materials can lead to drastic changes in the microelectronics industry. An important item on the microelectronics industry development agenda should be accelerating the industrialized production of silicon wafer materials, micromachining materials, polishing and grinding materials, and packaging materials, with a focus on advanced ULSI core processing techniques based on the latest progress and achievements worldwide in the area of microelectronic materials. We need to actively explore materials used in silicon-based photoelectric integrated chips and silicon-based mixed integrated chips and non-silicon materials,[31] which have great application potential, in order to create the technological conditions for making breakthroughs in power consumption and linewidth.

2. High-performance computing

Computing technology is the heart of the IT industry. Developing high-performance computing is an important strategic choice for strengthening our country's IT industry. We should think about mainly using high-performance CPU and GPU technologies, and high-performance

---

[31]Silicon-based new materials mainly include silicon-on-insulator, strained silicon and BiCMOS, and non-silicon-based new materials mainly include GaAs, InP and GaN.

super computer and network computing technologies to carry out the coordinated development of capability and capacity computing, significantly increase overall information processing efficiency and strive to reach the international advanced level of high-performance computing.

a. High-performance CPUs and GPUs   A computer's CPU directly determines the computer system's performance. To meet the requirements for the independent development of our country's computer industry, we need to pool efforts to tackle the problem of developing high-performance CPU chips. We need to adapt to the multicore trend and develop high-performance multicore, many-core, and embedded CPUs, so that our independently developed high-performance chips gain a foothold internationally. GPUs are used mainly for graphic processing. Their powerful floating-point computing performance has drawn wide attention recently, and we need to intensify our R&D in this area.

b. High-performance supercomputers   Supercomputers are an indispensable technological tool for complex large-scale computing tasks and play an important role in the national economy and cutting-edge areas of science. We need to carry out independent R&D on supercomputers with higher overall performance, master high-performance computing, mass storage and low power consumption technologies, and develop large-scale application systems that utilize these technologies. We need to develop better high-performance supercomputers in a timely manner to satisfy the demand of the national economy and national defense development for high-performance, high-speed computing. We should endeavor to make our country one of the world's leaders in high-performance computing capabilities (see Fig. 15).[32]

c. Network computing technologies   Using and relying on fast-growing and ever-expanding networks is a new, inexpensive, efficient and universal way to effectively improve computing capabilities and mass information processing capacity. This area has huge potential for development. Therefore, we need to improve the key technologies for high-performance

---

[32]Data for the period 2004–2008 are from http://www.top500.org, an authoritative international high-performance computer rating organization, and those for the period 2009–2012 are based on the estimates of planned research projects publicized by the concerned international companies.

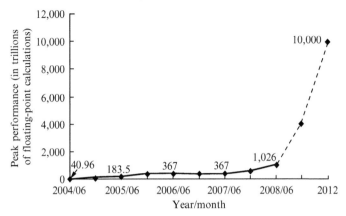

Figure 15   Changes in peak value of high-performance computers in the world.

scheduling, network resource management and secured resource sharing, undertake R&D on network-integrated computing systems based on heterogeneously distributed computing and storage, and enhance resource sharing and coordination in network environments, in order to create a virtual computing environment for developing and utilizing massive online information resources more effectively.

d. Non-traditional computing technologies   A major transformation in computing technologies and computer architecture capable of opening up huge development opportunities could be around the corner. Once we break through technological barriers in search of new bionic algorithms based on the human brain's cognitive abilities, computers will acquire capabilities such as super-large-scale parallel computing, hyper-powerful error tolerance and associative thinking, and a high level of self-adaptation and self-organization that are scarcely imaginable with traditional computers, leading to an unforeseeable IT revolution. Optical computers use an optical beam to replace electric current for calculation and storage, use different wavelengths to represent different data, and execute highly complicated computing tasks at great speed, thus greatly escalating both information processing speed and capability. Quantum computing makes use of qubits,[33] quantum states,[34]

---

[33]A qubit is a basic information unit of a quantum computer, in which basic particles, such as electrons, photons and ions, are called qubits.

[34]A quantum state is the state of atoms, neutrons, protons and other particles. It represents the energy, rotation, momentum, magnetic field, and other physical properties of particles.

and their transformation to speed up data searching and large integer decomposition and thus achieve super-high performance information processing. We need to increase research on biological, photon, and quantum computing, artificial intelligence and other cutting-edge technologies to promote the interconnection and convergence of disciplines such as informatics, physics, biology and cognitive science, and make great achievements and original innovations in multiband computing, semantic analysis, human brain structure simulation, machine learning and other key technologies.

3. Software

Software is the soul of the IT industry. Software has both technical and cultural properties. The software industry is a strategic, knowledge producing industry with zero pollution, low power consumption and a high employment rate. In order to expand the scope and raise the quality of our country's software industry, we should take full advantage of Chinese language processing and human resources, follow the international trend in open source codes, boost the industry through applications, attend equally to both internal and external factors, and cultivate dynamic comparative advantages in the international division of labor.

a. Basic software   Basic software is the foundation for all kinds of application software, and is therefore the cornerstone of support software systems. Multicore CPUs and high-performance computers all need support from operating systems, which presents a rare opportunity to develop operating systems from an advanced starting point. Highly reliable server operating systems for multicore CPUs; secure and user-friendly desktop operating systems; large general-purpose database management systems that are highly reliable, high performing, and highly secure; and middleware that supports network services should be the focus for development. Closely integrating basic software such as operating systems with CPU design is conducive to integrated software development.

b. Embedded software   Hardware and software integration and shifting software functions into firmware are important development trends. Our huge manufacturing industry offers favorable market conditions for developing embedded software. Focusing on integrating hardware and software technologies, improving the chain of coordination between hardware and software, and developing embedded basic and application software will facilitate the creation of a unique and practical product series with a high price/performance ratio, and increase the scope for growth in the software industry.

c. ***Software and information services***   SaaS is an important opportunity for the transformation of the software industry. Our country's software and information services industries stand to benefit greatly by fostering the culture of the Chinese nation and absorbing the outstanding achievements of other civilizations. Promoting digital cultural products and actively developing information services containing digital content will become new growth areas for the software industry. Faced with demand from all sectors of the national economy, we need to provide comprehensive IT solutions to carry out the restructuring, reengineering and optimization of business processes and solve specific problems restricting different sectors, industries and development stages. Nurturing and developing new Internet-based businesses in e-commerce, e-finance, distance education and value-added wireless Internet services, and mastering more distinctive and highly competitive service technologies and business models will be instrumental in the Internet industry's prosperity and the momentous growth of the network economy.

4. Networks

Networks form key infrastructure in the march toward an information society. Developing an advanced network industry is of great importance for enhancing independent innovation, safeguarding national information security, and driving IT industry transformation and upgrading. With the main trend toward the integration of telecommunications, computer, and radio/cable TV networks, it is an important strategic choice to take the initiative to adapt to the transformation of the network industry. Speeding up the research and deployment of a ubiquitous network and building a comprehensive national network infrastructure are necessary requirements for promoting economic and social informationization, and provide an important means to deal with emergencies such as extreme weather conditions, earthquakes, and geological disasters, as well as severe epidemic outbreaks. We need to continue to carry out R&D on next-generation network technologies and wireless broadband technologies, formulate standards for them, focus on research on terahertz technology, and strive to gain a competitive edge in technology, IPR, standards, and the market, try to take the lead in technology, and further enhance the core competitiveness of enterprises.

a. Broadband mobile wireless communications   Broadband mobile wireless communications are a primary means of offering large-capacity multimedia information communications access to anyone at any time and place. We need to make breakthroughs in key technologies, such as the new generation of wireless transmission and networking technologies, improve the utilization and transmission efficiency of the frequency spectrum and use "everything over IP" to seamlessly interconnect hetero-geneously structured networks. Commercial application of our independently developed 3G technology (TD-SCDMA) has already begun. We need to closely follow its technological evolution and seize the key opportunity to develop next-generation broadband wireless network technologies when it presents itself. We need to further intensify our research on future systems like TD-LTE[35] (see Fig. 16) and actively work out coop-eration models for coordinating the development of the whole industry chain with operations in order to provide more technology based on our own independent innovation for next-generation mobile communications standards and achieve a competitive edge in both technology and markets.

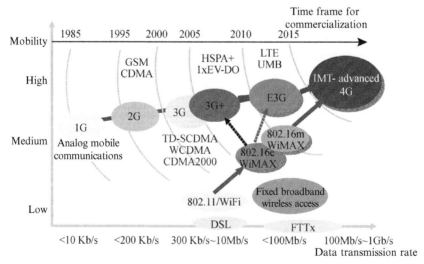

Figure 16   Evolution of mobile wireless technologies.

---

[35]TD-LTE means long term evolution of TD-SCDMA.

Furthermore, we need to pay special attention to keeping costs and power consumption low and to environmental friendliness as we develop key chips, core components and multifrequency, multimodel and multimedia terminals, among other products, to meet development needs.

b. Next-generation network   The next-generation network, which can provide a great variety of business services and significantly improve communication performance, is the direction in which our national information infrastructure must evolve. In conformity with the trend toward more diversified access technologies, integrated core architecture and the synthesis of application services, it is necessary to carry out research on the key technologies of network construction, organization and convergence for next-generation networks, develop key equipment such as high-capacity and expandable routers and signaling gateways, and build a secure and reliable carrier network. In addition, we need to attach great importance to sensor network technology and its application, intensify our research on ubiquitous heterogeneous networks, build a variety of stub networks in accordance with a unified network protocol, and speed up development of a trans-network, seamless ubiquitous network.

c. Network and information security   Network and information security is an important component of national security. When a network is designed or software is developed, security issues should be considered and proactive measures taken in order to create security architecture that provides effective information protection. Priority should be given to carrying out R&D on network and information security technologies such as network reliability, network security protection, content security, encryption and encryption keys; improving network and information security systems; building a network trust system and Internet event analysis system; enhancing specialized network and information security services; and better screening and filtering the vast amount of hazardous and junk audiovisual information, so that the Internet is effectively managed and develops soundly.

5. Key components and materials

Key components are a basic element of the IT industry. High-performance and high-reliability microelectronic, photoelectronic and vacuum electronic components are the basis for information acquisition, transmission, processing, storage, display and utilization. Key components are at the head of the product manufacturing chain in the information industry and therefore play a determining role in the performance of equipment. To promote the sustained development of our country's IT industry, we need to let demand for equipment fully play its guiding role, focus on breakthroughs for key components that constrain industrial development, and by developing new high-end components, comprehensively upgrade the structure and technology of our country's electronic components industry, form a components industry system for the production of a complete range of components that mutually support each other, and develop large-scale manufacturing capability.

a. New components and electronic materials   Miniaturization, modularization, enhanced precision, multifunctionality, and low power consumption components constitute our development orientation. To improve the level of the new components industry, we need to extensively adopt advanced design and manufacturing technologies, such as functional integration, micromachining, three-dimensional packaging and comprehensive system testing; make breakthroughs in key technologies for sensitive components and sensors; and develop components for high-frequency surface acoustic wave and high-frequency microwave media. Electronic materials are used to produce the components and serve as a medium for the realization of their functions. Development of new materials may lead to great innovations in components. Functional and structural electronic materials including semiconductors such as monocrystalline and polycrystalline silicon, green battery materials, advanced electronic ceramic materials, liquid crystal materials and flat panel conductive glass should be actively developed, and we need to give priority to the exploration of theories for and the development of new materials in order to achieve innovation and development.

b. High-end special-purpose components   High performance, high reliability, and a long life cycle are the basic requirements for high-end special-purpose components. We need to establish an industrial system for aerospace-grade special-purpose components and achieve major technological breakthroughs in microwave power components such as special traveling wave tubes, gallium nitride (GaN), and silicon carbide (SiC) power devices, signal processors such as analog to digital converters

(ADCs) and digital signal processors (DSPs), as well as high-precision detectors such as infrared focal plane arrays (IRFPAs). New electric and electronic components such as vertical double diffused metal-oxide semiconductor field effect transistors (VD-MOSFETs), insulated gate bipolar transistors (IGBTs), charge coupled devices (CCDs), and field-programmable gate arrays (FPGAs) should be developed in order to achieve self-reliance and meet the country's strategic needs.

c. Display and photovoltaic components   Display components are an integral part of the photoelectronics industry, and are indispensable information display elements of many IT products such as televisions, computers and mobile handsets. Digitization, flattening, higher definition, enhanced brightness, and lower power consumption are the directions in which display components are evolving. In order to speed up the development and transformation of our country's display components industry, we must satisfy the urgent need for key technologies and equipment for new flat panel display components[36] and integrate our domestic thin film transistor liquid crystal display (TFT-LCD) and plasma display panel (PDP) industries, expand their scale, and raise their level. The present task is to initiate research on new display technologies that best represent the future orientation of the industry, such as organic light emitting diodes (OLEDs) (see Fig. 17) and laser 3D stereoscopic imaging (see Fig. 18), in order to narrow the gap between the domestic industry and the world advanced level.

OLEDs are charge carrier double injection light emitting components. Their light emission mechanism is driven by external voltage. Electrons injected from the electrode and holes in the organic material combine with each other to generate energy. The energy is then transmitted to the molecules of the organic light-emitting substance causing them to jump from the ground state to an excited state. The excited molecules emit light when they relax from the excited to the ground state through the process of radiative transition.

---

[36] At present, the world's display components industry has completed the transformation to digitization, flat panels and high definition. The main kinds of flat panel displays are PDP, TFT-LCD and OLED, of which PDP and TFT-LCD are more mature technologies. Mass production has already begun, and this is rapidly driving down their costs, enabling them to gradually replace traditional CRT display components as the main display components worldwide.

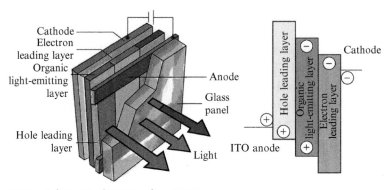

Figure 17   Schematic diagram of an OLED.

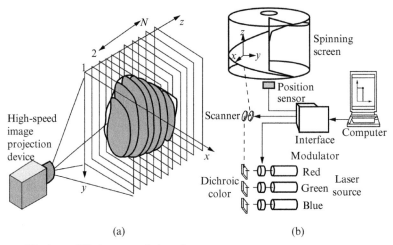

(a)   (b)

Figure 18   Laser 3D stereoscopic imaging.

Figure 18a shows how the moving screen in 3D space intercepts and captures the 2D image cast by the high-speed projector in different positions along the z-axis to form a true 3D image.

Figure 18b shows how the red, green, and blue laser beams combine into one beam, which is projected onto the spinning screen where it produces a colored spot. When the screen spins fast enough, it becomes transparent and the colored spot seems to be floating in the air and becomes a 3D pixel. A number of such 3D pixels can form a 3D object.

Photovoltaic components are the basic components for achieving photoelectric conversion. The solar-energy photovoltaic industry is developing an effective new way to develop clean energy. To expand and upgrade the solar-energy photovoltaic industry, we principally need to solve the problems of basic materials and complete sets of equipment, master material purification techniques, and develop processing techniques and key equipment such as cell modules and related instruments and meters. In addition, we need to look for new materials in order to further improve the efficiency of photoelectric conversion of cells and better utilize solar energy. New thin film solar cells (see Fig. 19) are highly efficient energy products and new building materials, which can reduce costs substantially and are therefore suitable for large-scale application. They have already become a new trend and focus of development in the international photovoltaic industry. Our country should focus on developing large-area, highly efficient, low-cost film solar cell technologies suited for mass production.

A copper, indium, gallium, and selenium (CIGS) thin film solar cell is composed of three parts—the bottom-contact electrode, p-n junction CIGS/CdS and top-contact electrode. The sunlight goes through the transparent and conductive ZnO:Al and CdS layers onto the CIGS on the light absorption layer to generate extra electron-hole pairs. In the electric field of the p-n junction, the extra electron moves to the external circuit through the top-contact electrode ZnO:Al layer and the hole moves to the external circuit through the bottom-contact electrode Mo, and thus photoelectric conversion is achieved.

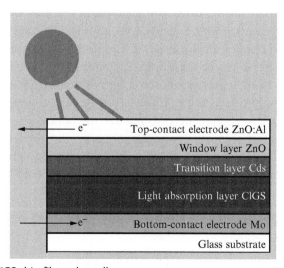

Figure 19   CIGS thin film solar cell.

V. POLICIES AND MEASURES FOR DEVELOPING THE IT INDUSTRY

Improving policies for the IT industry is a strategic initiative to meet international competition, accelerate industrial development and promote modernization in the new period. On the basis of our country's realities and the general trend in global development, we need to give high priority to policies for the IT industry, stress effective guidance by the government, clarify the strategic orientation, formulate rules for the marketplace, improve systems and mechanisms, and strengthen laws and regulations in order to create a favorable environment for industrial development.

A. Rely on major national projects to achieve breakthroughs in core technology

There are already success stories of relying on major national projects and special science and technology projects to achieve core technological breakthroughs in some industries. To implement projects, we should focus on key development areas of the IT industry, make the best use of limited resources and motivate everyone involved in order to tackle difficult technological problems and translate research results into actual productive forces. We need to combine science and technology closely with the economy, have the state play an important role in organizing, coordinating and guiding industrial development, formulate plans, marshal resources, make careful arrangements, nurture innovative groups, and actively seek out new ways of carrying out major national projects and special science and technology projects in a socialist market economy. We need to endeavor to master core IT of importance to the country's strategic interests, develop key information products with proprietary IPR, and undertake R&D on major information equipment that reflects the industry's technological capabilities. We should also promptly organize the implementation of major national projects and special science and technology projects already scheduled in order to seize the high ground for future competition.

B. Encourage the use of domestically produced original products

Domestically produced original IT products encounter a great degree of difficulty in entering the market. This is a major problem that constrains independent innovation in the IT industry and we need to solve it quickly.

Doing so requires amending relevant provisions of laws and regulations on tendering and bidding procedures and developing tendering and bidding procedures that support original products. We need to improve the policies for IT application, encourage innovation through government procurement initiatives, create a system under which preference is given in public spending on products based on independent innovation, and under equal conditions give priority to using innovative products and technologies. The government can support buyers of domestically produced original products by granting them appropriate subsidies from funds created for that purpose, giving them tax credits, extending them credit or giving them guarantees against risks. We need to promote high-quality and affordable products and services to satisfy demand in rural areas and the central and western regions. R&D and the application of domestically produced IT products need to be accelerated to facilitate the upgrading of industries through IT and the informationization of the national economy and society.

C. Energetically promote the integration of telecommunications, computer, and radio/cable TV networks

Integration is the development orientation of telecommunications, computer, and radio/cable TV networks and is an objective requirement for promoting interconnectedness and intercommunicability, putting a halt to redundant construction, and sharing resources. We should improve our overall plans and promote the integration of businesses, networks and terminals in an orderly way. We also need to accelerate the formulation of policies with respect to business licenses, interconnectivity and cross-network settlements, and allow telecommunications and radio/cable TV networks to expand into each other's fields. We need to look for new mechanisms for building networks and sharing information resources and promote innovation in business models. We need to strengthen cooperation between different areas, such as network operations, equipment manufacturing, application services and systems integration, and cultivate new forms of business such as the network information services industry. We need to deepen reform of the telecommunications management system and radio and television operational mechanisms and gradually establish an industry management system in which administration is separated from oversight, government administration is separated from enterprise management, and the functions of government are separated from those of institutions in order to standardize management content, improve management methods, strengthen oversight responsibility, and establish a scientific and reasonable supervision system.

D. Build international IT industry bases

The IT industry is highly internationalized. In order to enhance the international competitiveness of our IT industry, we should cater to both domestic and foreign markets, participate in more extensive international exchanges and cooperation at a higher level, rationally allocate and effectively utilize resources around the globe, and strengthen international economic and technological exchanges and cooperation in a comprehensive way in order to form an open industrial system. We need to adapt to the trend toward economic globalization and make full use of our country's comparative advantages to combine the commodity and service trades, further internationalize our information services industry, and build industry bases that have unique features and enjoy international leadership in the areas of microelectronics, computers, components, software, and service outsourcing. We need to fulfill our obligations and responsibilities as a member of the WTO, strengthen inter-governmental coordination and establish a coordinated response mechanism to resolve international disputes in the IT industry with respect to trade, investment and IPR in an appropriate manner.

E. Implement fiscal and taxation policies beneficial for industry development

Fiscal and taxation policies have a huge influence on industry development. The government needs to provide more fiscal and taxation support for the IT industry to encourage its development. Fiscal funds should be focused on supporting efforts to improve independent innovation capabilities and should especially go toward funding R&D on difficult core technologies in key areas. In addition, we need fiscal expenditure to properly play its role in guiding non-state investment. We must use policies such as tax reductions or exemptions and grants of soft loans to strengthen guidance and support to solve the problems of large enterprises lacking the motivation to innovate and small and medium-sized enterprises lacking the ability to do so. Measures such as VAT reform, accelerated depreciation, and differentiated export tax rebates can be adopted to support strategic priorities such as microelectronics, software and key components. For enterprises involved in transnational mergers and acquisitions or asset reorganization, we should do all we can to prevent double taxation and reduce their investment risks. We need to implement the policy of deducting R&D investment from taxable income and encourage IT enterprises to develop new products, processes and technologies.

F. Establish a venture capital mechanism to support innovation and development

High investment, high risk and high returns are distinctive features of the IT industry, and its development requires a relaxed financial environment. Supporting entrepreneurship and innovation through venture capital investment and striving for a sound cycle of industrial development are important approaches developed countries have adopted to develop their IT industries. The key to establishing a sound venture capital investment mechanism in our country is to stimulate the capital market, improve the investment entry and exit mechanism, accelerate development of the growth enterprise market to provide support for qualified enterprises to receive financing by going public, and open more flexible financing channels for IT enterprises, especially small and medium-sized enterprises. In addition, we need to actively set up venture capital investment funds and industry investment funds and encourage scientific research results to be used as production factors in investment so that a market operation based venture capital investment system that relies mainly on non-state capital and enjoys policy support can take shape.

G. Use IPR and relevant standards to provide assurances and support

IPR is the lifeline of the IT industry. Without IPR, an industry has no voice in the international community. We should protect IPR throughout the process of IT industry development, and cultivate an ethos of respect for and protection of IPR. We need to both protect our own IPR and respect others' IPR. We need to settle IPR disputes in a proper fashion, strengthen the protection of patents, trademarks, copyrights and commercial secrets, and guard against IPR abuse. We need to redouble our efforts to protect IPR, and strictly punish IPR infringements and instances of piracy in accordance with the law. We need to move faster to establish special IPR scrutiny mechanisms for enterprise mergers and acquisitions and technology transfers in order to prevent the loss of IPR. In the course of IT product R&D and production, due regard must be paid to making products compatible with existing international standards. We need to work harder to formulate our own technological standards and do all we can to get our technologies adopted as international standards and increase our influence on the formulation of such standards. In areas relating to national security, we need to strengthen the formulation and implementation of compulsory national standards. We need to ensure that enterprises have an important position in the application of IPR and in the development of standards in order to motivate them to hold more patents and other proprietary IPR.

H. Develop a talented group of industry and high-end technology leaders

Competition in the IT industry is competition between technologies and is ultimately decided by human talent. The focus of this competition is on highly competent industry leaders and high-end technology leaders. To develop industry leaders, we need to firmly establish the thinking that talent is the most important resource, further deepen the reform of the talent system to establish a placement mechanism that is open and mobile and allows everyone to use their talents to the full, and create an environment where talented people can stand out. We should rely heavily on talented young people, train young people who can make theoretical innovations, and have multiple skills and technical ability. We need to think outside the box and successfully identify talented people and give them appropriate jobs so that a group of industry leaders is formed through practice. We should explore how to standardize stock and option incentive mechanisms and work out distribution policies that help attract, retain and optimize the use of talented people. Enterprises, universities and research institutes should be encouraged to work together to cultivate highly talented people.

We need to actively participate in international competition for highly talented people and attract more of them to come and work in China, and encourage Chinese students studying overseas to return home and contribute to the motherland's development.

I. Improve laws and regulations that promote IT industry development

History and reality both demonstrate that the institutionalization of effective policies and measures of the IT industry into laws and regulations through legislative procedures is conducive to its development and technological advances. For cutting-edge fields that have not yet matured through practice, it is necessary to take actual conditions as our starting point, draw upon beneficial experience from foreign countries, and make the legislative process more scientific and foresighted. Focusing on the IT industry's development strategy and development priorities, we need to speed up formulation of laws and regulations on telecommunications, integrated circuits, software and IT applications, and amend and improve laws and regulations on IPR and standards when appropriate. We need to address the issues of information security, Internet crime and Internet governance by quickly organizing research and formulating laws and regulations on e-government, e-commerce, information security, personal information protection and online behavior protection for minors. We should intensify law enforcement and adopt stricter standards for judicial procedures so that all laws are strictly enforced and all violations punished, thereby creating a favorable legal environment for the development of the IT industry.

VI. CONCLUSION

The most important task for developing our country's IT industry in the new period is to make breakthroughs in core technologies and elevate our innovation capacity. Much of the time, it is not a lack of potential to make progress but a lack of nerve and knowledge to innovate that stands in our way. In many circumstances, it is not a lack of possibility for breakthroughs but a lack of confidence in victory that prevents us from achieving success. From an objective survey of the development history of our country's IT industry, we can perceive a buildup of energy, and we have every reason to expect that breakthroughs are on the way. Our country will undoubtedly become a world leader in IT as long as we persevere on the path of developing the IT industry with Chinese characteristics.

ACKNOWLEDGMENTS

I wish to thank Comrades Zeng Peiyan, Liu He, Lou Qinjian, Chen Dawei, Ning Jizhe, and Zhang Fuliang for their assistance in writing this article.

References

1 Moore GE. Cramming more components onto integrated circuits. Electronics 1965; 38(8):114–7.
2 Bresnahan TF, Trajtenberg M. General purpose technologies: engines of growth? Journal of Econometrics 1995;65(1):83–108.
3 OECD. OECD information technology outlook 2006. Paris: OECD Publishing, 03-10-2006.
4 Romer P. Increasing return and long-run growth. Journal of Political Economy 1986; 94(5):1002–37.
5 Abramovitz M. Resource and output trends in the United States since 1870. American Economic Review, Papers and Proceedings 1956;46(2):5–23.
6 Denison EF. Why growth rates differ: postwar experience in nine Western countries. Washington, DC: The Brookings Institution; 1967.
7 Ministry of Information Industry of the People's Republic of China. Review of information industry development during the tenth five-year plan period (Telecom Volume). Chin. ed. Beijing: Posts & Telecom Press, 2006.

PART Two

Report on an Inspection Tour of the US and Canadian Electronics Industries*

August 10, 1983

At the invitation of the Canadian Department of Communications, Hewlett-Packard and other US companies, a delegation of the Ministry of Electronics Industry visited Canada and the US from June 1 to 30, 1983. The objective of this visit was to explore the possibility of further expanding China's economic and technological exchanges with the two countries, and discuss cooperation with US and Canadian companies in the fields of integrated circuits, computers, communications equipment, and electronic instruments. In accordance with the planned itinerary, the delegation visited 34 production and research facilities, and attended the 37th International Exhibition on Military Electronics and Communications Equipment held jointly by the US and the European Community. During the visit and inspection tour, we gained an understanding of the basic situation of the electronics industries in these two countries and studied their experiences in development, research, production, operations, and management. We signed memoranda of understanding on joint ventures with Hewlett-Packard, Rainbow Electronics, and other companies, and met with Francis Fox, the Canadian Minister of Communications. Additionally, at the invitation of the US Department of Commerce, we met with Undersecretary of Commerce Lionel H. Olmer and Assistant Secretary of State William Schneider Jr., and learned from them the circumstances under which the US would ease restrictions on exports to China, thus fulfilling the desired objectives of the visit. I now present the following report on the main points regarding our inspection tour and our comments and suggestions on importing electronic technology from the US and Canada.

---

*Report submitted to the State Council after the first inspection tour of the US and Canadian electronics industries by a Chinese delegation headed by Jiang Zemin, then Minister and Secretary of the Leading Party Group of the Ministry of Electronics Industry.

I. CHANGES IN US POLICY ON EXPORTS TO CHINA AND DISCUSSION OF JOINT VENTURES WITH AMERICAN AND CANADIAN COMPANIES

Recently, US government export controls against our country have eased somewhat. Prior to our visit, we had invited a delegation led by Under Secretary of Commerce, Mr. Olmer, to visit China, so they could see the achievements our country's electronics industry had made independently. On June 15, we met with Mr. Olmer and Mr. Schneider at the US Department of Commerce. During the meeting they both expressed the profound impression China's electronics industry had left on the delegation, and said that the US was looking into transferring advanced technology to China and easing its policy concerning technology transfer in major areas such as semiconductor fabrication facilities, semiconductor devices, all-purpose computers, computer software, and communications equipment. On June 24, the Reagan administration officially declared it was easing restrictions on exports to China. In general, the scope of controls will be considerably more relaxed than the original restrictions, and if the US honors its commitments, this will remove many obstacles to importing American electronic technology and forming joint ventures with American manufacturers.

In accordance with this shift in US policy, we entered into joint-venture memoranda of understanding with Hewlett-Packard and Rainbow Electronics concerning advanced technology transfer. The plan is to create a joint venture with Hewlett-Packard to produce minicomputers and peripherals, microwave and digital instruments, and related components. With Rainbow Electronics we will begin by assembling microcomputers and gradually proceed to joint production of microcomputers.

The US has already stopped producing ordinary low- and medium-power electron tubes, yet there is still considerable demand for them. Therefore, we reached an agreement with a US company to assemble low- and medium-power metal-ceramic electron tubes in the US, making use of China's surplus ordinary electron tubes.

II. CONDITIONS AND CHARACTERISTICS OF DEVELOPMENTS TAKING PLACE IN THE ELECTRONICS INDUSTRIES IN THE US AND CANADA

Through our visit and inspection tour, we gained a better awareness and understanding of the conditions and characteristics of developments taking place in the electronics industries in the US and Canada.

The economic development of the US and its accomplishments in science and technology as well as national defense rely heavily on its advanced electronics industry. In 1981, the gross output value of the US electronics industry reached $113.8 billion; the export volume amounted to $23.6 billion, 20.7% of the gross output value; and the industry employed more than 1.6 million people. In recent years, the US economy has been in a recession, yet each year growth in the electronics industry has exceeded 10%. The electronics industry has already become a strong sector in the American economy, and predictions indicate that by the end of the 1980s its output value will exceed that of the steel, automobile, or chemical industries.

The wide application of electronic technology has considerably boosted productivity and work efficiency in both the US and Canada, thus giving a powerful impetus to economic development. Everywhere we visited—from factories to research institutes, banks, shops, hotels, and homes—we saw widespread use of computers and information terminals. Americans estimate that the work done by their computers is comparable to that of 400 billion people. Experts believe that the US is becoming an information society, and an important indicator of this is the widespread use of electronic technology.

The composition of the American electronics industry has already developed from its former state in which the communications and the radio and television industries dominated the sector to one in which the computer, communications equipment, and semiconductor industries form the backbone. In 1981, computers, communications equipment, components, and consumer electronics made up 38.2%, 30.4%, 21.4%, and 10%, respectively of the industry's gross output value. In the components industry, the output value of the semiconductor industry was $7.8 billion, and that of the passive components industry was $2.94 billion, constituting 32% and 12%, respectively, of the gross output value of the components industry. This product mix indicates that the US electronics industry has already completely shifted to a new technological foundation based on semiconductors and large-scale integrated circuits.

Based on our visit, we believe that the US and Canadian electronics industries have the following significant characteristics.

1. The industries are taking the path of intensive development. The construction of factories and research facilities is capital intensive and utilizes state-of-the-art technology and equipment. Plants generally

consist of self-contained, nonpartitioned spaces with large-area air conditioners to facilitate the fast introduction of new products. In terms of production methods, the focus is on large-scale industrial production, with widespread use of computer-assisted design, manufacturing and testing, and computerized production management to boost labor productivity, guarantee product quality, and reduce production costs. The productivity at Hewlett-Packard's integrated circuit factory is $90,000 per worker per year. Under large-scale industrial production, the prices of integrated circuits and all kinds of electronic products have fallen drastically. Currently, the price of a microprocessor's integrated circuit is roughly equivalent to the face value of a postage stamp; a 16 K memory circuit costs only $1; and a 64 K one costs $6–8. In 1970, a million-bit computer cost about $1 million, but by 1980 the price had already dropped to $40,000. The reliability of brand name products has also reached a very high level. At 55°C, the performance degradation of Intel Corporation's integrated circuits is only 10^{-7}.

2. The industries are following the path of development through research and taking scientific research and product development as their guide. The decisive reason the US electronics industry is one of the best in the world is that it has mastered the important link of R&D. In order to maintain their competitiveness, American companies put great effort into R&D, and each year R&D costs reach about 10% of their total sales revenue. Research facilities generally all use cutting-edge technological equipment and design and testing procedures, and their labs are full of instruments and equipment. In order to ensure that the development of its hard drive technology keeps pace with the development of IBM computers, Memorex Corporation invests $120 million each year in its 129-person research center, and its lab is full of instruments and equipment such as sophisticated scanning electron microscopes, Auger spectrometers, and electron probes, and it uses 1–2 micron linear microelectronic technology to develop and manufacture thin-film magnetic heads. While investing large sums in research, all companies also hire many top-level scientists and engineers. With strong research teams, companies make many scientific and technological breakthroughs, produce an extensive array of products, and frequently introduce new generations of products. Bell Labs holds 19,823 patents, of which 303 were issued in 1982 alone.

Between 1971 and 1981, Intel turned out four generations of microprocessor integrated circuits, with the level of integration increasing by 45 times. Hewlett-Packard has more than 5000 product types, with an R&D period of usually 2–3 or 3–4 years for its electronic instruments. In 1982, half of the products it produced were new types that had been developed during the previous 3 years.

3. R&D work is well integrated with industrial production. All corporations are able to rapidly make use of their technological achievements in industrialized production of products. Bell Labs has a highly successful partnership with Western Electric, which sets an example that many countries follow. Bell Labs' work is divided into the two major branches: basic and applied research, and product development. Research work is done at Bell Labs' research centers while product development is undertaken at seven separate Bell Labs research centers set up in Western Electric factories. The task of product development is to translate scientific and technological discoveries into products that can be manufactured in factories. The staff at Bell Labs' seven product development centers account for 30% of its total personnel. We inspected a Western Electric plant in Allentown, where Bell's product development center has 843 employees responsible for product development work. This arrangement eliminates duplication of work by the plant.

4. Software accounts for a large proportion of production in the electronics industry. As the use of computers and integrated circuits has spread, aside from hardware manufacturing, software has come to account for an ever-increasing share of production in the US electronics industry. In addition to system software that manages computer hardware, due to the general use of computers in the design, manufacturing and testing stages of the production process, it is also necessary to develop a wide variety of application software. Honeywell's minicomputer systems and peripherals factory told us that it has 800 technical personnel, 200 of whom design hardware and 600 who design software, and that 60% of its total output value comes from software. At Bell Labs, 40% of technical personnel are involved in software development and in 1982 it put into operation the 5ESS program controlled digital and electronic switching system, which has 29 million lines of code. In order to meet its development needs, Western Electric has recently established a

software development center staffed by 2000 engineers. According to predictive analyses, the output value for microcomputer software alone may reach $2 billion in 1985, and may surpass $25 billion in 1990.

5. Companies accelerate depreciation of fixed assets to ensure that they use high-level, new technology in production and improve their competitive market position. Hewlett-Packard's normal period for plant depreciation is 15–40 years, and the period for machine tools and equipment is 3–10 years. In the area of integrated circuit production, this period is even shorter, with equipment normally replaced every 4 years. For this reason, companies spend large sums of money to expand production, generally more than 10% of their sales revenue.

6. In order to maximize their business potential, electronics companies adopt a system under which product divisions carry out integrated product development, production, marketing, and technical service, with corporate headquarters exercising management to achieve a unified objective. In general, all American and Canadian electronics companies use a management system under which operations are distributed across product divisions. Companies are divided into a number of divisions on the basis of product type, with each division being an operational entity under corporate headquarters. Hewlett-Packard, for instance, has 50 product divisions, each of which enjoys relative independence and autonomy, and thus resembles a small independent company. These divisions all carry out independent accounting and try to attain the profit target set by the corporate headquarters. In order to maintain their vitality, the maximum number of staff in a division does not exceed 2000. In all their business activities, the divisions maintain intimate relations with the market, meticulously research user needs and energetically open up markets. The pattern they follow is to take market demand as their starting point and develop new products. They then mass produce superior products, introduce them into the market through sales networks, provide after-sales technical service, feedback any problems consumers encounter during use to production departments, and further improve products before reintroducing them into the market. This is a closed-loop control system from the market to the market that conforms to the objective laws of commodity production and has great vitality. For this reason, companies always hire talented people

who understand both technology and economics to do market development work. Texas Instruments has adopted a unique setup, having established 12 regional technical centers in the US, Europe, and Japan that serve as a bridge between the company and users. These centers deal directly with users, researching their business and user needs, and subsequently providing solutions to their problems.

7. Electronics companies give high priority to investment in knowledge, and they constantly update their employees' knowledge and enhance their creativity. Capital competition includes competition for knowledge and for talent. All companies focus on investing in knowledge, and constantly educate and train their employees in new knowledge. In addition to providing short-term rotational employee training, Wang Laboratories has also established the Wang Institute of Graduate Studies. Bell Labs spent $1.8 billion on employee training in 1982. Approximately one in four Hewlett-Packard employees receives some kind of training every year. It encourages employees to take university courses, and cooperates with Stanford University, using its television system to train employees to master's degree level.

8. The geographical concentration of companies facilitates cooperative development. In the US for example, the integrated circuit industry is concentrated in Boston on the east coast, the San Francisco area on the west coast and the Dallas area in the southwest. Santa Clara County, which is south of San Francisco, has 1375 electronics companies, and because it is famous for semiconductors, it is called Silicon Valley. The semiconductors and integrated circuits manufactured in the region account for 40% of total American production of these products. Revolving around semiconductors and integrated circuits, all kinds of specialty companies, from materials to equipment to analytical and testing instruments, link up to form an integrated whole. Furthermore, famous universities such as Stanford University and the University of California at Berkeley are located there, which creates advantageous conditions for cooperative development.

Canada's electronics industry has its own unique characteristics. The Canadian communications industry is relatively advanced. Because the country is vast and many regions are sparsely populated. Canada focuses on the development of domestic satellite communications, automated shortwave communications, and mobile wireless communications equipment, most of which employs American technology.

III. TECHNOLOGICAL DEVELOPMENT TRENDS IN THE US AND CANADIAN ELECTRONICS INDUSTRIES

From our observations of all aspects of the US and Canadian electronics industries during the inspection tour, we reached a general understanding of the technological development trends in the industries; the most notable points of which are as follows.

A. US and Canadian electronics companies have perfected the production of large-scale integrated circuits and are making rapid headway in producing very-large-scale integrated circuits

In the US, large-scale integrated circuits are already being produced industrially, with a total output value of approximately $4 billion in 1982. In addition, computer and communications equipment companies' production of integrated circuits for internal use was worth about $3 billion. The production lines for large-scale integrated circuits generally use 4-inch wafers, and newly built production lines are already starting to use 5-inch wafers. Production equipment makes widespread use of many kinds of new technologies such as projection lithography (including reduction projection step-and-scan lithography equipment), dry etching, ion implantation, magnetron sputtering, and ion depositions. Companies are constantly honing their techniques to improve product yield. One important development is that Western Electric and Mostek are using the laser probe rectification technique in their production of 64K memory, which greatly increases their product yield. They say that after such rectification of 64K chips, the product yield can reach more than 90%.

In the area of very-large-scale integrated circuits, 256K dynamic memory units are already being produced in fairly large batches and it is expected that large-scale production could begin in three years. Several companies are currently in the process of designing 1 M memory. A number of companies have successively developed and begun producing 32-bit microprocessors and single-chip microcomputers. In 1982, Bell Labs came out with its BELL-MAC-32 microprocessor, which has 32-bit word length, 150,000 transistors and a graphic line width of 2.5 microns. Hewlett-Packard has released its HP-9000 single-chip microcomputer, which has 500,000 transistors and a graphic line width of 1.5 microns.

In the area of very-large-scale integrated circuits, in addition to memory units, microprocessors, single-chip microcomputers and gate array circuits, the new Cell Array concept has been introduced in order to develop micro-systems and accelerate the pace of circuit design. Bell Labs is in the midst of designing 100 types of different cell arrays, with each having 75 circuit elements and its own functions. When designing dedicated circuits or micro-systems, it is possible to design a wide variety of products by assembling cells in different ways, and this is opening up new avenues in the development of dedicated circuits. For this reason, Bell Labs is designing the EBES-4 electron beam exposure system, which can directly deposit a filament 0.5 microns wide on a silicon chip and arrange 200 million circuit elements on a 5-inch wafer. Furthermore, it is in the midst of a program of basic research work for the development of micron- and submicron-scale microprocessing equipment.

B. The focus of computer development is shifting toward minicomputers, microcomputers, and the applications systems for them

As a result of the development of integrated circuit technology, the performance of minicomputers and microcomputers has already attained or is approaching that of normal large and medium-sized computers. With the ever-expanding application of computers, demand for minicomputers and microcomputers is steadily increasing. IBM, whose mainstay is production of large and medium-sized computers, has modified its development strategy and thrown itself into the competitive fray in the micro-computer market. According to information provided by Hewlett-Packard and the analysis of relevant data, the demand for large and medium-sized computers will drop in the coming ten years, and by 1985 their sales volume may fall to 33% of total computer sales. Minicomputer and micro-computer sales will rise considerably, and by 1986 microcomputer sales could reach $11 billion. Personal computers, which have burst onto the scene, can be divided into many types, such as professional computers, home computers and briefcase computers. The development of home computers in particular has turned electronic computers into consumer electronics and opened up a vast market. There were 300,000 home computers sold in the US in 1981 and 2 million in 1982, and it is estimated that the figure will reach 9 million in 1983.

C. Communications and computer technology are becoming integrated and rapidly developing toward digitalization

Bell Labs believes that zeros and ones are the language of the information age. The main direction of the development of communications technology is its integration with computer technology and the progress from analog to digital systems. Based on our observations during the inspection tour, we now feel that this trend is developing much faster than we originally thought. In 1981, Bell Labs formulated a plan for developing the Integrated Services Digital Network (ISDN), according to which all types of information such as telephone and television signals, telegrams, data, graphs, and documents would be digitally encoded before being transmitted in a common format. Considerable progress has already been made in implementing several aspects of this plan. In 1982, 55% of Bell Labs' subscriber lines used program controlled digital exchanges. More than half of interoffice trunk lines already use digital transmission, and this figure is projected to exceed 90% by 1990. In order to accommodate the huge increase in subscriber information and meet the demand for connecting to computer networks, Bell Labs has developed subscriber line digital transmission multiplexing equipment and carried out technological upgrading of its subscriber line circuits. In order to adapt to the requirements of distributed transmission control, Bell Labs has successfully developed the Class 5 telephone electronic switching system (5ESS, Bell Labs' second-generation electronic switching system), with a capacity of between several hundred and 150,000 lines, and it can be expanded at any time using a 3020B microprocessor distributed control system. Between each of the module boards on the switching system, there are fiber-optic communications links for internal information transmission. The first telephone exchange to use this kind of switching technology went into operation in March 1982.

D. Fiber-optic communications are developing rapidly and will gradually become a major means of transmission

In 1981, optical cable sales reached $65 million and sales of optical communications equipment reached $35 million, with an annual growth rate of 50%. In 1982, Bell Labs invested $210 million in development of fiber-optic communications, and 60 interoffice junction fiber-optic communications systems have already gone into use. Western Electric has installed an FT3C digital fiber-optic communications system between Newark and Philadelphia, which is already in use. This system uses an optical cable containing 144 optical fibers, and has a capacity of 240,000 telephone calls. Before 1985, Western Electric will install another 1600 km of high-capacity fiber-optic communications systems. Last year, Bell Labs completed a trial in which it laid 108 km of deep-sea optical cable (at a depth of 5000 m, and with a capacity of 40,000 digital telephone calls), and it plans to put this cable into operation as part of the trans-Atlantic submarine optical communications system by 1988. When new intra-city and long-distance communications systems are built, optical cables will be increasingly used in place of standard electrical ones.

E. Electronic office automation equipment will develop into an emerging industry

The electronic office automation equipment industry will undergo dramatic growth. This emerging industry integrates computer and communications technology and is a development trend well deserving of attention. Reportedly more than half of workers in developed countries work in offices. There are 42 million office workers in the US, receiving $892 billion a year in wages, and their employers spend $85.6 billion a year on office equipment. Raising office efficiency is increasingly becoming an important factor in maintaining one's competitive position. Currently, about 2 million American office workers use computer terminals, but it is predicted that the number could rise to 18 million by 1990. Experts project that the world market demand for electronic office automation equipment could reach between $300 billion and $400 billion in 1990. This is a huge potential market and many companies are energetically trying to exploit it. Wang Laboratories, for example, has decided on a development strategy of concentrating on office automation equipment.

The Canadian Department of Communications has formulated plans for Nortel, Maitaier, and other corporations to concentrate efforts on exploiting the electronic office automation equipment market.

F. A new generation of military electronic equipment is in the process of being developed

At the 37th International Exhibition on Military Electronics and Communications Equipment, we learned that the US is energetically developing a new generation of military electronic equipment, and several points are worthy of note.

Military electronic equipment is not only produced as stand-alone sets of equipment but is increasingly developing into a form of electronic systems engineering. A new generation of early-warning radar aircraft, third-generation defense communications satellites, and naval aviation global tactical satellite systems were among the equipment shown at the exhibition.

Exploitation of the electromagnetic spectrum is rapidly progressing in the direction of using higher frequencies. Thompson Ramo Wooldridge Inc. announced that its microwave electronic components can already reach 200 GHz, and it is already using its millimeter wave technology in space communications, short-distance all-weather radar, missile homing guidance, radar electronic warfare, and top-secret communications.

Electronic computer technology is increasingly being applied in all kinds of widely used military electronic equipment, and it is becoming a key link in command, control, communications, and information processing. Most computers used by the military are reinforced civilian computers, and the software systems of both are compatible.

Radar technology is developing in the direction of entirely solid-state components. General Electric has already successfully developed the TPS-59 L-band, solid-state, phased-array, 3D radar. Texas Instruments is in the process of developing and producing 2000 units of next-generation airborne phased-array, solid-state radar systems for the US Air Force.

A US company, International Telephone and Telegraph Corporation (ITT), announced that its avionics equipment division was doing R&D on the Integrated Communications, Navigation and Identification Avionics (ICNIA) system for the US Air Force. According to sources, this system will replace 14 non-integrated pieces of electronic equipment currently used for communications, navigation and identification, and reduce the cost, size, weight and power consumption by 50%. It uses a fast transversal filter radio frequency tuner, a high-efficiency solid-state amplifier module, and ultra-high-speed integrated-circuit digital signal processing technology, and it can operate on multiple channels at different frequencies at once.

Rockwell Collins exhibited an AN/ARC-182 (V) airborne transceiver, which operates in the 30–400 MHz frequency band and weighs only 4 kg.

In the area of tactical communications, many kinds of digital tropospheric scattering communications equipment, automated shortwave communications equipment and frequency-hopping, anti-jam portable transceivers were exhibited. ITT exhibited the SINCGARS-V airborne radio system that operates in the 30–80 MHz frequency band, capable of randomly hopping frequency to any of the 2320 channels.

IV. COMMENTS AND SUGGESTIONS FOR MAKING USE OF THE FAVORABLE INTERNATIONAL SITUATION TO IMPORT US AND CANADIAN ELECTRONIC TECHNOLOGY

Our country's electronics industry lags behind in science and technology. While adhering to the policy of self-reliance, we should also make use of the favorable international situation by attempting to bring in advanced technology and skilled personnel from abroad. This is an important measure for moving the starting point of our work forward and speeding up the development of our electronics industry.

1. We need to actively import US and Canadian electronic technology. Integrated circuits and computers are the development priorities of our electronics industry, and we need to make breakthroughs in these areas first. It is our intention to import the production technology for large-scale integrated circuit products, particularly 64K memory and 16-bit microprocessors, and production technology for large and medium-sized computers, super minicomputers, microcomputers, and high-capacity disk drives from the US; and also to import from Canada the production technology to build a satellite communications ground station.

2. We need to explore how to set up an R&D company in the US to provide an important avenue for us to absorb and import American technology. There are a lot of Chinese-American experts in Silicon Valley, and they have many small companies of their own. We need to look into setting up an R&D company in this area with either a foreign company or a Chinese-American owned company, and send personnel there to undertake design and development work. This would be very helpful for making full use of favorable conditions to import technology and secure market information.

3. We need to increase personnel exchanges, initiate cooperative research, and send people to American and Canadian electronics companies and universities for work-study programs. In this way, we can send more people abroad to study, which will help speed up our development. We also need to attract talent and invite professional and technological personnel from American and Canadian universities, companies, and research facilities to come to China to give lectures on new technology, develop academic exchanges, and carry out short-term research.

4. We need to set up joint ventures in order to import technology, study operations and management methods, gain entry into the international market, and learn how to compete in order to constantly raise the level of our electronics industry through competition. Therefore, it is our intention to initially set up a joint venture with Hewlett-Packard to produce electronic instruments and computers, as well as a joint venture with Rainbow Electronics in Canada to make micro-computers, and acquire experience before progressively expanding our efforts.

Revitalize Our Country's Electronics Industry*

*Originally published in the *People's Daily* on September 11, 1983.

September 11, 1983

Since the beginning of this century, and particularly since the end of World War II, the electronics industry has developed rapidly. The widespread application of electronic technology and products has led to a transformation in production technology and social activities. Economically developed countries generally attach great importance to the electronics industry and give high priority to its development.

I. ENSURE THAT THE ELECTRONICS INDUSTRY PLAYS ITS ROLE IN THE FOUR MODERNIZATIONS

The report on the Sixth Five-Year Plan for National Economic and Social Development stated that the electronics industry plays an extremely significant role in modernization, and we should place great emphasis on its development and progressively use electronic technology in all sectors of the national economy. After more than three decades of development, our electronics industry has begun to reach a good economy of scale and become an emerging industrial sector with a relatively complete range of specialties that combines military and civilian applications and the efforts of both central and local authorities. As our country's four modernizations progress, electronic science and technology will be extensively applied in all areas, including industry, agriculture, transportation, culture, education, health, and national defense, and will produce immense social and economic benefits. For instance, the use of automatic safety controls and regulators in the power industry can significantly reduce coal consumption and losses due to power outages. The use of electronic energy management technology in the steel industry can save large quantities of energy. If computers are adopted to manage railways, transport efficiency can greatly increase. If computers are also used to manage logistics and financing, inventories will decrease and the turnover of funds will accelerate. The list goes on and on.

Revitalizing the national economy has to depend on technological progress. Electronic technology is an important indicator of modernization. In this sense, without the electronics industry, there would be no four modernizations. Our electronics industry, however, lags far behind the world's advanced level and has a long way to go to meet the needs of domestic development. We therefore need to develop this industry more quickly, so that it can supply the army and the national economy with electronic technology and equipment, and provide the people with electronic products to enrich their cultural lives.

II. ESTABLISH A RATIONALLY STRUCTURED ELECTRONICS INDUSTRY

At present, the major structural problem with our country's electronics industry is that the proportion of electronic capital goods is too low. In economically developed countries, the proportion of the output value of big-ticket electronic products (including capital goods and military products) is generally about 50% of the industry's gross output value, or even 70% in certain countries; whereas in China, the figure is around 20% and the output value of electronic capital goods accounts for only 10% of the total. Therefore, it has become an urgent task for the electronics industry to rigorously develop capital goods to meet the needs of economic development.

In accelerating the development of electronic capital goods, we ought to persistently give high priority to military products and successfully develop civilian applications of military technology. The development of electronic military equipment has a bearing on national security and therefore must be our top priority. In addition, we need to actively implement the policy of integrating military and civilian technologies and use similar military technology to develop electronic equipment for civilian use.

Development of electronic capital goods must adhere to the orientation of serving the needs of key development areas and technological upgrading of all industries and sectors. We need to gain an understanding of demand in all sectors of the economy, tailor our research and production according to their needs, and strive to develop and provide them with whole electronic devices.

Electronic capital goods are expensive, incorporate complicated technologies, have long production cycles, and require investment of relatively high levels of technological resources and funding. Therefore, we can produce inexpensive quality products and meet demand only by improving operations and management, raising product quality, and reducing costs.

While speeding up development of electronic capital goods, we should continue to emphasize developing production of electronic consumer products. On one hand, we need to increase their variety and improve their quality, and on the other we need to expand into new areas and develop new types of products.

III. CONCENTRATE ON KEY PROJECTS

Our electronics industry has a weak foundation and a low level of production technology and product quality, and the country's financial resources are also limited and lag far behind developed countries. In developing the electronics industry, we must proceed from our country's actual conditions, do some things while setting others aside, and concentrate our resources on key areas, the most crucial technologies, the most important products, and projects with the greatest impact on the overall situation.

What are the electronics industry's key areas? At present, we need to focus on electronic military equipment, large-scale integrated circuits, and electronic computers. If these three areas are developed, they can stimulate the development of the entire industry.

While developing electronic military equipment, large-scale integrated circuits, and electronic computers, we also need to prioritize tasks; it is impossible do everything at once. In developing computers, we need to focus on minicomputers and microcomputers, develop all kinds of application systems, and achieve balanced development between minicomputers and microcomputers on one hand and medium-sized computers on the other, between host computers and peripherals, and between hardware and software. In the short run, the development of integrated circuits needs to focus on the industrialized mass production of low- and medium-grade large-scale integrated circuits, thereby establishing a foundation for the intensive mass production of computers and integrated circuits, significantly reducing costs, expanding areas of use, and opening up domestic and international markets.

At the same time as we focus on key areas, it is also important for us to achieve balanced development in other fields such as the radar, communications, radio and television, and components industries. We need to consider all fields from an overall strategic perspective, resolutely narrow the scope of our activities, determine priorities, and successfully carry out the overall planning.

IV. PROMOTE SCIENTIFIC AND TECHNOLOGICAL PROGRESS AND KNOWLEDGE DEVELOPMENT

The electronics industry is dependent on research and development (R&D). Scientific and technological progress and knowledge development are the foundations for its development.

To advance technological progress, we plan to focus on developing, disseminating, and applying microelectronic and computer technologies representative of the advanced world level around 1980s during the Seventh Five-Year Program period. In order to better integrate research with production, we need to reorganize the research institutes we now have, set up a number of technology development centers in the industry, and then progressively establish consortiums of research institutes and manufacturers, thus integrating research, design, testing, production, and business operations, and bringing research facilities in close association with manufacturers.

In recent years, the electronics industry has imported some technologies and equipment from abroad, and this has greatly helped to improve the research and production conditions in the industry. In the future, to meet the needs of technological upgrading, we will continue to import equipment, run joint ventures, and engage in license trade to bring in appropriate and advanced technologies. Some components, spare parts, or even ready-to-assemble kits badly needed for research and production, but which we currently cannot make on our own, can also be imported, subject to the necessary controls, in order to gain time and satisfy user demands.

Human resource development is the key to developing the electronics industry. Skilled personnel training needs to begin with giving equal weight to increasing numbers and improving quality. Over the Seventh Five-Year Program period, we intend to increase the proportion of scientists and engineers in the electronics industry workforce from 16% to 20% at the central level and from 6.4% to 10% at the local level. In addition, we will work hard to train high-caliber scientists and engineers, find a way to help workers update their knowledge, and constantly improve the professional, technical, and cultural levels of scientists, engineers, managers, and other employees through various forms of education.

Accelerate the Development of the Electronics Industry and Meet the Challenges of the New Technological Revolution*

February 10, 1984

The new technological revolution is eliciting heated discussion both in China and abroad. Although everyone calls it by various names, they all agree that a major breakthrough in the productive forces is likely by the end of this century or the start of the next. Electronic computers, bioengineering, fiber-optic communications, lasers, marine exploitation, and new materials are a group of emerging technologies that will rapidly permeate all aspects of production and daily life, thus triggering profound changes in human society. Despite the fact that disagreements exist about what this new technology encompasses, it is widely agreed that electronic technology, especially microelectronic technology, will play a leading role in these emerging technologies.

While some traditional industries in Western countries have struggled in recent years, a number of high-tech industries, particularly the IT industry, have enjoyed rampant development that has initiated changes in social and economic structures. There is a qualitative difference between changes caused mainly by IT and those brought about by textile machinery, steam power, and electrical technology in the past. While traditional technologies merely increased people's physical power, IT has expanded their intellectual power. Some Western academics believe that this is the key feature of the new technological revolution.

In the field of modern science, electronic technology is employed in almost all advanced scientific instruments. Abroad, computers are widely used to aid design, manufacturing, and testing. Research in our country also employs

---

*Excerpt from an exclusive interview with an *Economic Daily* reporter.

electronic computers to do large quantities of complex calculations beyond human capabilities. Electronic technology permeates everything it touches and has a wide range of applications, and in combination with other industrial technologies has generated a number of new products and expanded into many new markets. The use of this technology can also save huge amounts of energy. According to statistics, there are now nearly 200,000 industrial boilers in China, consuming hundreds of millions of tons of coal annually. If microprocessors were employed to control their combustion, 5% of that coal could be saved. This alone represents a considerable amount of coal saved nationwide each year, and there are countless similar examples I could cite.

In today's world, technological development yields something new every day. How to seize the opportunity and make the right technological choice to develop emerging industries while carrying out technological upgrading in traditional ones, so as to take a reliable path of rapid economic development suited to one's country's conditions, has become an issue that every country must address. What should we do on the eve of the new technological revolution? Over the past several months, we have been considering the development strategy and technology policy we will adopt in the development plan for the next 10–20 years. This is the challenge we now face. In my view, there are only two possibilities, each leading to a different kind of future. One possibility is that we make the correct policy decision, grasp this opportunity, and use it to the full to accelerate the development of our electronics industry, thereby narrowing the gap between our country and developed countries. The other possibility is that we formulate poor policies, give improper guidance, and forfeit this golden opportunity, thus affecting the course of our four modernizations and widening the gap between us and developed countries. Needless to say, we must do our utmost to pursue the first possibility and bring about the future it promises and avert the second possibility and the future it would bring.

At present, a new trend is emerging in the development of the electronics industry nationwide. In 1983, the industry's gross output value increased by 27% over the previous year and profits also rose significantly; the only time in recent years the industry has achieved such impressive results. In addition, the enthusiasm of all regions in the country for developing the industry has risen to unprecedented levels, and many regions have given high priority to progress in electronic technology and the development of the electronics industry. For example, Shanghai has determined to give the industry the vanguard status in its economic development, and Guangdong has proposed developing the industry into a pillar of its provincial economy. Beijing, Tianjin, Fujian, Jiangsu, and other provinces and municipalities directly under the central government have also given high priority to the development and application of microcomputers and are striving to make high-level breakthroughs in order to stimulate the development of other advanced technologies and their entire regional economies. Some industry sectors are also vigorously developing electronic science and technology and importing and assimilating advanced scientific and technological achievements from abroad. This situation is extremely conducive to the electronics industry's development. In developing this industry, however, we need to stay grounded in reality, respect science, focus on priorities, choose the proper line of attack, and proceed in a down-to-earth manner. We need to avoid trying to make uniform progress across all regions with no sense of precedence, and guard against the tendency of every region to strive to be self-sufficient and to compete to expand production facilities and get new ones approved. We must bear in mind that developing and utilizing high technologies like microelectronics is vastly different from producing television sets and radio/tape recorders and that not everyone can do this work effectively in a short period. Rather, it requires those who have more scientific and technological knowledge and have received a certain amount of training. Therefore, we also need to train large numbers of hardware and software professionals in order to meet the needs of industrialized production and widespread application. According to a preliminary investigation, development of microelectronic technology demands more than 70 types of specialists. In terms of hardware, in addition to host computers, we also need a wide variety of peripherals, including many precision electronic machines. Some aspects of developing peripherals can be even more difficult than the problems faced in building host computers. As for software, in addition to system software, software engineers need to constantly engage in the secondary development of application software in order for users to make full use of their computers. Therefore, we need to develop software applications from the perspective of systems engineering and develop microelectronic software in a planned, proportional, and multilevel way. For investment- and technology-intensive projects that have strict environmental requirements, such as the building of integrated circuit factories and research institutes, we need to carry out unified nationwide planning and follow a path of intensive development concentrated in a few suitable locations and not let the industry become dispersed, thus wasting human and material resources.

We can make arrangements to increase production of microcomputers by an appropriate amount. We need to more extensively spread applications of electronic technology. Generally speaking, to develop microelectronics in China, research institutes, manufacturers, and end-users need to fully collaborate with each other and divide the work among themselves so that they all have their own emphasis and the mistakes of low-level redundant development do not get repeated. In addition, we need to energetically train skilled personnel and work hard to propagate microelectronic technology.

Silicon Valley in California is a world-famous electronic research center and important electronics industry production base. It was not established on the basis of a plan; rather it formed naturally as a result of a variety of favorable conditions prevailing there, for example, the presence of Stanford University, whose main orientation is cutting-edge science and engineering as well as a host of research facilities and related manufacturers. Furthermore, California's policies and laws provide a number of preferential conditions, and Silicon Valley has pleasant weather and clean air. All this provides favorable conditions for its development, and the area has gradually become a high-tech research center and industrialized production base.

We also need to consider concentrating our microelectronic industry to an appropriate degree in a location with suitable conditions. For example, the Yangtze River Delta has many electronics factories, strong technological resources, and favorable conditions for collaboration, and its weather is also suitable for developing high-tech industries, so it should become a key area. However, capabilities there are still scattered for various reasons. Therefore, we need to undertake further rational planning, promote consortiums, and do all we can to concentrate our microelectronic industry bases in accordance with actual conditions.

This year and next, the electronics industry needs to focus on the following five areas of work: giving high priority to ensuring that the army obtains the electronic equipment it needs; speeding up the manufacturing and application of microcomputers and developing the technology for small-, large-, and medium-sized computers on the basis of our needs; vigorously developing electronic capital goods; continuing to steadily develop electronic consumer products; and intensifying efforts to develop basic products with the focus on large-scale integrated circuits and military components. If we do well in these areas, we will lay the groundwork for the future development of the electronics industry.

The rapid development of electronic technology worldwide both poses a challenge and offers an opportunity. By learning from the experiences of other countries and directly adopting their new technological advances, we can skip certain traditional development stages and develop faster.

Gradually Explore a Chinese Style Development Path for the Electronics Industry*

February 21, 1984

The main aim of this meeting is to discuss and determine the main thrust and objectives for the electronics industry in the last 2 years of the Sixth Five-Year Program period, and also to exchange views on the approach for developing the industry during the Seventh Five-Year Program period and beyond. At this meeting, we need to gain a clear understanding of the situation, unify our thinking, and coordinate policies and actions, so that this year and next we can concentrate our efforts on breakthroughs in key areas that will help initiate a new phase in the development of the electronics industry.

I. THE NEW SITUATION CONFRONTING OUR COUNTRY'S ELECTRONICS INDUSTRY

At present, our electronics industry faces the following new circumstances and trends that deserve close attention.

The new technological revolution, a subject of intense debate both at home and abroad, is intimately related to the electronics industry's development, and we should give it our full attention.

The new technological revolution, though called by various names, implies that at the end of this century and the beginning of the next, a series of new technologies already developed or to be developed— electronic computers, bioengineering, fiber-optic communications, lasers,

---

*Report presented at a national working meeting of heads of departments and bureaus of the electronics industry under the title of "Welcome the New Technological Revolution and Accelerate the Development of the Electronics Industry."

marine exploration, and new materials—will become widely used in production and society, greatly stimulating the productive forces and bringing great changes to society, the economy, and social activities. Western economists and sociologists call this the "third wave" or the "Fourth Industrial Revolution." No matter what they call it, all agree that having reached a high level of industrialization in the 1950s and 1960s, developed countries are now shifting from an industrial society to an information society, or so to speak, a knowledge society. They say, "The productivity of knowledge has already become the key to productivity, competitive strength, and economic achievement." The emergence of this kind of situation and viewpoint reflects a major trend in economic and social change in postindustrial capitalist countries. In recent years, a number of traditional industries in Western countries are facing hard times while at the same time, a number of high-tech industries, especially the IT industry, have experienced spectacular growth, changing the social and economic structure. This is a well-known fact.

Frederick Engels said, "Science was for Marx a historically dynamic, revolutionary force." The history of production in human society tells us that great developments in science and great technological inventions have given rise to profound revolutions in social production and activities. Past industrial revolutions all began with the invention of new technologies, leading to comprehensive social change. This is a lesson from history as well as an objective law governing the course of events. Because of this, the new technological revolution has already become the focus of worldwide attention, and countries of all kinds, each with its own objectives, are studying it and adopting measures to meet it. We are now focused on carrying out the four modernizations, so we should place greater emphasis on studying the new technological revolution.

First, we need to fully appreciate the position and role of electronic technology in the new technological revolution. We need to realize that an important hallmark of this revolution is the widespread application of electronic technology and that electronic technology, especially microelectronic technology, plays a leading role in it. Electronic technology is the leading technology of our times, and it typifies the new productive forces. Its widespread application will open up for the human race a vast high-speed, high-efficiency, and high-value world, and will provide an advanced technological foundation for us to attain a high degree of socialist material progress, and cultural and ethical progress. The development and application of electronic technology, especially microelectronic technology, is closely related to the breadth and depth of a country's new technological revolution and the level of economic development. We must fully understand that the electronics industry bears a great deal of responsibility as our country carries out this new technological revolution. Its five most fundamental responsibilities are as follows:

1. Provide advanced military electronic equipment to modernize national defense;
2. Provide various kinds of equipment necessary to create high-speed, accurate, and free-flowing information systems;
3. Use microelectronic technology to upgrade production equipment and raise its technological level;
4. Provide the most effective information tools for intelligence development and scientific research; and
5. Provide a large quantity and variety of electronic products that promote cultural and ethical progress and enrich people's material and cultural lives.

Second, the new technological revolution requires that our country's electronics industry must first undergo revolutionary transformation. Based on our present understanding, our country's electronics industry must institute the following changes.

1. We need to strategically transform product technology by shifting from a focus on discrete components to an emphasis on integrated circuits, from an emphasis on analog technology to a focus on digital technology, and from human control of processes to the use of intelligent tools.
2. The industrial structure needs to undergo massive transformation from light industry (with output value dominated by ordinary consumer electronics) to heavy industry (where electronic capital goods occupy a larger share); from the foundation of traditional manufacturing technology to a new foundation of microelectronic manufacturing technology, such as micromachining, precision analysis, and automated

monitoring; and from the production of individual accessory products to providing services for complete systems engineering.

3. Major changes need to be made in the human resources structure. It is becoming increasingly evident that the electronics industry is an R&D industry, and that the pace of technological progress is constantly increasing, and the kinds of skills people have and the types of research undertaken are also increasingly important in determining the course of development of the electronics industry. To accommodate the development of the microelectronics industry, we require more experts in more fields. Especially since software development has entered the domain of the electronics industry, it has become an important part of it and the proportion of software engineers must dramatically increase.

4. The kinds of knowledge every type of worker has must change accordingly; otherwise, they will be unable to adapt to the demands of the development of the microelectronics industry. Therefore if we do not promptly carry out education to update people's knowledge, we will miss the opportunity to adapt.

Third, we need to calmly analyze the significant effects this new technological revolution can have on our country's electronics industry. In developed countries, electronic technology has already progressed to a very high level, is widely applied, and is still progressing rapidly. A number of important characteristics that typify the new technological revolution have already begun to manifest now. This kind of situation is both an opportunity and a challenge to the development of our country's electronics industry. It is an opportunity because, given the development of the new technological revolution, the government has granted a strategic position to the electronics industry and is providing more support to its development. In addition, international technological exchanges will further expand, making it possible for us to directly utilize a number of foreign advanced scientific and technological achievements to skip some traditional development stages in some areas of our electronics industry and thereby accelerate the pace of the industry's development and narrow the gap between us and the advanced world level. It is a challenge because, under the conditions of the new technological revolution, we face fiercer competition from foreign electronic products, so our research and new-product development work must adapt to the demands imposed by the rapid development of microelectronic technology. Faced with this situation, there are two possibilities for the development of our country's national electronics industry, each leading to a different kind of future. One possibility and the future it would bring are that we make the correct policy decision, and grasp this opportunity and use it to the full. We will actively import and use new technological achievements, energetically push our country's progress in electronic science and technology forward, and accelerate the development of our electronics industry, thereby constantly narrowing the gap between us and developed countries, while gradually adapting to the requirements of the four modernizations and claiming a share of the international market. The other possibility and the future it would bring are that we will stick to our old ways of thinking, formulate poor policies, give improper guidance, develop slowly, and forfeit this golden opportunity. The result of this would be a constantly widening gap between us and developed countries, which would affect the course of our four modernizations. However, generally speaking, the new technological revolution is an effective stimulus to the development of our country's electronics industry, and we should energetically pursue the first possibility and bring about the future it promises while averting the second possibility and the future it would bring.

Fourth, we need to actively research and adopt policies to meet the challenges we face. The present situation indicates that the new technological revolution is still in its infancy, and that its decisive influence on the world economy will only genuinely manifest itself in the 1990s. Many countries are making the most of this opportune moment to research policies. The US has invested huge sums to create a powerful computer industry, and is still pouring money into research and manufacturing of next-generation computers in an effort to maintain its high-tech dominance. Japan has taken the path of government–public collaboration, enacted a law to invigorate its information industry, and formulated a plan for nationwide cooperative research and manufacturing of fifth-generation computers in order to do all it can to compete with the US for high-tech dominance. Western European countries are also active in this area, and are planning the creation of a European electronic consortium to strengthen cooperation and create areas of superiority in order to become better able to develop technology and compete in the market.

There is a great disparity between our country's technology base and economic strength and those of developed countries, and the Chinese government is now studying and discussing what kinds of policies we should adopt concerning this new technological revolution. However, one matter has already been decided: we need to give high priority to the electronics industry and give it greater strategic importance. The key to the electronics industry playing a role in promoting our country's new technological revolution is for it to revolutionize itself. It cannot just grow quantitatively; rather, it should take the lead in using microelectronic technology to upgrade all kinds of existing products, that is, to improve qualitatively. This should not only be our objective, but also become our development principle. On our development path, we need to take independence and self-reliance as our starting point, and actively import advanced and appropriate technologies in an effort to save time by skipping a number of traditional stages of industrial development. We need to keep an eye on and study developments of the new technological revolution abroad and not lose the opportunity to adopt corresponding policies. In this manner, we can gradually explore a Chinese style development path for the electronics industry.

In recent years, inspired by the new technological revolution, all regions of the country have manifested an unprecedented enthusiasm for developing the electronics industry, and many provinces and municipalities directly under the central government have given high priority to developing electronic technology and the electronics industry in their area. This is an extremely favorable situation. We should not only highly value their enthusiasm, but also actively help localities draw up development plans. However, it would be all too easy for a situation to develop in which localities strive to be self-sufficient and compete to get new facilities approved. We must endeavor to avoid such a scenario and prevent new incongruities.

As a result of the guidance of a series of principles and policies adopted since the Third Plenary Session of the Eleventh CPC Central Committee and the Twelfth National Party Congress, the current domestic political and economic situations are both very favorable, which is very beneficial for the development of the electronics industry.

First, due to the whole Party and the people of all ethnic groups uniting as one and working hard, our country's national economy continues to grow steadily, our political situation is more stable, and we are making greater socialist cultural and ethical progress. Our country's achievements in all areas are very heartening, and encourage the whole Party and the people of all ethnic groups to continue to accelerate the pace at which we enter a new phase of socialist modernization.

Second, Party rectification work is now in full swing, and this will inevitably promote improvement in the Party's work style, increase the militancy of the Party's organizations, and become a powerful driving force that provides impetus to production and all of our work.

Third, as the national economy steadily develops and greater effort is put into developing key projects, all sectors of the national economy are accelerating their pace of development and giving an important place to promoting technological progress and intensifying technological upgrading in enterprises, thus creating new demand for electronic capital goods. As the living standards of the masses, particularly the rural population, rise, their purchasing power for consumer electronics increases dramatically. This provides a new impetus for the development of the electronics industry.

The electronics industry has made major progress in production, R&D, and facilities construction, all of its economic indicators have reached historical highs, and an inspiring new development situation has emerged.

In 1983, the target set in the national plan for the gross output value of the electronics industry for the year was reached with 2 months to spare. The total output value for the entire year was 14.026 billion yuan, 126.4% of the target for the year set out in the plan, and an increase of 27.4% over 1982. Furthermore, this figure met the target for the last year of the Sixth Five-Year Program period with 2 years to spare. In 1983, the profits of enterprises in the electronics industry nationwide grew much faster than production, and totaled 1.536 billion yuan, an increase of 70.5% over 1982, and the profitability of enterprises directly under the Ministry of Electronics Industry exceeded the target set for the last year of the Sixth Five-Year Program period. In the vast majority of provinces and municipalities directly under the central government, the output value, sales revenue, and profits of the industry all simultaneously increased. There were 15 provinces and autonomous regions in which the industry recorded overall losses in 1982, 14 of which earned a profit in 1983. In contrast to previous years, the targets for variety, quantity, and quality of electronic products were all fully met, which is an achievement unmatched in recent years and represents the emergence of a new phase in which great increases are made on the basis of a complete recovery.

All key projects achieved good results. Many achievements came in research and new product development. Some production methods were improved through the use of imported technology. Leading bodies at all levels were replenished and strengthened through institutional reform, making their cadres more revolutionary, younger, better educated, and more professionally competent. The work of comprehensively rectifying enterprises, with the focus on improving economic performance, raised their quality. These are the conditions that enabled us to make such great progress last year, as well as laid an invaluable foundation for us to win new victories in the future. However, we need to acknowledge that the successes achieved hide problems we cannot overlook, the most important of which is that the increase in output value and profits still comes mostly from consumer electronics such as TVs, radios, and radio/tape recorders, while electronic capital goods that serve the national economy still amount to just over 10%, and this irrational industrial structure still needs to be changed at the root level. Therefore, the foundation for the successes achieved in 1983 is relatively weak and it will be difficult for the industry to withstand market shocks. In the course of future development, the industry will need to not only continue to deal with old problems, such as redundancy and dispersion, but also address the new challenges of short supply and rising prices of energy and materials, and it will be very difficult for the industry to further improve its economic performance amidst falling electronic product prices. Faced with the rapid progress of global electronic technology, we must make even greater efforts in order to face this situation squarely and close the gap. We absolutely cannot afford to be blindly optimistic and treat this matter lightly.

II. MEDIUM- AND LONG-TERM PLANNING AND TASKS FOR THE LAST 2 YEARS OF THE SIXTH FIVE-YEAR PROGRAM PERIOD

Since the middle of last year, we have constantly explored and studied the issue of how to accelerate the development of the electronics industry, and have also formulated a medium- and long-term development program on the basis of the new situation. In August of last year, we presented a report on the program to the State Council and in October submitted the Report on Accelerating the Development of the Electronics Industry, which makes suggestions on goals, strategic priorities, and the main development principles and measures for the Seventh Five-Year Program period and up to 2000.

The overall thinking is (assuming the government adopts corresponding measures) to octuple the 1980 gross output value of the electronics industry by 2000 (an average annual increase of 10.9%), raise the industry's proportion of the country's gross industrial and agricultural output value from its 1980 level of 1.4% to about 3%, basically adapt to the requirements of the four modernizations, elevate the level of major products and production technologies to the level the world's advanced industrialized countries must have reached around 1990, and raise the level of a number of technologies to the world's advanced level prevailing at that time.

Based on the above thinking, we need to complete solid groundwork and build a good foundation in the Seventh Five-Year Program period. The goals are to double the 1980 gross output value of the industry by 1990, an average increase of 9.5% a year; increase its proportion of the country's gross industrial and agricultural output value to about 2%; and elevate the level of major products and production technologies to the level the world's advanced industrialized countries reached around 1980.

In 1983, we reached the target set in the Sixth Five-Year Program for the 1985 gross output value 2 years ahead of schedule, and the manner in which we carry out our work this year and next will have a great effect on whether we complete the tasks of the Seventh Five-Year Program and attain the strategic objectives set for 2000. We believe that in guiding the work during the last 2 years of the Sixth Five-Year Program period, we need to focus on making good preparations for developing the electronics industry during the Seventh Five-Year Program period. For projects that will go into operation and produce results in 1985 and afterwards, we need to adopt systems engineering methods and wage a number of tough campaigns to make breakthroughs in product development and the level of production technology in order to lay a good foundation for future development.

A. Give top priority to ensuring the upgrading of military electronic equipment

In accordance with the principles of "shortening the front, focusing on priorities, tackling research, and accelerating upgrading" and "transforming equipment, improving procedures, raising quality, and lowering costs," in the near term we need to focus on supplying the ground forces with electronic equipment, actively develop electronic equipment for the air force and navy, and improve electronic equipment in our strategic armaments and satellites.

In the last 2 years of the Sixth Five-Year Program period, we need to continue to adopt new technology and endeavor to improve the performance and quality of existing military electronic equipment. We need to stress priorities, pool all of our resources to achieve complete success in crucial areas, and develop a quantity of new equipment. We also need to accelerate scientific research and the development of new technology, develop military electronic equipment in the direction of systematization, integration, and digitalization, and make it more intelligent and highly reliable, as well as create conditions for solving the problem of aviation equipment functioning poorly at low altitudes and for developing rapid response electronic combat equipment.

B. Spare no effort to produce basic products, with the focus on large-scale integrated circuits and military-use components

We need to assiduously develop highly reliable, high-precision, low-power consumption, microminiaturized products, and increase production quantities without compromising product quality, in an effort to satisfy the demand of all sectors.

To develop integrated circuits, we need to accelerate the development of bases in both north and south China, and begin establishing research and production consortiums spread over Shanghai, Wuxi, and Shaoxing to create the conditions for large-scale development during the Seventh Five-Year Program period. Before 1985, we need to focus on mastering the technology for industrialized mass production of small- and medium-scale integrated circuits and achieving a breakthrough in the technology for the industrialized mass production of medium- and low-grade, large-scale integrated circuits. We need to strive to solve the difficult problem of ensuring the quality of small- and medium-scale integrated circuits having anywhere from several tens up to a thousand components on a wafer produced on a large production line and do everything possible to increase yield and decrease the failure rate. Products made in accordance with the seven special standards[1] should have tolerances of 10^{-7} m and consumer electronics should have tolerances of 10^{-6} m. In addition, one or two production lines should have the capacity to produce more than 10 million items per year and the whole country should be able to produce 50 million per year at a cost that enables them to sell at the same price that imported integrated circuits cost in the late 1970s. We need to attain stable batch production of circuits for memory, 4- and 8-bit microcomputers, computers, instruments and meters, communications equipment, electronic clocks and watches, and TV speakers, all of which have a degree of integration of around 10,000 components, and we need to produce a total of 3–5 million of them per year. At the same time, we need to

---

[1]The seven special standards are special batches, special technology, special personnel, special equipment, special materials, special inspection, and special cards. "Special batches" refers to the practice in researching and manufacturing electronic components used in national defense projects, weapons systems, and military electronic equipment that have rigorous reliability requirements of producing them in special batches. For these components, "special batch" supervision is strictly carried out for the entire production process, including materials feeding, assembly, testing, and delivery. "Special technology" refers to specially formulated technological standards to ensure high reliability. "Special personnel" refers to the selection of personnel with a strong sense of responsibility and a high level of technical and managerial ability for training in reliability technology and management, and for production or managerial jobs in the manufacturing of high reliability products after they have been certified. "Special equipment" refers to the selection of advanced equipment and instruments that meet high-reliability requirements to be used in the research and production of military products. "Special materials" refers to the selection and use of the best raw materials and parts, and the adoption of a strict system for storing, inspecting, maintaining, and using them in accordance with the principle of using specified materials and processing them at specified factories under specified technical conditions. "Special inspection" refers to the formulation of special inspection criteria and the carrying out of inspections of raw materials, parts, semifinished products, and finished products by professional inspectors. "Special cards" refers to the printing of special flow-path cards and quality-tracking cards, which record the production of products, either by batch or individually. The cards should completely record the actual conditions of every step of a product's production from materials feeding to the time it leaves the factory and should be signed by every person responsible for each step of the process.

actively carry out R&D on high-grade, large- and very-large-scale integrated circuits. We need to finalize the design of 16K single-supply NMOS dynamic memory cells and 4K CMOS static memory cells and put them into production, and build satisfactory prototypes of 16K NMOS static memory cells, 64K NMOS dynamic memory cells, 16-bit microprocessor circuits, and ultra-high speed GaAs circuits.

We need to endeavor to produce accessories for products utilizing integrated circuits in accordance with priorities set by the government. By 1985, our country will produce more than 1,000 kinds of integrated circuit products, including more than 300 kinds of small and medium-scale integrated-circuit auxiliary equipment that meet MIL standards for military use, thereby ensuring completion of the task of producing new key auxiliary equipment. All kinds of small and medium-scale integrated circuits needed for small, large, and medium-sized computers, microcomputers, and industrial control computers already listed in the government series and type spectrum, and small, large, and medium-scale integrated circuits with 10,000 components or less needed for program controlled switchboards and digital telephones will essentially all be produced. Linear circuits and amplifier circuits needed for TVs, radios, and radio/tape recorders will also all be in production.

With regard to components used in the defense industry, we need to decrease the failure rate, overcome the negative temperature problem, promptly solve the present problem of the low quality of urgently needed components for key military electronic equipment, and gradually adopt MIL standards. At the same time, given the need to finalize the design of key next-generation equipment for the Seventh Five-Year Program period, we need to make every effort to conduct preparatory research on new technologies and strive for breakthroughs in millimeter wave and broadband electronic vacuum components, photoelectric devices, military-grade high-speed large-scale integrated circuits, and high-reliability components. Technological breakthroughs need to be made in electronic components widely used in large quantities in order to solve the problems of stability and conformance, and we need to actively promote IEC standards. In 1985, high-power semiconductor components will reach ultra-high frequencies, photoelectric devices will be produced in small batches, black-and-white and color picture tubes will be produced essentially using domestic technology, and the total number of electronic components produced will reach about 10 billion for the year.

C. Accelerate the development of microcomputers and correspondingly develop small, large, and medium-sized computers

In the last 2 years of the Sixth Five-Year Program period, we need to focus on establishing a technological foundation for the industrialized production of microcomputers, become better able to produce complete systems, strive to do things domestically, and actively try to expand the range of applications in order to promote and stimulate the development of microcomputers.

We need to energetically develop 8- and 16-bit machines, develop typical products such as general-purpose systems for serial single-board computers, microcomputers, and development systems for microcomputers, and concentrate our efforts on building some trial production lines for microcomputers nationwide. In 1985, we will achieve large-scale production of single-user systems and small-scale production of multiuser systems, with a national system assembly capacity of around 30,000 units. Significant progress will be made in our ability to do this work domestically, and we will begin to use domestically produced components in some microcomputers and seek to ensure their prices are the same as those for microcomputers in the early 1980s. At the same time, we need to promptly develop bases for the computer industry in north, south, and east China, and start work on establishing computer research and manufacturing consortiums in Shanghai, Nanjing, and Hangzhou to create the conditions for significantly developing computers during the Seventh Five-Year Program period.

We need to use the development of microcomputers as the point of attack for stimulating the development of small, large, and medium-sized computers. The focus for small computers should be on bringing out new DJS-100, DJS-180, and S16 models, completing research into 32-bit super minicomputers and creating the capability to produce them in quantity. At the same time, we need to quickly research and manufacture a number of large and medium-sized computers that fit our country's needs. Primarily, we need to develop the 8000 series computers compatible with IBM 370 software ourselves and import systems testing technology for DPS8 distributed computers to create the capability for small-scale production.

We also need to develop peripherals. In the last 2 years of the Sixth Five-Year Program period, we need to formulate a type spectrum for microcomputer peripherals, accelerate the development and manufacturing of peripherals such as monitors, displays, printers, and 5 inch floppy disks, strive to create the capability to assemble around 5000 microcomputers, speed up the process of becoming reliant on domestic capabilities, and gradually develop complete mainframes.

We need to throw ourselves into applications and strive to become better able to develop them. In the next 2 years, we need to strive to develop around 200 effective data processing and real-time control applications. We need to focus on disseminating relatively mature application systems for monitoring looms, managing hotels, monitoring power plants, managing power grids, making hydrological forecasts, and monitoring, storing, and transporting gas. We also need to focus on applied systems for office automation, enterprise management, computer software application, inventory control and financial management, and energetically spread local-network technology.

We need to speed up software development. In the next 2 years, we need to import 40–50 application software programs and develop 5–10 Chinese character software programs for each of the key computer models, strive to harmonize software and hardware development, actively strengthen the information processing industry, and get the software, training, and repair services industries, and the computer sales network to reach a good economy of scale.

D. Energetically develop electronic capital goods needed by all sectors of the national economy

By 1985, we need to aim to complete the 11 major equipment engineering projects and 279 important construction projects designated by the government, actively arrange for the contracting and development of complete sets of electronic equipment, and provide advanced electronic equipment, systems and software technology for the coal, oil, electric, metallurgy, chemical engineering, railway, transportation, post and telecommunications, machine building, light industry, textile, civil aviation, meteorology, education, public security, and radio and TV broadcasting sectors.

We need to actively develop modern communications technology and equipment systems in the fields of fiber optics, satellites, digital microwave communications, program controlled switchboards, mobile communications, data and image transmission, and multifunction telephones. We need to develop systems engineering and equipment such as satellite broadcasting, color TV broadcasting, and stereo broadcasting. By 1985, the Jinan Shanghai 120-line digital microwave communications system and the Fengtai-Shacheng-Datong railway mountain terrain dispatching system will go into operation, the postal and telecommunications services will be supplied with small capacity cross-bar switchboards, and the main research work on communications and navigation equipment for ships we build for export. We need to ensure progress in developing equipment and systems needed for offshore oil exploration; the second phase of the Baoshan Iron & Steel General Plant, the Datong-Qinhuangdao heavy-duty, double-track, electric railway; the nationwide coalmine system; the east China section of the 500,000 volt extra-high-voltage transmission station; the air traffic control system; the expansion of radio and TV reception; and other areas in order to ensure that research, production, and supply deadlines specified in the plan are met.

We need to strengthen development of electronic measuring instruments, and machinery and equipment used in electronics. We need to vigorously raise the quality and reliability of electronic measuring instruments, implement and enforce the new standards of the Ministry of Electronics Industry for environmental testing of instruments, actively adopt new technology, accelerate R&D on 38 key government-designated projects and new component testing instruments that meet IEC standards, and develop intelligent instruments that use microprocessors and automated testing systems that use microcomputers or desktop computers. We need to concentrate our efforts on making breakthroughs in equipment technology for large-scale integrated circuits and on assimilating imported equipment technology, accelerate development of microfabrication, picture-tube production, and environmental testing equipment, actively develop and apply computer-aided design, manufacturing, and testing technology, and expand the application of microprocessors in electronic testing instruments and specialized equipment.

At the same time as we strive to develop various kinds of systems engineering, we need to actively spread the application of electronic energy-saving devices, microwave energy and solar energy, as well as control, testing, and warning equipment needed in industry, transportation, farming, animal husbandry, fisheries, and the service industry, in order to help upgrade technology in all industries and sectors.

E. Continue to develop consumer electronics

What's most important in developing consumer electronics is coming out with more new products, developing new areas, improving quality, and expanding functionality, as well as increasing the application of integrated circuits and 1- and 4-bit microprocessors in consumer electronics and striving to promote specialized mass production.

Prior to 1985, we need to energetically research and produce equipment for TV reception of live broadcasting via satellite, full-frequency spectrum integrated color and black-and-white TV receivers, and high- and medium-grade multifunctional radios and radio/tape recorders equipped with computers. We also need to accelerate the development of new electrical appliances such as clocks, calculators, entertainment products, and home appliances, and strive to open up new areas for product development, such as healthcare, study aids, electric cooking utensils, safety products, and labor services.

We need to increase the production capacity in a planned way. In 1985, annual production of TV sets will reach 8 million, including 1.2 million color TV sets. Production of radios will remain stable at around 20 million sets, over one-third of which will be high- and medium-grade sets with integrated circuits or microprocessor controls. Production of tape recorders (radio/tape recorders) will reach 5 million units. Electric clocks, electronic watches, electronic toys, electronic calculators, and home appliances should all achieve a significant production capacity based on market needs.

Product quality needs to rise significantly. The mean failure-free operating time should exceed 5000 h for black-and-white TVs and 15,000 h for color TVs.

III. POLICIES AND MEASURES FOR ACCELERATING DEVELOPMENT

To attain the short- and long-term objectives for the electronics industry, we must implement the following principles, policies and measures.

A. Stress priorities and develop comprehensively

Concentrating financial and material resources to ensure development in key areas is a strategic policy decision for national economic development and also a guiding principle we must adhere to while developing the electronics industry. Without priorities, it would be impossible to direct our efforts effectively; however, ignoring comprehensive development could result in production imbalances. We urgently need to accelerate development of the electronics industry, but government fiscal and material resources are limited, so we must develop realistically and adhere to the principles of working within our capabilities and doing some things while setting others aside. We need to concentrate our efforts on the most important products and the most crucial technologies, and make breakthroughs that will spur overall development.

Military products must take precedence over civilian products. On this point, we can never waver. From the perspective of which key products and technologies have a decisive influence on electronics industry development, large-scale integrated circuits are the technological foundation of the industry today. If we can quickly fabricate them and develop an industrialized mass production capability, we can shift our electronic products onto this new technological foundation and thereby comprehensively raise the technological level of the electronics industry.

Of all modern technological devices, electronic computers have the widest application and greatest utility for modernization, and accelerating their research, production, and widespread application will have extremely important strategic significance for spurring development of the whole electronics industry and carrying our country's modernization forward. Having taken a broad view of the overall situation and analyzed the interests of all sectors, we have decided that electronic equipment for the army, large-scale integrated circuits, and electronic computers are strategic priorities for the development of the electronics industry.

The purpose of stressing priorities is to give impetus to other areas, not to displace them. Therefore, it is imperative we handle the relationship between priorities and ordinary tasks well. Focusing on priorities, we must successfully develop products and technology in the areas of radar, communications, navigation, radio and TV broadcasting, electronic components, and instruments and meters in a planned way and in good proportion so that they constitute a well-balanced whole, allowing us to achieve comprehensive balanced development.

B. Make comprehensive plans that take all factors into consideration

All sectors of society have been inspired by the new technological revolution to develop the electronics industry, and we must adhere to the principle of making comprehensive plans that take all factors into consideration if we are to guide their enthusiasm so that we can achieve sound and proportionate development in line with our plans.

First, we need to coordinate plans for central and local enterprises. During more than 30 years of development since the founding of the People's Republic, our country's local electronics industries have already become mature and robust, and possess good research and new product development capability, and thus constitute an important force in the electronics industry. In order to adapt to this change, we must adhere to the view of the country as an integral whole, strengthen the centralized and unified leadership of the country's electronics industry, emphasize research into problems relating to the development of local electronics industries, and unleash the enthusiasm of both central and local enterprises under the guidance of comprehensive planning that takes all factors into consideration. In our work of formulating development plans, allocating production quotas, and deciding what capital construction and technological upgrading projects to undertake, we need to set out with the overall picture in mind, consider what is necessary and what is possible, comprehensively consider matters on the basis of the same conditions and standards, and treat central and local enterprises alike. Key central and local enterprises need to make the most of their technological strengths and actively support small- and medium-sized local enterprises.

Second, industries and localities need to coordinate planning. In organizing professional collaboration, the production of auxiliary products and combined operations, we need to break down barriers and actively promote industrial and regional consortiums and cooperation.

Third, planning needs to be coordinated between the coastal and interior regions. We need to ensure that advanced regions support more backward ones and promote the transfer of advanced technology from the coast to the interior. At the same time, we need to conscientiously make adjustments and improvements in hinterland regions and get the enterprises and institutions there to fully play their role.

Fourth, we need to make overall plans that coordinate centralization and decentralization. For large-scale integrated circuits and electronic computers, which are technology and capital intensive, we need a significant level of centralization and need to take the path of intensive production when we set up research and production bases. For products that many localities and companies have the capability to produce, we need to select the best based on nationwide apportionment, market demand, as well as enterprises' production and technological conditions. We need to encourage enterprises to expand production of readily marketable brand name products and eliminate backward, low-quality, high-priced, and energy-inefficient products from the market through competition.

C. Comprehensively rectify enterprises and improve economic performance

Improving economic performance is the starting and end point of all our economic work. Improving economic performance involves many factors; for example, we must organize production based on social demand, rely on technological progress, excel at operations and management, and increase output while decreasing input and energy consumption. However, the key is to effectively and comprehensively rectify enterprises. Particularly today, when the prices of raw and semifinished materials are rising, electronic product prices are falling and we are under considerable foreign competitive pressure, the fundamental approach to ensuring that the electronics industry's economic performance improves significantly is to effectively rectify enterprises and raise their quality.

In rectifying enterprises, we need to maintain high standards and impose strict demands; we cannot do this perfunctorily. Enterprises already certified as meeting rectification standards need to consolidate their accomplishments, continue to improve, and strive to meet the six objectives for enterprise rectification.[2] By 1984, 70% or more of enterprises should be certified, and we need to ensure that the work of rectifying enterprises is complete by the end of 1985.

Enterprises need to focus on four things to raise their quality. First, they need to create good leading bodies based on the principle of making their cadres more revolutionary, younger, better educated, and more

---

[2]The six objectives of enterprise rectification are the basic requirements for improving enterprises in the course of rectification put forth in the Decision of the CPC Central Committee and the State Council Concerning Comprehensively Rectifying State-Owned Industrial Enterprises, issued on January 2, 1982. The decision states that through comprehensive rectification, enterprises should gradually create a leadership system that is both democratic and centralized; create a workforce that is both politically reliable and professionally competent; create a management system that is both scientific and civilized; become able to correctly handle the economic relations between the government, the enterprise, and its employees; fulfill the state plan in an outstanding manner; and achieve the goals of balancing the interests of the government, the enterprise and its employees, producing good-quality products, achieving good economic performance, maintaining good labor discipline, operating in a civilized manner, and doing political work well.

professionally competent, as well as improve the ranks of second- and third-echelon cadres. Second, they need to effectively rectify all aspects of basic management work, continue the good work of making the transition and changes, formulate and implement quota standards, put original records in order, further improve their internal economic and technological accountability systems, actively implement modern management, and use microcomputers for the management of their business. Third, they need to provide good employee training in the areas of politics, technology, and culture to raise the political, technological, and professional quality of their staff. Fourth, they need to strengthen the analysis of their economic activities and their economic accounting to eliminate losses and increase profits. By 1985, all enterprises with operating losses must earn a profit.

D. Adjust the industrial structure and increase the proportion of electronic capital goods

The present composition of our country's electronics industry is as follows: consumer electronics, 43%; components, 37%; military products, around 10%; and electronic capital goods, about 10%. In developed countries, the gross output value of military products and electronic capital goods generally exceeds 40% of electronic production, and reaches as high as 70%. In comparison, our country's proportion of electronic capital goods is much too small. This situation makes it difficult for China's electronics industry to shoulder the heavy responsibility of providing the national economy with the electronic technology equipment it needs, and may even hinder modernization of the national economy. We have therefore decided that developing electronic capital goods should be a major principle in initiating a new phase in the electronics industry, and the tasks arranged for the last 2 years of the Sixth Five-Year Program period particularly emphasize development of these products. We envisage that, after several years of hard work, we can raise their proportion to more than 30% of electronic production. Every industry and locality needs to take an application-oriented approach, actively adjust their industrial structure, energetically develop application services, accelerate the development of electronic capital goods, and genuinely incorporate these objectives in their planning and arrangements, organization and leadership, investment guarantees, and allocation of resources on the basis of the unified planning by the Ministry of Electronics Industry.

E. Rely on scientific progress to accelerate technological upgrading

The electronics industry is an emerging R&D industry. We must firmly apply the principle of relying on technological progress to speed up the replacement of old products with new ones and raise the overall level of technology.

First, we need to steadfastly push scientific research to the fore and organize efforts to tackle key scientific and technological problems and spread the application of new technologies. While focusing on raising the technological level of product development and industrialized mass production, we also need to concentrate our efforts on the R&D of next-generation military electronic technology and equipment for command and control in electronic warfare. We need to carry out R&D on the following areas: new technology for next-generation information products such as electronic computers, software, fiber optics, and satellite communications products, as well as new radio and TV technology; new products whose electronic components incorporate microelectronic, microwave, and photoelectric technologies; electronic systems engineering technologies such as data acquisition, process control, and industrial inspection; and micromachining and high-reliability technology and technology for industrialized electronic mass production. We need to integrate research with production more closely, strengthen pilot-testing methods, attempt to shorten the time spent on R&D and trial production, formulate and implement specific technological and economic policies on transferring scientific and technological achievements, and put such achievements into industrial production more swiftly.

Second, we need to actively adopt domestic and foreign advanced technology to accelerate the technological upgrading of existing enterprises and research institutes. We need to focus on improving research methods, create a specialized mass production base, raise the technological level of industrialized mass production, and focus our efforts on developing and upgrading research and production bases for key products as well as core enterprises and institutions. We need to promptly and effectively carry out technological and economic feasibility studies of all development and upgrade projects, and strive for maximum returns, while minimizing the time and money needed to implement projects. We need to actively use electronic technology to transform the electronics industry. We need to take the lead in using computers in research, production, and management. We need to stress and strengthen the research, trial productions, and full productions of electronic instruments and meters and specialized equipment, as well as the research, testing, and widespread application of new techniques and materials. We need to integrate the importation of foreign technology with domestic efforts to tackle key technological problems and produce complete equipment systems, and we also need to combine technological upgrading of complete production lines with input from the masses who run them.

Third, environmental protection is a strategic task in our country's modernization drive and a basic state policy. We need to further implement the principle of putting prevention first while integrating prevention with control, and take advantage of technological upgrading to comprehensively prevent and control industrial pollution. We need to intensify scientific and technological research on the environment and rely on scientific and technological progress to solve environmental problems.

Fourth, we need to further strengthen standardization in our work and introduce a standardization system. We need to stress and strengthen technological and economic intelligence work, and strive to do well in gathering, analyzing, and compiling intelligence. We need to break through technological barriers, promote technological exchanges, and make them better serve to promote technological progress in the electronics industry.

F. Institute reform actively yet reliably, and set economic relations of all kinds in good order

In welcoming the new technological revolution, we must reform those aspects of the superstructure unsuited to it at the same time as we solve problems concerning the orientation of and policies for technological development. The basic guiding thought for future reform is to strengthen macro guidance, facilitate horizontal relations, create a matrix management system, adjust production relations in accordance with the economic laws of socialism, and rationalize the production, research, and distribution areas. To this end, we need to continue to do well in the following aspects of our reform and work.

First, we need to continue to improve the system of hierarchical management. We need to make new progress in facilitating horizontal relations and strengthening unified planning and guidance for industries and regions, and for central and local enterprises.

Second, we need to accelerate the development of technology development centers for the industry, electronic systems engineering institutes, professional engineering companies, and the China Academy of Electronics and Information Technology, and gradually set up technology development, and technological and economic research divisions in institutes where conditions permit.

Third, we need to make new breakthroughs in the areas of reorganization, association and cooperation to promote specialization. Lenin once observed, "Technical progress must entail the specialization of different parts of production." The accelerated development of new productive forces and technological progress coming in the wake of the new technological revolution require us, in our reforms, to give high priority to the division of labor and enterprise reorganization based on specialization. First of all, we need to make breakthroughs in the specialization of general production techniques and the production of common products. We need to consolidate and develop industrial and regional specialized companies and consortiums; vigorously promote socialized, industrialized mass production; promote the integration of research, production, operations, and services; and seek to develop specialized transportation and lifestyle service enterprises in cities with a high concentration of electronics enterprises.

Fourth, we need to continue to reform the planned management system and strengthen management of the distribution field. We need to reform the planned management system, strive to unclog distribution channels, and achieve overall balance between production, supply, and marketing. We need to conduct market research, have a good grasp of market conditions, link production with marketing, strengthen product marketing work, and strive to provide good repair services. We need to strengthen the planned management of materials and equipment, strive to shorten distribution chains, exploit resources, reduce inventories, and guarantee supplies. We need to further reform and strengthen the management of prices, capital, and costs, maintain strict financial discipline, use capital effectively, and raise its rate of return.

Fifth, we need to formulate economic policies and vigorously work on economic laws. We need to conscientiously review the experience from trials in which enterprises pay taxes instead of remitting their profits to the government and trials for implementing a responsibility system, and to formulate corresponding economic policies on that basis. We need to continue to do well in trials for adjusting and reforming enterprise salaries and study ways of improving the system and measures for granting incentives.

G. Always put quality first and ensure product quality

In the defense industry, research, and production tasks must be allocated to carefully chosen factories and institutes with the best technological capabilities and equipment. We need to continue to practice total quality management, strengthen quality control in the production process, do our reliability work well, and establish a sound system of quality assurance. We need to make the final product inspection system stricter, strictly enforce regulations concerning routine and periodic tests, and firmly put a stop to substandard products being put on the market. We need to improve after-sales service, help users use products correctly, provide good repair services, and manage information from feedback on quality well. We need to actively adopt international standards and strive to improve product performance and quality. We need to continue to do well in creating quality products and evaluating products in order to identify the best. We need to implement the policy of producing quality products at a good price, limit the production of inferior goods, encourage excellence, and spur all producers to strive for higher product quality. We need to strengthen the quality supervision system, promote supervision and inspection work, and firmly stop the small number of enterprises that churn out inferior products from doing so. The system for certifying the quality of electronic components needs to gradually spread from trials to general application. We need to expand the system of production licensing to cover more products and accelerate its implementation on the basis of trials last year. We need to promptly develop a system for licensing the production of equipment and gradually begin trials of it.

H. Integrate technology with trade and expand technological and economic exchanges with other countries

Our import–export work must serve to promote our country's new technological revolution and spur technological progress in the electronics industry. Guided by the principle of opening to the outside world and invigorating the domestic economy, we need to adopt a variety of flexible measures such as combining technology and industry with trade, operating joint ventures, undertaking joint development, engaging in processing with supplied materials, and assembling products for resale in order to vigorously expand technological and economic exchanges with other countries and import advanced and appropriate technologies. We need to do our utmost to include advanced foreign technology in the equipment and components we import, particularly when we import items for key government projects. We need to focus on importing technology, but not rely on doing so. There are many cutting-edge technologies and key equipment and components that foreign countries refuse to sell us, so we can only obtain them by our own efforts. We can import key components and assemble key equipment while producing some components ourselves in order to speed up the development of electronic products, but we must not content ourselves with just doing assembly work. We must do everything we can to promote domestic production. We need to conscientiously assimilate and transplant technology and equipment we have already imported, and do all we can to become more self-reliant.

We need to assiduously expand the export of electronic products. We will adhere to the principle of using imports to stimulate exports, using exports to finance imports, and exporting products to spur industrial production, and make expanding the export of electronic products a strategic task. We need to surpass the target set by the government to increase the 1981 export volume of machinery and electronic products three- or four-fold by 1985, and increase their export value by more than 60% a year in the last 2 years of the Sixth Five-Year Program period. We need to strive to increase the proportion of medium- and high-grade assembled machinery and military products in the composition of export products. We need to set up relatively concentrated factory sites devoted to producing products for export, carry out technological upgrading and product design with the focus on key export products, do all we can to adopt international standards, focus on raising the quality of products, improving their packaging, and presentation, and strive to reduce costs. We need to increase our investigations and studies of international markets, and actively open up the export market by first gaining a firm foothold in third-world countries in places such as Southeast Asia, and then attempt to gain entry to markets in Europe and America.

We need to strengthen the unified leadership of import and export work. We need to adhere to a unified policy and present a united front to the outside world. In importing, we need to avoid unnecessary duplication, and in exporting we need to prevent competing against ourselves and driving prices down in disguised form, and also pay attention to protecting the rights and interests of enterprises and institutions. We need to strengthen overall planning and supervision of export-oriented agencies and factories in the electronics industry located in the Shenzhen Special Economic Zone and other areas, and get them to fully play their role as a link between China and the world. We need to focus on raising the quality of workers in the foreign trade field, train them well, and raise their professional level.

I. Stress intellectual development and strengthen talent training

Promoting intellectual development and talent training is an extremely important strategic measure for vitalizing our country's electronics industry. At present, only 9.7% of the industry's workforce consists of technological personnel, and the figure drops to only 6.4% for local electronics industries. Moreover, the mix of specialties and the classifications of technological personnel are unsound and not suitable for the present and future development of the industry. We must take a strategic perspective, adopt effective measures, and expand investment channels to arouse the enthusiasm of all sectors to provide education and train talent. In order to quickly change the present situation, in which the knowledge of leading cadres at all levels and managerial and technological personnel is becoming outdated, we must adopt a variety of measures to improve on-the-job training. The Ministry of Electronics Industry needs to accelerate the development of colleges for management cadres in the electronics industry and education centers for updating the knowledge of technical cadres in the industry. All sectors, regions, and large and medium-sized enterprises need to set up employee training centers to train technological personnel and management cadres in rotation so that they quickly grasp new theory, technology, and knowledge, and adapt to changing research and production conditions in the industry. We need to strive to run universities and colleges well, accelerate their development in a planned way, strengthen specialties in short supply, improve teaching conditions, recruit more students, improve teaching quality, enroll more graduate students, and send more students abroad in order to produce more high-level technical personnel. We need to appreciate the importance and accelerate development of specialized secondary technical schools, and gradually change the unfavorable situation in which there are fewer students in specialized secondary schools than in specialized junior colleges. We need to train more specialists in all areas through a variety of means such as evening universities, TV universities, correspondence courses, employer sponsorship of employee education, and self-study. In addition, we need to further strengthen and improve the management of the of technical workforce, continue to implement our policy on intellectuals well, use talented people well, and make full use of the technical personnel we currently possess.

J. Strive for cultural and ethical progress while making material progress

At the Second Plenary Session of the Twelfth Central Committee, Comrade Deng Xiaoping said, "Now that we have shifted our emphasis to economic development, all our members in the Party should consider how to strengthen ideological work and adapt it to the new conditions, so that it is not neglected in favor of economic work." Government agencies at all levels in the electronics industry must steadily promote both material progress and cultural and ethical progress, give ideological and political work an important position, and handle it well.

First, we need to carry out Party rectification work well, closely integrate Party rectification work with economic and other work, get them to spur each other, make improvements in the course of rectification, and use Party rectification as a stimulus to promote progress in all of our work. Newly formed leading bodies need to have a new mental outlook and work attitude, be adept at learning new knowledge, studying new situations, and solving new problems, and pay particular attention to studying and resolving issues of principle and policy that affect the overall situation.

Second, we need to investigate the characteristics and laws pertaining to ideological and political work in the new period, and vigorously strengthen ideological and political work concerning industry employees. We need to foster the fine traditions of our Party's political work, improve organs engaged in political work and their work systems, and improve the quality of political cadres. We need to intensively carry out activities to promote the five areas of emphasis (culture, civility, cleanliness, order, and morals), the four sources of beauty (heart, language, actions, and the environment), and the three objects of ardent love (the motherland, socialism, and the CPC), activities to get people to emulate exemplary individuals, and cultural and sporting activities that benefit workers' physical and mental health, so that people become model employees with high ideals, moral integrity, a good education, and a strong sense of discipline, and become more active and creative in their research and production.

Third, we need to intensify discipline inspection work, continue to crack down on economic crimes and other criminal offences, and resolutely correct all kinds of bad practices.

Promote Rapid and Balanced Development of Our Country's Electronics Industry*

March 1, 1984

This meeting has been successful and productive. To phrase it in the words of those present, the meeting had a good central theme, rich content, and ideological vitality; it stayed on schedule and had the three virtues of being held at the right time, having a good topic and having a good atmosphere.

This meeting was held at the right time. We all believe that at this critical moment when the development of our country's electronics industry is on the eve of a new technological revolution, we have indeed grasped the opportunity to unify our thinking and discuss what measures to take by holding this meeting.

This meeting had a good topic. Proceeding from the fact that the electronics industry plays a leading role and bearing in mind the objective requirement for it to have a higher level of development than the rest of the national economy, you have conscientiously studied and set forth the tasks for the last 2 years of the Sixth Five-Year Program period, the targets for the Seventh Five-Year Program, and the strategic objective of ensuring that by 2000, the 1980 gross output value of the electronics industry is octupled and its general technological level is 10 years ahead of the rest of the national economy. This has brought your thinking more in line with the general tasks and objectives set forth at the Party's Twelfth National Congress.

The atmosphere was very good. The meeting has improved its style in accordance with the requirement the Party Central Committee set forth for Party rectification work that the Party's work style should be improved in the course of rectification. Service attitudes have also improved at this meeting, a circumstance that was welcomed by participants.

In short, the meeting made achievements in the following four areas.

---

*Speech at the conclusion of a national working meeting of heads of departments and bureaus of the electronics industry.

First, it has deepened our understanding of the new technological revolution and increased our sense of responsibility and urgency for accelerating the development of the electronics industry. The meeting participants reached consensus on three points.

1. The new technological revolution has given new tasks to the electronics industry, and we need to accelerate development of the electronics industry without delay.
2. Both central and local authorities have immense zeal and unprecedented enthusiasm for developing microelectronic technology, which is very encouraging.
3. New improvements in developing the electronics industry have occurred in all provinces, autonomous regions and municipalities directly under the central government in the past year or so.

Everyone here agreed that the situation is good, the burden is heavy, and pressure is great. This pressure derives from a sense of responsibility and urgency.

Faced with the new technological revolution, all provinces, autonomous regions and municipalities are actively considering what measures to take and how to rise to the challenge. During the discussion many comrades raised the question: How can we better unleash the initiative of all localities and accelerate the electronics industry's development in this excellent situation? It is widely agreed that there are two points especially deserving of attention.

1. We need to fully value initiative, strive to do our work well and promote the development of the electronics industry.
2. Given the premise of unleashing the initiative of all localities, we need to steadfastly view the country as a whole, strengthen unified planning and guard against blind action.

Those of us active in the electronics industry need to advise the country's leaders effectively; this is a major responsibility.

Second, the meeting has clarified our objectives up to 2000 and unified our thinking. On the basis of work that took most of last year, we have set the objective to octuple the electronics industry's 1980 gross output value by 2000. Comrades at this meeting have achieved a considerable degree of consensus on this objective and believe it is attainable. Some comrades at the meeting stated that by 2000, it will be more difficult to reach the technological level the world's advanced industrialized countries will have reached around 1990 than to octuple our gross output value. In particular, they consider it unrealistic to expect us to reach this world advanced level in all respects. Other comrades stated that if by 1990, our country's major products and production technologies reach the level the world advanced industrialized countries reached around 1980, and if by 2000 they reach the level those countries will have reached around 1990, then our development level will always lag 10 years behind the world advanced level. We can understand this issue as follows: Reaching the level advanced industrialized countries will have reached around 1990 is our general objective, but it is a sliding scale and does not apply uniformly; rather, it is one that is possible for some products and product types to attain. For example, some types of integrated circuits will reach the world advanced level by 2000. In brief, at this meeting we have defined the short-term and long-term objectives toward which we will strive and, in particular, we have come to understand the urgency and importance of technological progress.

Third, we have discussed the situation, increased understanding and established closer relations. During the meeting, comrades from provinces, autonomous regions and municipalities discussed their respective plans and arrangements, increased mutual understanding and exchanged information. Leading comrades from the Ministry of Electronics Industry and comrades from the ministry's departments, bureaus and supervisory bureaus participated in discussions, expressed their views openly, and fully exchanged comments and opinions, leading to increased mutual understanding. We tried our best to solve all the problems we could at the meeting as you raised them, and when we could not do so or believed that we required more information, we explained the situation. In short, the meeting's atmosphere was positive, and you studied and explored issues concerning the development of the electronics industry with a positive attitude, and put forward many constructive comments and suggestions that will benefit our future work enormously.

Fourth, many excellent comments and suggestions have been put forward concerning the nationwide development of the electronics industry and Party rectification work in the Ministry of Electronics Industry. This will greatly promote efforts to rectify Party organization in the ministry's agencies and improve the ministry's work style. We will certainly take these comments and suggestions seriously and deal with them systematically and in accordance with their particular circumstances. Some of the less complex issues were resolved at the meeting, while others will be studied further and then resolved. As for the comments and suggestions concerning the ideology, work, and work style of the ministry's leaders and agencies, we will make it our priority to resolve these issues during our ministry's Party rectification efforts. With regard to comments and suggestions concerning our current work, as long as the ministry is able to solve the problems raised, we will assign the relevant departments and personnel to promptly do so. As for comments and suggestions regarding long-range programs and macro-policy decisions, some will be referred to higher level authorities for resolution, while others will be designated as special projects for investigation, study and resolution according to overall planning.

Regarding the long-term tasks in the electronics industry, we have summarized our discussion at the meeting as follows: We must build a foundation, raise our level, improve quality, pursue profits, octuple the gross output value and get 10 years ahead of the rest of the national economy. This is both a statement of our tasks and our slogan for appealing to and mobilizing employees in the electronics industry.

Now, I would like to express my views on several issues that were raised during the meeting.

I. ON IMPROVING ECONOMIC PERFORMANCE

During the meeting, we informed you of the guiding principles of the recent National Economic Work Conference, whose central theme was to improve economic performance. The State Economic Commission has set clear objectives and requirements, and we must conscientiously implement them on the basis of conditions in the electronics industry. We need to put more effort and care into studying how to increase both production and economic performance. We must first of all rely on technological progress and successfully carry out technological upgrading and innovation in enterprises. In addition, we need to pay attention to developing talent and promoting education to universalize electronic technology such as computers. We need to earnestly seek to turn enterprises' losses into profits. The government has prescribed that by 1984, 35% of enterprises operating at a loss must rectify this situation and all industrial enterprises must essentially eliminate their operating losses, and that by 1985, they must turn a profit. In the electronics industry, we should meet this target ahead of schedule. We not only need to work hard to turn around unprofitable enterprises but at the same time increase the profits of profitable enterprises. Profitable enterprises also need to achieve turnarounds with regard to their unprofitable products. We need to prevent a recurrence of losses.

We need to vigorously expand production of high-quality and brand name products. There is great market demand for some products, but customers want brand names. This means we need to produce "brand name dishes." Quanjude roast duck and Donglaishun mutton hot pot restaurants in Beijing are famous because they offer unique products. When we produce goods, we cannot just prepare generic "big pot dishes"; we also need to produce brand name products. To expand the production of high-quality brand name products, enterprises in close proximity to each other can work together provided quality is guaranteed and good brand names do not become tarnished.

II. ON THE ISSUE OF COMPREHENSIVE, OVERALL PLANNING

Facing the new technological revolution, all localities are immensely enthusiastic about promoting the electronics industry, and this will greatly benefit its development. Presented with this excellent opportunity, central and local authorities need to make overall plans and work in unison. This needs to be the case within the electronics industry, and the industry should also fully cooperate with other sectors. We need to devise sound programs for the whole industry, taking the overall situation as our starting point. At this meeting you have thoroughly discussed this issue and reached consensus. We must value everyone's initiative and use it in order to promote the rapid development of the electronics industry. At the beginning of this meeting, I suggested we should not rush headlong into action and initiate too many projects at once. Some comrades felt that this message was inappropriate and feared it could have a negative effect, an objection that has some merit. The premise for such a suggestion is that when everybody is highly enthusiastic, it is necessary to guide their enthusiasm toward developing the electronics industry in a planned, proportionate and sound manner, and avoid proceeding blindly. This is absolutely not intended to tie anyone's hands. With regard to microcomputers, for example, not everyone should assemble host computers. On the contrary, everything should be developed in a coordinated manner according to plan, with some playing a leading role and others in a supporting position. The same holds true in producing generating equipment in the machinery industry; while some produce main units, others should produce equipment, and still others should make parts. Equipment manufactured with any of these links missing will not work and will not generate electricity. When we stress key areas, this does not mean we do not need to deal with ordinary areas. On the contrary, key areas must promote ordinary ones; they cannot replace them. We cannot say minor areas are dispensable and unimportant. The same thing is true in an opera; it has lead roles, supporting roles and bit parts.

You have all agreed with the proposal for treating central and local electronics industries alike. We need to enshrine this as a principle. The Planning Department of the Ministry of Electronics Industry distributed to you for your comments copies of a draft version of a document on principles and policies concerning local electronics industries, which attracted everyone's attention and interest. We will revise the document on the basis of the results of discussion of it at this meeting, and will then promulgate the final version for implementation. Effective implementation will require a certain period of time, and we need to gradually feel our way and gain experience. Should problems arise in the implementation of this document, we hope that localities will report them to us, inform us about them and keep in close contact with us so that the problems may be solved as we move ahead, so that the central and local electronics industries develop in a more coordinated manner.

III. ON ISSUES OF ORGANIZING AND SUPERVISING CIVILIAN SYSTEMS ENGINEERING AND ELECTRONIC CAPITAL GOODS

At this meeting, comrades expressed support for vigorously developing electronic systems engineering and electronic capital goods, and agreed this was an excellent suggestion of the Ministry of Electronics Industry. However, the organization of this work has not been carried out effectively and there is a lack of a specialized supervision agency and a contingent of specialists, which has affected progress in this work. Therefore, it has been proposed that the ministry establish a comprehensive supervision agency in charge of organization and implementation. On the basis of your comments and suggestions, the Leading Party Group of the ministry has made the tentative decision to establish an agency in charge of electronics systems engineering and establish a contingent of specialists in the fields of project contracting, consulting, construction, installation and services. At this time we have only defined the orientation and objectives for the development of electronic capital goods, and have not sufficiently worked out specific plans, so each locality must formulate specific plans for developing and widely applying these goods on the basis of their own conditions. These kinds of products are difficult to develop and often fail to earn significant profits, but they are indispensable in the four modernizations, so we must work hard to produce them. The electronics industry's competent authorities in provinces, autonomous regions and municipalities should study how to implement these plans and organizational measures on the basis of their local conditions, complete all aspects of their work effectively and attain positive results.

IV. ON THE QUESTION OF AVOIDING REDUNDANT IMPORTS

At this meeting I talked of the need to avoid redundant imports, citing the example of the import of carbon film resistor production lines. Some provinces and municipalities have not imported too few of them, but rather more than they can possibly use. This is the case only in some provinces and municipalities such as Shanghai, Jiangsu, and Fujian; other areas have not imported enough production lines. Our overall production capacity suggests that supply outstrips demand. We must avoid redundant technology imports, especially in capital- and technology-intensive projects. We can import a little more for projects that require low capital input and produce quick results. With regard to imports, we also encourage different areas to offset each other's wants and needs. For example, the coastal region and other areas have imported too much and they should pass some of this on to places that have too little. The relevant departments of the Ministry of Electronics Industry should inform various localities as to China's electronics industry imports at regular intervals. I would like to particularly emphasize that before importing anything, we must carry out feasibility studies. We need to study and master foreign trade knowledge and acquire skills for doing business with foreign entrepreneurs. We need to make a point of importing key equipment and software technology and then vigorously work to assimilate, absorb and spread them.

V. ON SEVERAL SPECIFIC ISSUES THAT AROSE DURING DISCUSSIONS AT THE MEETING

1. The issue of establishing local leading agencies of the electronics industry. At present, there are many types of such agencies. According to statistics, nine of the 28 provinces, autonomous regions and municipalities in China that have an electronics industry have kept their departments and bureaus of the electronics industry as they were, 12 of them have turned them into corporations, and seven of them have merged them with their departments and bureaus supervising the machine-building industry or other industries. Many comrades object to this situation on the grounds that in the new technological revolution, it makes it difficult for these agencies to exercise effective leadership over the electronics industry under their jurisdiction. With regard to the establishment of agencies, our attitude is as follows. (i) Institutional reform is subject to unified arrangements by the central authorities. Conditions vary from region to region, so uniformity cannot be imposed, and agencies need to constantly improve through practical experience. (ii) Comrades in all localities need to work well within the existing agency structure, serve as good advisors to local Party committees and governments, exercise effective leadership and supervision of local electronics industries, and strive to minimize the effect of unsuitable agencies on development and growth of their electronics industries. (iii) The Ministry of Electronics Industry needs to report the situation to the State Council, and comrades need to report to their local Party committees and governments in order to make the establishment of leading electronics industry agencies more rational. As the productive forces develop, the relations of production are constantly adjusting and changing. The establishment of leading electronics industry agencies will inevitably improve as the industry develops.
2. The issue of investment channels for local electronics industries. Many comrades report that now that the revenue-sharing system for the

central and local authorities is in place, local electronics industries have great difficulty arranging any investment locally. Many factors contribute to this situation. The situation will improve if the issue of the electronics industry's strategic position is resolved. Local government agencies of the electronics industry need to do their best to explain the importance of their industry to local Party committees and governments.

3. The issue of production centers for color TV sets. All localities are eager to produce color TV sets; over 30 factories in more than 20 provinces, autonomous regions and municipalities throughout the country have sought permission to produce them. In order to avoid unnecessary duplication of imports, trial production and production, the Ministry of Electronics Industry has distributed its draft Methods for Authorizing Factories to Produce Color TV Sets at the meeting for your comments and suggestions. The document will be revised and promulgated after this meeting. In the future, only factories meeting the requirements specified in this document will be authorized to produce color TV sets. Where conditions are similar, preferential treatment will be given to factories in remote areas and areas with weak electronics industries.

4. The issue of improving and upgrading routine testing centers for electronic products. In the past we used Soviet standards for electrical products, but we are now shifting to IEC standards and MIL standards, and we require corresponding agencies and equipment in order to carry out tests and experiments. At present, every province has a routine testing center, but most of them have obsolete or defective equipment and instruments and they have difficulty functioning properly. The Ministry of Electronics Industry plans to establish a team to undertake a fact-finding mission and prepare a special report to the State Council so that this problem will be solved in a planned and systematic manner. At present, it is difficult to have a testing center in every province, so our preliminary idea is to establish one in every greater administrative area first in order to improve testing and testing procedures. In addition, we must make full use of the existing testing capability of key enterprises.

5. The issue of improving methods for approving electronics products. In the past, many meetings were held on approving electronic products by the central authorities, the Ministry of Electronics Industry, the ministry's bureaus, provincial and municipal governments, as well as factories

and research institutes. Many comrades reported the shortcomings of these meetings, believing some engendered unhealthy tendencies, while others were costly and failed to achieve their intended purpose. In the future, we will gradually reform this approval method. We can hold fewer meetings and rely mainly on testing and experimental data from authoritative agencies. When the data satisfies requisite conditions, the competent authorities will issue a certificate of approval. Reform measures will have to be worked out through joint research by concerned parties.

6.   The issue of hinterland enterprises opening offices in the coastal region. The Party Central Committee and State Council affirm the strategic policy of developing the hinterland, with the overall policy being to maintain stability there. Naturally, in the course of developing the hinterland, some enterprises situated deep in the mountains will have difficulty surviving. The government now has a planning office for adjusting and improving development of the hinterland, and it is studying ways of adjusting and upgrading enterprises there. Not all of these enterprises can open offices in the coastal region. The principle here is that we will support offices that help consolidate hinterland bases and oppose those that weaken them. We cannot allow all of them to open such offices. This very much involves government policy and we need to formulate specific regulations concerning it.

I would also like to offer some guidelines for our work in 1984.

At this meeting we discussed the tasks for the last 2 years of the Sixth Five-Year Program period and the Seventh Five-Year Program, but we did not focus specifically on our work in 1984. Generally speaking, in 1984 the electronics industry needs to continue to implement the Party Central Committee's principle of readjusting, restructuring, consolidating and improving the national economy. It needs to strive to improve economic performance, accelerate its pace of development and inaugurate a new phase of development. The Ministry of Electronics Industry will issue an outline plan of specific work to be done. The draft plan is now being discussed and revised, and the final version will be issued shortly. The tentative idea is to accomplish work in 12 areas. I will not elaborate on each of them, but I want to emphasize several areas.

1. Effectively rectifying enterprises

Rectifying enterprises is the key to improving economic performance. The government requires that about 70% of state-owned electronics industry enterprises, including all large and medium-sized leading enterprises, covered by the state program and budget must pass a rectification inspection by the end of 1984. It will take a great deal of work to attain this objective. We need to avoid both formalism and bribery in this campaign. When their rectification efforts are examined for acceptance, some enterprises show they have formulated many rules and regulations. I do not think that "the more rules and regulations there are, the better." What counts is that they are well defined, succinctly worded, and feasible. What counts even more is that they are conscientiously implemented. When we rectify enterprises, we must considerably improve economic performance, make notable progress in turning enterprises around and increasing profits, fundamentally end operating losses in industrial enterprises, minimize policy-related losses, and ensure profits, taxes and production all increase simultaneously.

2. Improve product quality effectively and promptly

The greatest concern for users of electronic products is quality; it has a direct bearing on the reputation of the electronics industry. The electronics industry is now in an excellent situation of rapid development, but we must never place one-sided emphasis on quantity to the neglect of quality when our products are in high demand and are selling well.

In 1983 we chose 27 enterprises whose electronic components were considered to be of relatively high quality and carried out quality certification in accordance with the standards of the Ministry of Electronics Industry. Although certification in accordance with one standard was postponed, four enterprises failed to pass the certification. Many other enterprises still have a long way to go to meet the ministry's standards and even farther to go to meet international standards. This shows that we have to work extremely hard to improve product quality.

We need to focus on ensuring the quality of military products, continue to improve the quality of components subject to the seven special standards,[1] and effectively guarantee the quality of key projects and military equipment. Our satellite communications equipment has been instrumental in China's communications satellite launches, and received praise. However, we must guard against complacency and be aware that we still lag behind other countries. In the future we will continue to launch satellites and guard against mishaps. Many quality problems are not caused by technical faults but by deficient management. If components factories earnestly improve their management, the quality of their products will improve considerably.

3. Continue to promote institutional restructuring and enterprise reorganization and consortiums

We need to continue to effectively restructure enterprises and the product mix, follow the path of specialization, and focus on ending scattered small-scale production and increasing specialized mass production. Where

---

[1]The seven special standards are: special batches, special technology, special personnel, special equipment, special materials, special inspection, and special cards. "Special batches" refers to the practice in researching and manufacturing electronic components used in national defense projects, weapons systems and military electronic equipment that have rigorous reliability requirements of producing them in special batches. For these components, "special batch" supervision is strictly carried out for the entire production process, including materials feeding, assembly, testing, and delivery. "Special technology" refers to specially formulated technological standards to ensure high reliability. "Special personnel" refers to the selection of personnel with a strong sense of responsibility and a high level of technical and managerial ability for training in reliability technology and management, and for production or managerial jobs in the manufacturing of high reliability products after they have been certified. "Special equipment" refers to the selection of advanced equipment and instruments that meet high-reliability requirements to be used in the research and production of military products. "Special materials" refers to the selection and use of the best raw materials and parts, and the adoption of a strict system for storing, inspecting, maintaining and using them in accordance with the principle of using specified materials and processing them at specified factories under specified technical conditions. "Special inspection" refers to the formulation of special inspection criteria and the carrying out of inspections of raw materials, parts, semi-finished products and finished products by professional inspectors. "Special cards" refers to the printing of special flow-path cards and quality-tracking cards, which record the production of products, either by batch or individually. The cards should completely record the actual conditions of every step of a product's production from materials feeding to the time it leaves the factory and should be signed by every person responsible for each step of the process.

conditions permit, surface coating, heat treatment, casting and forging, tools and dies, plastic compression, and printed boards must be brought under unified planning, mainly by provincial and municipal governments, with specialized production in concentrated factories.

Progress needs to be made in creating consortiums of enterprises. We need to review the experience gained by existing economic consortiums, make better use of their advantages to solve problems on our way forward, and promote their sound development. We need to use reforms and consortiums to strengthen the relations and cooperation between central and local enterprises, between coastal and inland enterprises, and between enterprises in advanced and backward regions. Although central and local enterprises have different investment channels, they can establish joint ventures.

4. Step up technological, economic and policy research

China's electronics industry is in an important period of change, and it faces many new circumstances and problems that require study and exploration. We cannot guide people's work only on the strength of our experience. In order to stand higher and see further, we must have a foundation of scientific analysis. To this end, leading departments need to free themselves from some of their specific work, and organize technological, economic and policy research in order to make sound macro policy decisions. This is the weak link in our work. To strengthen this work, the Ministry of Electronics Industry has established the China Academy of Electronics and Information Technology. In the future, technological and economic research centers will also be established in some industries. This matter has been made a priority in our work this year, and I hope you will do it well.

After this meeting concludes and you return to your respective localities, you need to make good reports to the leaders of provinces, autonomous regions and municipalities where you live, and implement the guiding principles of this meeting under the leadership of local Party committees and governments. As we face new challenges, we need to take new steps in order to win new victories.

Foreign Trade in the Electronics Industry and Its Development Policy*

August 20, 1984

China's electronics industry began trading with the outside world in the 1950s and this trade has now been going on for 30 years. Since the adoption of the reform and opening up policy, our country's electronics industry has rapidly developed its foreign trade. China National Electronics Import and Export Corporation was established with the approval of the State Council in 1980 in order to further expand the electronics industry's foreign economic and technological exchanges. It integrates industry with trade and has four subordinate branches in Guangzhou, Shenzhen, Shanghai, and Tianjin. It also has branches in provinces and municipalities such as Beijing, Jiangsu, Fujian, and Guangdong, which are linked with the electronics industries in each of these areas and directly engage in importing and exporting. This measure has strongly promoted the development of foreign trade in China's electronics industry.

In 1983, the export volume of China's electronics industry increased by 55.6% and its import volume grew by 11.9% over the previous year. Export products evolved from pocket radios, electronic components and devices, and specialty electronic materials, to over 80 different types of equipment. In the past we imported mainly TV and radio/tape recorder parts and components, but nowadays 75% of our imports consist of production technology and complete or stand-alone manufacturing equipment. In the past, we exported mainly to Hong Kong and Macao, but we now export to over 70 countries and regions including the US, Western Europe, Southeast Asia, and Africa.

Several hundred Chinese electronics enterprises have imported foreign advanced technology and equipment since 1979 and in the past three years alone they have imported $600 million worth of technology and equipment from Japan, the US, and Western Europe. In all these projects,

---

*Originally published in the journal *Intertrade*, No. 8, 1984.

whether they involved technology transfer, joint ventures or compensation trade, both sides cooperated well and were satisfied with the results.

The electronics industry is a rapidly developing emerging industry. To a great extent, the technological condition of a country's electronics industry determines the country's technological progress; therefore, it is essential for the electronics industry to develop before other industries. In order to invigorate all areas of the national economy, the Chinese government has given an important place to the electronics industry and resolved to accelerate its development. Our tentative thinking is that by 2000 the industry's 1980 gross output value should be octupled to reach 80 billion yuan, and that major products and production technologies should reach the level advanced industrialized countries will have reached around 1990. The latter objective is 10 years more ambitious than the objective the government set for the national economy as a whole of reaching the level those countries reached around 1980.

To attain the above objectives, we will focus on both developing key projects and upgrading technology, and accelerate the modernization of research and production in the electronics industry. In the course of developing key projects and upgrading technology, we will actively utilize foreign capital and import advanced technology. Any production technologies urgently needed at home that we are currently unable to develop on our own will be imported from abroad whenever they are needed through various means on the basis of investigations, studies, and unified planning, in order to make our country more self-reliant and accelerate technological progress in its electronics industry. This is a long-term strategic principle for developing our country's electronics industry, and will not change.

In accordance with the Chinese government's principles and policies concerning technological imports as well as the characteristics of the electronics industry, our general requirements are: technology imports must (i) be suitable for the actual conditions of our electronics industry, (ii) be technologically advanced and reasonably priced, (iii) and be beneficial for increasing our self-reliance. We need to select the best technologies, and import them through various channels on the basis of equality and mutual benefit. In the future, we need to continue to adhere to the principle of linking technology imports with trade expansion, and extend preferential trade conditions to countries and firms that grant us preferential treatment for technology imports.

Our country has clear objectives and a clear orientation for importing electronic technology. The general requirements are to focus on products; set enhancing scientific and technological capacity, accelerating the updating and upgrading of products, lowering consumption, and conserving energy as our objectives; import advanced and appropriate foreign technologies; and promote technological upgrading of manufacturers and research bodies. Our orientation for importing technology at present and for the foreseeable future is to focus on the technological upgrading of the microelectronics and microcomputer industries as well as the efficient mass production of electronic components and devices, though we also have to make appropriate arrangements for importing technologies for manufacturing modern communications equipment, electronic measuring instruments, and consumer electronics.

Countries with an advanced electronics industry have long industrial histories, many unique features in their technology, and a wealth of operational and managerial expertise. All this provides the conditions for diversifying our bilateral economic and technological cooperation into more areas. In importing technology, we will not only target "hardware" such as stand-alone equipment and production lines, but also pay more attention to "software" including technical know-how, patents, technical data, and manufacturing drawings. Our country has already enacted the Patent Law and we respect international principles for technology transfers and will ensure that our partners enjoy the benefits they deserve.

We will adopt a number of flexible methods for importing technology in accordance with common bilateral intentions and requirements. We welcome our foreign friends in the electronics industry to carry out economic and technological cooperation with us through various means such as joint ventures, cooperative production, compensation trade and license trade; we also welcome them to set up factories under sole ownership in China. In order to cultivate closer bilateral cooperation, we hope that joint ventures and joint development will be adopted as much as possible. The Chinese government has decided to open another 14 coastal cities, most of which have a certain foundation in the electronics industry, and they are preparing to make the industry a focus for accelerating development and attracting foreign capital. Even those cities that have a weak electronics industry are currently drawing up long-term development plans that will create favorable conditions for foreign partners and investors. Furthermore, we recently decided to concentrate our strength in the short term on establishing some model joint ventures in open coastal cities that will be satisfactory to both Chinese and foreign parties, in order to lay the foundation for further foreign cooperation.

When we import technology, our foreign friends often fear that once China masters their advanced technology, this will affect their market. In point of fact, this will not happen. Because technology is developing rapidly and international contacts are increasing by the day, we always need to have a mutual exchange of needed products, and Chinese products also have to enter the international market and be put to the test. Every country has its advantages and features, and no country can monopolize every aspect of the international market. Moreover, China has a population of one billion with a huge market potential. Recently our country has adopted a more flexible policy to open portions of our market to the outside world when necessary and allow Chinese-foreign joint ventures to sell some of their products in China. I therefore believe our foreign friends may be rest assured.

In short, prospects are promising for China's electronics industry to further develop foreign trade and international economic and technological cooperation. We welcome our international friends in the electronics industry to carry out even more extensive, economic, and technological exchanges and cooperative projects with us.

Accelerate the Development of Our Country's Computer Industry*

September 5, 1984

More and more people now recognize the important position and role of electronic technology, especially computer technology, both in the new technological revolution and in modernization. Both the Party and the government are paying great attention to its development. All regions and departments have demonstrated their enthusiasm for using computers, particularly microcomputers, and this has created excellent conditions conducive to developing the computer industry and computer use.

Under these conditions, accelerating the development of the computer industry to satisfy the needs of the country's modernization is an important task and duty entrusted to us by the Party and people. The Ministry of Electronics Industry has designated computers as one of the strategic priorities in the development of the electronics industry and selected microcomputers as an area of focus in order to promote the comprehensive and balanced development of the computer industry. Accordingly, we must adopt a number of specific policies and measures.

I. UNSWERVINGLY ADHERE TO THE PRINCIPLE OF BEING APPLICATION ORIENTED AND USE APPLICATIONS TO PROMOTE RESEARCH AND PRODUCTION

The guiding ideology and principles for developing the electronics and computer industries are to serve the overall objectives for economic development by the end of this century as set out at the Party's Twelfth National Congress, the key strategic development priorities of the national economy and national defense, and the technological upgrading of traditional industries.

---

*Excerpt from a speech at a press conference for a computer exhibition; it originally appeared in the *China Computer World* on September 23, 1984.

The main orientation for computer R&D, production, and application from now until 1990 is: to extensively use computers, particularly microcomputers; digitize manufacturing process controls, engineering design, economic management, and all kinds of electromechanical equipment; ensure development of key national defense projects and weapon systems; expedite the upgrading of national defense equipment; set up economic information systems at all levels; and provide government agencies at all levels with modern business tools.

The goals for computer applications before 1990 are: to have computers widely used in all large enterprises and institutions of higher learning; give high priority to spreading their use in medium-sized enterprises, research institutes, secondary specialized schools, storage and transportation facilities, and government offices responsible for economic management; equip some small enterprises, secondary schools, business management organizations, and hotel service providers with computers; and get selected township and village enterprises, primary schools, government purchasing centers, and wholesale and retail businesses to either use computers on a trial basis or partially install them.

II. STRIVE TO IMPROVE RESEARCH, DESIGN, AND PRODUCTION TECHNOLOGY, INCREASE DOMESTICATION OF COMPUTERS, AND ESTABLISH OUR OWN COMPUTER INDUSTRY

It would be impossible for us to modernize without electronic computers. As the four modernizations progress, the demand for computers is growing rapidly, and we cannot rely on imported computers in the long run. This is not only because it saps our national strength, but also because genuinely advanced foreign products are not for sale and adequate supplies of spare parts and technical services for imported computers are not guaranteed, not to mention the additional oversight they are subject to, which imposes limitations.

At present, our country's computer industry—consisting of R&D, production, application, and personnel training—has established a significant foundation, and has in particular gained superiority with respect to the Chinese character system and technical service packages. We still need to speed up technological upgrading on the existing foundation; organize efforts to tackle major scientific and technological problems; strive to improve research, design, and production technologies and our domestic auxiliary support capability; and resolve to improve the price/performance ratio of our domestically produced computers.

At the same time, we need to work out limited protectionist policies to support the development and growth of our computer industry.

III. ADOPT THE INNOVATION STRATEGY OF SKIPPING DEVELOPMENT STAGES, AND TAKE A PATH OF MODERNIZING THE ELECTRONICS INDUSTRY WITH CHINESE CHARACTERISTICS

In line with the demand for applications, we will formulate a development plan suited to our country's conditions. We will take application requirements and improved economic performance as our starting point, work hard to achieve socialized mass production, and refrain from blindly striving to reach high technical targets.

In research, we will aim to reach advanced levels achieved in foreign countries and organize research on different levels to tackle key scientific problems.

On the basis of the experience we have gained in developing television sets and tape recorders, we will start with end products and concentrate on production technology, basic components and the domestic production of parts and components, in addition to concentrating on product technology. Whatever products we can produce domestically, we will do so and no longer import them. Any products we cannot produce ourselves will be imported from abroad and from end products onward we will progressively expand the production chain and become more self-reliant.

IV. VIEW THE COUNTRY AS A WHOLE, REMOVE DEPARTMENTAL AND REGIONAL BARRIERS, FORMULATE OVERALL PLANS AND SELECT THE BEST TO RECEIVE OUR SUPPORT

As the authority responsible for the computer industry, the Bureau of Computer Industry of the Ministry of Electronics Industry needs to proceed from our national interests and view the country as a whole, make overall plans, and organize the main research and production forces in all departments, regions, local enterprises, and enterprises directly under the ministry on the basis of merit and set them on a track of nationwide professional collaboration.

We must vigorously promote collaboration and the formation of consortiums of central and local enterprises and institutions, invest in partnerships through various means, and establish all forms of associations in R&D, production, education, business operations, and services. We must judge all consortiums on uniform criteria, select the best and grant them preferential treatment in financing, tariffs, and industrial and commercial taxes so they can become more competitive.

V. ADHERE TO THE OPENING UP POLICY AND BRING IN TECHNOLOGY AND CAPITAL TO ADVANCE TECHNOLOGICAL PROGRESS

Opening up provides favorable conditions for our country to attract foreign capital, import technology, and use both international and domestic markets and resources. It enables us to see clearly how far we have fallen behind the world's advanced industrialized countries, and it arouses our spirit of struggle.

We need advanced technology and sincere cooperation. We welcome and are ready to engage in technological and economic cooperation and trade with large foreign companies that have considerable technological and economic strength, and we are also willing to cooperate with small and medium-sized foreign companies.

We operate on the principle of equality and mutual benefit. We will open portions of our market to the outside world in return for truly advanced and appropriate technologies. Under the same conditions we will establish cooperative relations with foreign companies based on their technological and economic strength, sincerity in cooperation and attitude toward China.

We will make the most of favorable conditions in special economic zones and open cities to attract foreign funds and import technology by allowing the development of wholly foreign-owned enterprises, in addition to already existing forms of cooperation such as joint ventures, compensation trade and cooperative production. All departments, regions, enterprises, and institutions may, subject to government approval, experiment in running manufacturing enterprises that are wholly Chinese owned or joint ventures in developed countries.

To facilitate technology imports and the integration of technology with trade, we need to integrate the national plan for importing computers with that for importing technology through overall planning.

VI. ADHERE TO THE PRINCIPLE OF PURSUING LIMITED OBJECTIVES AND FOCUSING ON KEY AREAS, CONCENTRATE ON USING AND MANUFACTURING MICROCOMPUTERS, AND DEVELOP SMALL, MEDIUM-SIZED, AND LARGE COMPUTERS IN LIGHT OF ACTUAL NEEDS

Microcomputers are the most widely used products with the most conspicuous economic returns, and China urgently needs to spread this new technology. We must proceed from our country's actual conditions and give high priority to their production and application, and devote sufficient attention to this matter. At the same time, we must also refrain from rushing headlong into action.

We must concentrate our funds and efforts to make the key 0520, 0310, and ZD-2000 microcomputers the focus of our efforts to foster international cooperation, develop product technology, and build our industrialized production capability.

From now until the Seventh Five-Year Plan period, we will make full use of existing conditions to focus on developing three computer industry bases in north, east and south China, and progressively establish an industrialized mass production system for host computers, peripherals and software involving specialized cooperation and coordination over the whole range of R&D, production, application, marketing, services, personnel training, and maintenance.

We need to improve market research and forecasting, make overall plans, divide work rationally, make the most of our strengths while compensating for our weaknesses, and fully exploit our advantages. We will develop all kinds of general-purpose application systems for microcomputers and equip them with Chinese character processing capability so that our users can use them right out of the box. We need to satisfy the needs of our domestic market by supplying products having a price/performance ratio approaching the world's best and strive to enter some of our products into the international market.

We need to concentrate our efforts on developing large-scale integrated circuits for microcomputers, introducing advanced technology from abroad, carrying out technological upgrading, and developing our capability for industrialized production, so we can provide large-scale integrated circuits that approach the world advanced level of microcomputer manufacturing.

While focusing on developing microcomputers, we also need to develop minicomputers and maintain sufficient research and financial resources to track advanced technology used in small, large and medium-sized computers abroad. We will set super minicomputers as the focus of our development of small computers and focus on disseminating the 3000 series of computers for widespread use. Before 1990, we will organize the unified importation of components to assemble large and medium-sized computers and super minicomputers in China, stimulate the development of systems and production technology, and organize maintenance and secondary development at home so that we can lay the preliminary groundwork for industrialized production.

VII. INTENSIFY DEVELOPMENT OF THE COMPUTER SERVICES INDUSTRY

For an extremely complicated product like a computer we must have a strong supporting services industry. We can obtain greater benefits from computer use only by providing good technical training, repair and maintenance, and carrying out secondary development.

At present, China Computer Technical Service Corporation and China Software Technology Corporation together with branches of them across the country have been established, and China Computer Systems Engineering Corporation and branches of it will also be established. This signals the creation of our country's computer services industry. Yet, it still falls short of the needs of the rapidly growth of computer use. Greater development is still necessary, and we need to encourage some computer producers to shift to the services industry in order to strengthen its development.

While research and production of computer products should be concentrated, application development and technical services can take the form of widespread development. We will encourage more state-run and collective enterprises and individuals to engage in software development, technical services, and systems development in order to create a nationwide computer technology service network. We will also provide preferential treatment in taxation, loans and depreciation in accordance with state regulations.

We will support the founding of the China Software Industry Association to stimulate our software industry development.

VIII. CONTINUE TO IMPLEMENT REFORM, SIMPLIFY ADMINISTRATION, AND DELEGATE POWER

We will implement the Provisional Regulations on Granting More Autonomy to State-Run Industrial Enterprises promulgated by the State Council and the supplementary regulations of the Ministry of Electronics Industry, and provide guidance tailored to the situation in order to invigorate our enterprises.

We will institute a responsibility or contract system for attaining economic and technological targets in all enterprises and institutions, reward the diligent, sanction the indolent, and fundamentally eliminate the problem of everyone eating from the same big pot, thereby arousing the initiative of the workforce and stimulating the development of production.

We will promptly carry out institutional reform in enterprises and institutions and integrate research with production more closely. We need to shorten the period of trial production of new products and promote faster application of scientific and technological advances in production.

On the basis of the nature of computer technology, we will speed up the establishment of trans-regional and trans-departmental economic and technological consortiums or joint stock companies on a trial basis, and grant them significant autonomy in order to accelerate their development.

Accelerating the development of our computer industry requires the strong support of concerned departments and industries nationwide. The support of the news media in generating publicity is especially important. I therefore hope you will give us greater support in the future to invigorate our country's electronics industry.

Revitalize the Electronics Industry and Promote the Four Modernizations*

September 16, 1984

I

Fierce debate currently rages both at home and abroad regarding the new technological revolution, and opinions are divided. However, the common view holds that electronic science and technology, particularly microelectronics and electronic computers, occupy a position of crucial significance in the new technological revolution. This is due to the fact that electronic technology meets the requirements of current and future social progress.

Electronic science and technology are comprehensive disciplines that study the laws governing the motion of electrons and electromagnetic waves and their effects and are physical means used in information processing, energy conversion and a wide range of other fields. They can turn many kinds of natural energy and information into electrical signals, and absorb, reproduce, detect, differentiate, transmit, switch, store, compute, control, process or mimic them in order to use them in various ways. At present, people can install an electronic circuit that contains thousands, tens or hundreds of thousands or even a million electronic components on a fingernail-sized semiconductor chip to make a large-scale or very-large-scale integrated circuit. Although these kinds of microelectronic devices are small, they are very powerful. The rapid development and widespread application of integrated circuits marks the beginning of a new phase in the electronics industry based on microelectronic technology, in which electronic products become miniaturized, digital and intelligent. In particular, since the use of microelectronic technology in computers began, the performance of computers has increased considerably and their prices have dropped significantly, opening up new fields of potential utilization.

---

*Originally published in the journal *Red Flag*, No. 18, 1984.

One could say that in the history of the development of production in human society, the manufacturing and application of machine tools extended and augmented human hands, and that the invention and application of steam and electrical engines extended and replaced some physical labor, leading to the rapid development of the productive forces. Similarly, it may be said that the invention and application of electronic computers that use microelectronic technology, with functions such as memory (information storage), computing, control, and a certain degree of logical judgment, are capable of aiding people's thinking, and have thus extended their brains and replaced certain mental labor. The use of electronic computers based on microelectronic technology has raised IT and automation technology to an entirely new level and become the technological foundation of modern society. All this constitutes tremendous progress of epoch-making significance in the history of the development of natural science and technology and is an important hallmark of the new technological revolution.

Because of the ease of integrating electronic science and technology with other sciences and technologies and their permeation into other areas, their widespread application can promote advances in other aspects of science and technology and bring about profound changes in the entire social and economic structure, even in human life itself. For example, through the photoelectric effect, electronic technology is integrated with optics to produce optoelectronic technology, providing a more effective physical means of information processing. The integration of electronic technology with mechanical engineering technology leads to qualitative changes in traditional industries such as machinery, light industry and textiles, as well as the development of a series of new electromechanical products and the opening up of new markets. All the automation equipment needed in the so-called 3A Revolution (factory, office and home automation) in modern society uses microelectronic technology and computers as its core technology. Electronic technology is now being applied in the economy, sciences, culture, military affairs, and all aspects of people's lives on an unprecedented scale and at an unprecedented speed, bringing a new look to many areas of society.

Electronic products have many characteristics—they are highly reliable and low in power consumption, and save energy, materials, space and human effort. They have high value added, and their use can significantly increase production and work efficiency, lower consumption of energy and raw materials, and produce considerable economic returns. Therefore, in most developed countries the electronics industry has developed rapidly, demand for electronic products has increased sharply and the electronics industry's proportion of the gross output value in the national economy has expanded. Many countries have designated the electronics industry a priority for investment and development.

II

Faced with the challenges posed by the new technological revolution, people are paying great attention to the development of China's electronics industry. Most comrades advocate stressing the development and application of new technology in China, giving the electronics industry a leading position in modernization and adopting effective measures to accelerate its development. They believe that only in this way can we create and develop high-tech industries, apply advanced electronic technology to upgrade conventional industries, establish a material and technological foundation for our country's modernization, catch up with the scientific and technological level of advanced industrial countries, and create the conditions requisite for revitalizing the economy. Others, however, think that China's top priority should be to focus initially on developing traditional industries and waiting until they are functioning well to provide a foundation before we develop the electronics industry. Still others think that given our country's large population, pursuing automation will create employment problems, and so on. We believe that in these new circumstances in which the new technological revolution is taking off throughout the world, we need to deeply understand a statement made by the State Council in the Sixth Five-Year Plan, "The electronics industry performs a vital function in modernization, and we should place great emphasis on its development and progressively apply electronics to every sector of the economy." In line with this spirit, we must also emphasize the development of the electronics industry.

Admittedly, our country's traditional industries are certainly not fully developed; their technological level is not very high, and energy and transportation are the weakest links in the four modernizations, so we should focus on them and accelerate their development. However, how can we improve traditional industries to strengthen the weak links? The key lies in relying on technological progress and placing traditional industries on an advanced material and technological base. In some sense, the core of such a base is modern electronic science and technology. Energetically developing and applying electronic science and technology can provide advanced technical equipment for the development and technological upgrading of traditional industries and inject them with new production capacity, while at the same time enabling more efficient use of energy resources and reducing the pressure economic development puts on them. This is one effective way of overcoming shortages of energy and transportation. According to forecasts, the use of computers for automated monitoring and control in the electric power industry can reduce losses caused by power outages alone by more than 2 billion yuan annually. In 1980, China's thermal electricity generation was over 240 billion kilowatt-hours. If we had used advanced technology such as electronic controls to reach the advanced level achieved in foreign countries, this could have reduced coal consumption by 23 million tons. If electronic technology were used for automated control and economic management in production in the coal, petroleum and chemical industries, their productivity would be greatly increased. The experience of foreign countries suggests that if railroads universally adopted this technology to manage transport, shipping efficiency could be raised by 25–30%. Even if we are overestimating by 10%, we could still save a large number of freight cars, and we could ship an additional 200 million tons of goods and materials a year, bringing in more than 1 billion yuan in additional revenue for the railroads, with considerable additional social and economic benefits accruing from a more rapid turnover of goods and materials. If the machinery, light and textile industries used electronic technology, they could upgrade products and introduce new models more quickly, raise the technological level of production and effect major industrial restructuring. Therefore, in the process of modernization, the electronics industry requires traditional industries as a base, and the development and upgrading of traditional industries cannot dispense with the support of electronic technology. Accelerating the development of the electronics industry and rendering it suitably future-oriented accords with the law of economic development.

China is a country with a large population and vast labor resources; this provides good conditions for developing labor-intensive industries. However, we cannot ignore the necessity of automation just because of this. In China, the primary purpose of automation is not to replace human workers, but to raise product quality, productivity and increase economic benefits, and to expend the same amount of labor to create more material wealth in order to satisfy the people's ever-increasing material and cultural needs. In addition, in our scientific experimentation and social production, there are many projects and tasks that people cannot do with their bare hands and can only be done with the help of modern electronic equipment. For example, the processing of vast quantities of data, the observation of micro-scale and cosmic-scale structures, control of production and monitoring of high-precision products, the guidance of strategic weapons, and the transmission and processing of large quantities of rapidly changing social data all depend on electronic equipment to meet the requirements of speed, precision and accuracy. Automation will reduce the workforce required for some production processes or positions, but displaced workers can be transferred to new jobs in new fields. After achieving a high level of automation, large numbers of workers may well be needed to monitor technical equipment; write programs; and provide maintenance, repair and support services. Automation can stimulate the transformation of the workforce from a reliance on physical to mental labor. The development of a number of new professions in the electronics field will provide new employment opportunities for even more people. For example, the rapid development of new professions like software engineering and information processing will require a large increase in the number of workers in the fields of software engineering, information processing and technical services.

Rigorously developing and extending the application of electronic technology will effectively promote development of socialist culture and ethics, and more quickly raise the scientific and cultural level of the whole country. The electronics industry can provide a great variety of advanced experimental scientific methods, educational facilities and publicity tools for scientific research, cultural education, and broadcasting and publicity work, and thus promote the spread of science, technology and culture, expand the scope of education and raise its quality. The electronics industry also supplies an ever-increasing array of household electronics to society, thereby gradually improving people's material and cultural standard of living.

III

At present, the prominent problems that China's electronics industry faces in its development are having a weak foundation and backward technology and lagging far behind the world-class level, all of which make it difficult for it to fulfill its heavy responsibilities in the four modernizations. Faced with the challenges of the new technological revolution and the urgent need for electronic technology in modernization, the electronics industry is in a key period during which it needs to concentrate on accelerating development. However, the state's financial capabilities are currently limited, and the financial and material resources that can be devoted to developing the industry are few and scattered. The inspiration and stimulus that the new technological revolution provides have given localities and departments an unprecedented and valuable enthusiasm for the electronics industry, but without strong leadership, the problem of rushing headlong into indiscriminate development might arise. Further implementation of the opening up policy has given us more opportunities to import and use world-class technology and accelerate technological progress, but at the same time it subjects Chinese electronic products to intensified competition by products made abroad. At present, China's economic management system is beset by the problems of lack of separation between government administration and enterprise management, and disconnection between higher and lower levels, and between different departments or regions; these are detrimental to the overall planning and balanced development of the country's electronics industry and make it difficult for enterprises to take initiative. In light of these factors, if we wish to accelerate the development of our electronics industry, we must proceed from our country's actual conditions, draw on beneficial experience from abroad, adhere to reform, innovate boldly, and conscientiously solve the following several problems.

1. We need to effectively solve the problem of placing the electronics industry on a strategic footing and formulate corresponding policies and measures. The four modernizations assign the industry the important tasks of providing the army with modern electronic military equipment, providing all sectors of the economy with modern electronic equipment, and supplying the people with consumer electronics. As the new technological revolution progresses, the electronics industry will take on a greater role in developing the economy and promoting social progress. Therefore, I believe that, when considering economic development, we should accord the same importance to the electronics industry as we do to energy and transportation, give priority to fostering it, and accelerate its development. At the same time, we need to study

the industry's development strategy and formulate corresponding policies and measures concerning such issues as investment; new technology and products R&D; importing technology; importing and exporting electronic products; the geographic distribution of production, electronics applications and equipment; and knowledge development. We need to put these specific policies and measures into practice in our actual work.

2. We need to look at the country as a whole, draw up a comprehensive plan and strengthen management in the industry. The electronics industry is a high-tech, multifaceted industry, requiring the combined development of basic industries and products and whole systems, hardware and software, stand-alone equipment and engineering systems, and production and technical services. It also requires close interaction between scientific research and production, as well as coordination of production with market demand. China's electronics industry is in its nascent phase; all regions and departments are actively developing it, and the situation is very positive. It is worth noting, however, that everyone is scrambling to manufacture products such as color TV sets, radio/tape recorders and microcomputers that require little capital, generate quick returns and find a ready market, but there is a lack of enthusiasm for basic products and important projects that require large investment, are difficult to complete and have a limited range of applications. This may lead to imbalance within the industry. To guide the enthusiasm of all sides to achieve planned, proportional and sound development of the electronics industry, it is necessary to look at the country as a whole; draw up good plans for the industry, break through departmental and regional barriers in the context of an overall plan; organize electronic research, production, education and use nationwide, and divide the work rationally so that all sides have their own emphasis and everyone works in concert. On the basis of the guiding principles of emancipating our minds, seeking truth from facts, grounding ourselves in practice, and making steady progress, we need to carry out a systematic and thorough reform of the leadership and management system of the electronics industry, simplify administration and delegate power with the goal of separating government administration from enterprise management, take

economic measures, and promote the reorganization and association of enterprises and economic and technological restructuring.

3. We need to implement the principle of pursuing limited objectives and focusing on key areas. There are numerous areas of electronic science and technology and branches of the electronics industry and the tasks of research, trial production and full production are onerous, but the country's financial and material resources are too limited for the many demands placed thereon. This circumstance requires us to stay grounded in reality, act within our capabilities and focus on key areas. This means we need to determine limited objectives for each stage of development, concentrate on the most important products and the most crucial technologies, promote the overall situation with breakthroughs in key areas, and obtain the best possible benefits from limited investment. In our strategic arrangements for developing the electronics industry, in the short and medium term, we should concentrate on developing microelectronics and microcomputers to establish a microelectronics foundation during the Seventh Five-Year Program period, in order to accelerate the development of electronic military equipment, computers, communications equipment and other important capital goods; accelerate the shift to a foundation of microelectronics in these goods; and coordinate the comprehensive development of the electronics industry on a new technological foundation.

To focus our energy on ensuring that the most important tasks get done, it is necessary to correctly balance centralization and decentralization. Research and production of products such as large-scale integrated circuits and computers, which are highly technology and capital intensive, need to be concentrated in areas that have abundant research, education and production capabilities, as well as superior resources and natural environments. We need to establish major centers and implement intensive production there, and we should develop extensive applications for these products. Production facilities for other electronic products whose technology is easy to master and that have wide application, such as consumer electronics, can be relatively dispersed, but the industries require overall planning and the work needs to be distributed reasonably on the basis of consumer demand and the quality of the enterprises, with the focus on helping enterprises with outstanding brand name products to expand production. In this area, planning and guidance need to be combined with competition.

4. We need to further implement the opening up policy and actively import and exploit the fruits of the world's advanced science and technology. Modern electronic science and technology are undergoing great changes and progressing rapidly. To reduce the gap between where we are and the world-class level, we need to boldly scale the heights of science and technology and adopt a step-by-step development strategy to achieve different development objectives at various stages within a specified time period in order to maintain relatively stable development. In these new circumstances in which the state is further implementing the opening up policy, we need to further expand economic and technological exchanges with foreign partners and adopt a variety of measures through various avenues, such as linking trade with both technology and industry, import and adopt world-class technology and modern management methods, strive to leapfrog some traditional development stages of electronic technology and accelerate technological progress. In some areas and for some projects, we can adopt a reverse development model, in which we first import whole equipment or components and assemble them into products which we badly need but currently cannot produce on our own, and begin by developing applications and providing technical services, then assimilate and absorb the technology and make improvements and innovations, and finally gradually become able to produce the products on our own and thus become more self-reliant. We need to let open coastal cities and special economic zones fully serve as conduits for foreign economic and technological exchanges, and at the same time give a number of well-chosen key enterprises more decision-making power in their foreign business activities in order to carry out foreign economic and technological exchanges and cooperation more effectively. Because further opening to the outside world will intensify competition from foreign electronic products, we should formulate interim policies for electronic technology and equipment for each stage and appropriately protectionist policies for domestically produced electronic products to facilitate the sound development of our national electronics industry.

In addition, we need to devote attention to developing intellectual resources and training personnel effectively. We need to strengthen and improve management of the scientific and technological workforce, continue to implement our policy on intellectuals well, make good use of skilled talent, and get the scientists and engineers we already have to fully play their role.

We also need to focus on developing new materials to provide a material basis for expanding the electronics industry. From now on, we should emphasize development of single crystal silicon wafers with a large diameter, high purity, and high integrity together with other supplementary materials; promote the industrialized production of gallium arsenide and other semiconductor compounds; and accelerate R&D on information recording materials, specialized production of sensitive materials, and development of fiber optics and fiber optic components and products.

We believe that with the attention and concern of the Party and government, the full cooperation of all regions and departments, and the implementation of correct development strategies and policies, our country's electronics industry can surely be invigorated, develop and make its proper contribution to the four modernizations.

Write a New Chapter in Our Country's Computer Industry*

December 1984

China's electronic computer industry first emerged in 1956. Over the past 28 years, it has come into being and grown from small to large. It has undergone a tortuous course of development to become an emerging industry that has a significant impact on our national economy and social activities. Because of its key function in the new technological revolution and in national economic development, it has drawn the attention of every field and profession, and an increasing number of people are seeking to fully understand its development.

Our country's computer industry has, in general, gone through three stages of development.

During the period 1956–1965, arduous pioneering efforts laid the initial foundation for the industry. Our country started to develop computers by copying Soviet computers and then by drawing on Western technology before we gradually began our own design and manufacturing. By 1965, computers developed in China had entered the second generation and research on and production of small and medium-sized integrated circuits for the third generation had begun. At that time, our country's level of computer development lagged only several years behind just a few countries, including the US and the USSR. During this period, the industry provided a quantity of computers to our military, research and educational sectors, and some industrial sectors, contributing to our national defense development, economic development, and research work. Despite embargoes imposed by foreign countries, we managed to create the electronic computer industry by fostering a spirit of self-reliance and hard work to make the country stronger. This was a great achievement. However, because the prevailing conditions limited us and we placed too much emphasis on self-reliance to the neglect of absorbing advanced foreign

---

*Foreword to the book *A General Survey of China's Computer Industry*. The original title of the foreword was "Revitalize the Computer Industry and Strive to Serve the Four Modernizations."

technology, our computer industry developed somewhat blindly. This subsequently had an adverse effect on our country's development of computers.

During the period 1966–1976, tortuous headway was made in the decade of turmoil and catastrophe brought on by the Cultural Revolution. At that time, normal research and production were severely disrupted and the introduction of foreign technology was blindly rejected. All this severely undermined our computer development. Yet, urgent national defense needs still provided some opportunities and conditions for computer development. Our engineers, technicians, cadres, and workers made strenuous efforts under extremely difficult conditions to carry our country's computer development and manufacturing to the third generation, and began to do R&D on and manufacturing of serial computers, carry out R&D on microcomputers, and develop applications for them. This was a praiseworthy accomplishment. However, during the same period, foreign computer industries developed by leaps and bounds. Although our computers also developed, the gap between us and the world advanced level, which had narrowed earlier, widened again.

Since the Third Plenary Session of the Eleventh Party Central Committee, our computer industry has gradually revived and entered a new stage of development. During this time, the Party and the government have placed great emphasis on electronic computer development and given it high priority. Influenced and stimulated by the new technological revolution and national economic development, society has increasingly recognized the position and role of electronic computers, and expanded their use into more and more fields, creating a broad market for computer development. Furthermore, implementation of the opening up policy has stimulated technology imports, raised the starting point for China's technological development and accelerated the pace at which the electronic computer industry makes technological advances. Consequently, our computer research and production have entered the fourth generation; we have begun to develop complete peripheral devices; new progress is constantly being made in developing computer software and expanding its use; the production of computers and accessories has grown considerably; and microcomputers in particular have been developing rapidly. Overall, the vigorous development of the electronic computer industry is very heartening.

Reviewing successful experience and learning lessons from our failures in the history of our computer development will no doubt benefit the future development of our computer industry and give us a relatively correct understanding of the relationships between application and manufacture, host computers and peripherals, software and hardware, and self-reliance and technology imports.

The electronic computer industry is on a development upswing and is continuing to grow. Promulgation and implementation of our development strategy for the electronics and information industries will set a clear direction for their further development. To consolidate and build on this great situation, I would like to offer the following proposals.

I. STEADFASTLY IMPLEMENT THE POLICY OF EXPANDING COMPUTER USE TO STIMULATE COMPUTER DEVELOPMENT AND ENCOURAGING COMPETITION TO PROMOTE IMPROVEMENTS

Historical experience tells us the reason the computer industry has thrived for so long is that its powerful vitality comes from the constant expansion of computer applications. In developing the computer industry, we must give top priority to expanding computer use in all sectors of society. Raising the computer industry to a new level through application development will not only generate enormous economic returns for society, but can also open a broad market for computers and create favorable conditions for the development of the computer industry. To expand computer use, we need to stress software development and continuity. Software specialists are the heart and foundation of software development and we should provide multilevel and multichannel education to train a large body of software specialists.

Computers are products of an emerging industry, and there is an enormous potential demand in society for them in terms of variety, quantity and quality. Since all regions and departments are highly enthusiastic about developing computer products, competition should be allowed, and consortiums should be created for the purpose of upgrading or eliminating products having low quality, poor performance or high prices. The level of the industry can be raised through competition. Moreover, we should actively give guidance, foster reputable brands and set up industrialized mass production so that the computer industry will undergo sound development.

In the near future, we should focus on developing microcomputers while still developing small, medium-sized, and large computers. We should develop serial computers that are compatible with the best foreign-made ones. We should stress upgrading production and testing technology.

In application development, we should support key national application programs, and satisfy the demand for computer applications in planning, economic, scientific, and technological, and information management at all levels, as well as in automated military command and office automation. We should actively spread the use of computers for the operation and management of industrial and mining enterprises, computer-aided design and testing, and the automation of production processes, as well as in efforts to conserve energy, reduce consumption and control quality.

II. TAKE THE DEVELOPMENT PATH OF IMPORTING, ASSIMILATING, DEVELOPING, AND INNOVATING

Implementation of the opening up policy has provided excellent conditions for us to import foreign advanced technology and raise the starting point for developing domestic computer technology and products. We have gained successful experience in this respect but we must continue to eliminate "Left" influences. We should break free from our old practice of doing everything from scratch by ourselves. We should change our old ideas about being self-sufficient. We should become adept at making full use of both international and domestic markets and resources, and actively pursue technological exchanges, joint ventures, and cooperative production with other countries through various channels and by flexible means on the basis of the principle of equality and mutual benefit. We should stress both the importation of advanced product and manufacturing technology and the introduction of foreign advanced management technology, including advanced technology standards. At present, our technology imports should center on the development of microcomputers. Although we should stress the introduction of foreign technology, we should not completely rely on it, let alone follow it slavishly. While importing technology, we should also effectively organize our key technological personnel in all fields to use the intelligence and wisdom of the Chinese nation to further develop and innovate on the foundation of what we have already absorbed and assimilated in order to constantly make our country more self-reliant.

Large-scale integrated circuits are the foundation of modern computers. Therefore, in addition to developing computer technology, we should successfully carry out R&D on and production of large-scale integrated circuits by using imported advanced technology in order to lay a foundation for China's independent development of computers.

III. CREATE A MANAGEMENT SYSTEM FOR THE COMPUTER INDUSTRY SUITABLE TO OUR NATIONAL CONDITIONS

We are currently implementing reform of the existing management system for our computer industry. On the basis of streamlining administration and delegating autonomy to enterprises, we are breaking down departmental, regional, and ownership barriers to further adjust the industrial structure and product mix. We should also create consortiums of various kinds in large and medium-sized cities, centered on key enterprises, and led by brand name products. We should coordinate with the government's overall plans for key development and technological upgrading projects to create a number of computer research and manufacturing centers, which have the power to make their own operational decisions, intimately integrate R&D, production, education and services, and make the most of their respective strengths. Information services and high-tech tertiary industries should be set up and developed more rigorously. We should further strengthen the development of computer technical services, software technology, and systems engineering companies at all levels, and ensure they improve their service and raise its quality. We should energetically develop application software that can yield quick results and is highly profitable and easy to popularize. We should adopt the policy of loosening controls to invigorate the computer industry, and encourage state-run and collective businesses and individuals to provide better comprehensive technical services that are more convenient for customers in order to alleviate their concerns about using computers. We should change the situation wherein government agencies directly manage enterprises by separating government administration from enterprise management. On the one hand, this should invigorate computer enterprises and allow them to expand boldly and quickly by taking advantage of their own strengths and operational ability. On the other hand, it should allow government supervisory agencies of the electronics industry at all levels to concentrate on improving management of the electronics industry and create the conditions for accelerating its development by formulating principles and policies, making overall plans, maintaining overall balance, and providing organization, coordination, oversight and services. This work should result in the gradual establishment of a management system for the electronic computer industry that suits our national conditions and has Chinese characteristics.

IV. TRAIN COMPUTER PERSONNEL AND INCREASE COMPUTER LITERACY

As computers become widely used, we need to increase computer literacy. New advances in computer technology occur every day and even those who are already computer literate still need to study to keep pace with developments in computer technology. We must fully appreciate the fact that skilled personnel have a decisive impact on the development and spread of computer technology. We should adopt a variety of methods and means to train skilled personnel. We should rely on schools to train new recruits while carrying out on-the-job training to supplement and update workers' knowledge. At the same time, we should make use of all available modern tools to spread computer knowledge to every field and profession and all sectors of society, particularly our youth. Hopefully, computer knowledge will gradually become a general-purpose intellectual tool that everyone can learn to use, just as primary and secondary schoolchildren learn languages.

The new global technological revolution is changing patterns of production and the way business is conducted in society as well as people's work and lifestyle. This profound and wide-ranging transformation presents our computer industry with both opportunities and challenges. Looking ahead, if everyone working on computer-related R&D, manufacturing, application, and business services conscientiously follows the Party Central Committee's principles and policies concerning economic reform and opening up and does their jobs well, it will not be long before we have in place a computer industry system with Chinese characteristics. This system will be technologically advanced, well structured, adaptable, and trusted by consumers. It will be able to provide all kinds of computer products, develop various types of computer engineering systems, keep pace with world advanced technology, and make breakthroughs in artificial intelligence, network systems, robotics, and especially in software engineering and new Chinese character technology. It will serve the four modernizations and all social activities more effectively and write a new, brilliant chapter in our computer industry.

Initiate a New Phase in the Electronics Industry's Services for the Four Modernizations*

January 28, 1985

The current economic situation in our country is excellent. Under the guidance of the decision on economic restructuring adopted at the Third Plenary Session of the Twelfth CPC Central Committee, economic restructuring is deepening in a wide range of areas, the national economy is dynamic, and reports of success are constantly pouring in from all over. The situation is also encouraging in the electronics industry. In 1983, the industry attained its production and profit targets for the last year of the Sixth Five-Year Program period 2 years ahead of schedule. In 1984, it achieved new breakthroughs, production and profits increased in tandem, both doubling their 1980 figures, and the main economic and technical indicators reached their highest ever level.

The Report on the Development Strategy of Our Country's Electronics and Information Industries recently approved and issued by the State Council not only gives a great boost to the present encouraging situation, but will also surely have far-reaching significance. This meeting of heads of departments and bureaus is being held to discuss and arrange our present and future work on the basis of the new situation. Through this meeting, we will further emancipate our minds and unify our understanding and efforts in order to promote the sustained and sound development of the electronics industry; to attain the objectives of "building a foundation, raising our level, improving quality, pursuing profits, octupling the gross output value, and getting 10 years ahead of the rest of

---

*Report presented at a national working meeting of heads of departments and bureaus of the electronics industry, originally titled "Accelerate Reform, Make the 'Two Shifts' and Initiate a New Phase in the Electronics Industry's Services for the Four Modernizations."

the economy"[1] more quickly; and to initiate a new phase in the electronics industry's services for the four modernizations.

I. FURTHER ADJUST THE IDEOLOGY GUIDING OUR WORK AND COMPLETE THE "TWO SHIFTS" MORE QUICKLY

The development strategy approved by the State Council for our country's electronics and information industries specify that we need to make two shifts during the Seventh Five-Year Program period. One is to shift the focus of these industries' services to the national economy, the four modernizations, and all social activities, and the other is to shift the development path of the electronics industry to one based on microelectronic technology and dominated by computers and communications equipment. Therefore, we need to develop a new generation of basic components and strengthen the foundation of the entire industry. We need to accelerate the development of new electronic products needed for military equipment and for technical equipment used in production for the civilian economy. In addition, we need to greatly increase the production of consumer electronics. Making the two shifts is the road we must take to establish an electronics industry system with Chinese characteristics.

A. Be user-oriented, emphasize applications, and continue to change the service orientation of the electronics industry

The overall work for the entire country is to promote socialist modernization and attain the grand objectives set forth at the Twelfth National Congress of the CPC. The electronics industry needs to develop more quickly and become invigorated so that it can support efforts to achieve

---

[1]This is a summary of the electronics industry's development tasks for the foreseeable future made at a national working meeting of heads of departments and bureaus of the electronics industry. "Octuple the gross output value and get ten years ahead of the rest of the national economy" means by 2000, the 1980 gross output value of China's electronics industry should be octupled and major products and production technologies should reach the level advanced industrialized countries will have reached around 1990, with certain technologies reaching the world's advanced level prevailing at that time. The latter objective is 10 years more ambitious than the objective the government set for the national economy as a whole of reaching the level those countries reached around 1980.

these objectives and accomplish this overall goal. Therefore, the electronics industry must adjust the ideology guiding its work and shift the orientation of its services. Hence, it needs to properly manage the following relationships in its ideological understanding and practical work.

1. The relationship between the application of electronic technology and the manufacturing of electronic equipment

We need to steadfastly give equal weight to both, but give application a more important position. Electronic technology is widely applicable and permeates all areas of society, so developing applications is an enormous task. However, this aspect of our work remains weak. The authorities responsible for the electronics industry at all levels and the departments engaged in electronics research and manufacturing need to orient themselves toward the application of electronic technology, make application their objective and driving force, and better serve the national economy, and accelerate the development of the electronics industry by developing applications.

In order to strengthen the intermediate links between R&D and production and between manufacturing and application in the electronics and information industries, and promote the flow of technology, products, talent, equipment, and funds, we should consider the characteristics of these industries and further strengthen or establish specialized systems engineering companies and all-purpose electronic systems engineering companies. We should also vigorously develop high-tech tertiary industry services in the areas of information, consulting, technological development, technical training, and talent exchange, and make these services horizontal and vertical bridges and links connecting companies, so that they help enterprises develop production and invigorate the economy, and assist all sectors and industries in the use of electronic technology. Software development directly affects the breadth and depth of computer applications, so we need to focus on developing, carrying forward, and protecting software, emphasize the development of software applications that achieve significant results for industries and projects, and coordinate and manage our work successfully in order to promote the development of the entire software industry.

Sectors of the electronics industry should rid themselves of the parochial view that they can be self-sufficient and instead actively cooperate with end-users, research institutes, and universities; carry out joint investment, technological cooperation, and common development; and arouse everyone's enthusiasm. Spreading the application of electronic technology, opening up markets, developing technology, and accumulating funds will create more favorable conditions for developing the electronics industry and bring about a virtuous cycle encompassing manufacturing and application.

2. Relationship between the emerging electronics industry and traditional industries

The electronics industry needs to steadfastly serve traditional industries by providing them with modern electronic equipment so that they can accelerate their pace of technological upgrading, and develop production and improve their economic performance on the basis of this new technology, and thereby help the entire national economy to take off. In order to better provide services, the electronics industry must accelerate its technological progress and genuinely play a leading role in the new technological revolution. We must ensure that this emerging industry and traditional industries are closely integrated, support and reinforce each other, and make common progress.

3. Relationship between military and civilian products

The ideology guiding the electronics industry is to ensure the production of military products and find civilian applications for military technology. The electronics industry needs to ensure it completes its work for the military industry, while also actively engaging in national economic development and better serving the four modernizations and social activities. Therefore, manufacturers of military products should make appropriate adjustments in their arrangements for research and production capabilities and their product mix. We need to promptly carry out R&D for next-generation military electronic equipment, with emphasis on its technological level. In addition, we need to make full use of the existing talent, equipment, and technology to vigorously develop civilian products, boost production, and invigorate enterprises and research institutes, so that they contribute more to national economic development. This will enable us to better promote the development and production of military electronic equipment and combine military with civilian production.

B. Build a foundation, raise our level, and accelerate the development of key revitalization projects

For the electronics industry to effectively serve the four modernizations, it must develop in advance of other sectors of the national economy. It must not only keep production growing at a rapid pace, but even more importantly, take the lead technologically. In accordance with our country's development strategy for the electronics and information industries, we need to successfully develop key areas such as integrated circuits, computers, communications equipment, and software, build a foundation for our country's electronics industry, make the second shift, and provide better services for other sectors of the national economy.

Specific policies have already been formulated and the production scale, technological level, and main types of products have been specified for the development of the above key areas in our country's development strategy for the electronics and information industries. We need to implement these policies, build a foundation, raise our level, and make the second shift more quickly. To this end, we need to mainly adopt the following measures.

1. Give high priority to key projects and select the best to receive our support. With respect to key products, we need to provide significant human, material, and financial support and ensure that during the Seventh Five-Year Program period, we produce 400 million integrated circuits, 200,000 personal computers, 1 million computer peripherals, 500 satellite communications ground stations, 10,000 km of microwave communications cable, and over 2000 km of fiber-optic communications cable per year. We will strive to use microelectronics in computers, radars, communications products, instruments, and meters and to miniaturize electronic components. We need to actively organize bidding for major revitalization products and grant more autonomy and preferential conditions to successful bidders and enterprises responsible for key projects, so that they can attain the prescribed technological objectives and economic performance.

2. Strengthen the integration of research with production and successfully establish bases. We need to focus on key projects, tasks, and products, establish consortiums of research institutes and manufacturers, and set up R&D and product technology development centers to closely integrate production with research. Based on the

development strategy for our country's electronics and information industries, which designates the establishment of two microelectronic bases (one in the north and the other in the south), Shanghai, Wuxi, and Shaoxing should form the backbone of the southern base. We need to further improve the Wuxi Consortium of Research Institutes and Manufacturers so that it starts industrialized mass production at an early date. Electronics industry organizations need to actively explore ways to make the northern base a success, and create the conditions for forming consortiums of research institutes and manufacturers capable of carrying out R&D on microelectronics and producing high-end, large-scale integrated circuits. On the basis of the geographical distribution of manufacturers and institutes and existing local advantages, we need to establish a number of sound consortiums of research institutes and manufacturers or technological development centers in the areas of computers and peripherals, software development, systems engineering, digital microwave communications, fiber-optic communications, and satellite communications. We need to start organizing our R&D and production capabilities in order to make the production of products and the development of technology more efficient.

3. Foster an awareness of overall interests and take the initiative in developing cooperation. When carrying out key revitalization projects, in addition to completing their own work, organizations working on these projects need to extensively cooperate with and assist each other. These projects impact the overall development of China's electronics and information industries, so the organizations engaged in auxiliary work need to take overall interests as their starting point, voluntarily cooperate, and provide good services. In particular, they need to give high priority to producing auxiliary products needed by their partners in these key projects.

C. Encourage competition, provide correct guidance, and spur the enthusiasm of the entire electronics industry

Propelled by the new technological revolution, regions, departments, universities and colleges, and research institutes are increasingly enthusiastic about developing electronics. Fully unleashing their enthusiasm is an important way of promoting technological progress in the electronics industry and achieving balanced development. In the past, we underestimated this enthusiasm and often tried to restrain it for fear of instability and disorder, thus adversely affecting the development of the electronics industry to some extent. In the future, in order to preserve the enthusiasm for developing electronics, we will stimulate it instead of trying to rein it in. We will correctly balance centralization and decentralization, encourage competition under unified planning, and be careful to guide the way competition develops.

For electronic products whose technological foundation is shifting to microelectronic technology, are capital and technology intensive, and have a long production cycle (such as large-scale integrated circuits, large- and medium-sized computers, SPC exchanges, and color picture tubes), production must be relatively centralized and subject to unified planning in order to avoid blind development and waste of time and human and material resources. However, we need to be careful to unleash the initiative of all parties, make full use of favorable conditions, determine who should develop what on the basis of merit identified through competition, and accomplish more undertakings with our limited financial resources. When identifying organizations to carry out key projects, we need to put an end to the existing phenomenon of organizations competing with each other for projects and investment, and launching projects unprepared. We need to replace the existing allocation system with a bidding system, whereby key projects are awarded to bidders who have lower investment costs, shorter production cycles, and technological strength, and who provide quality service. When organizations are researching and producing the same key products, we need to not only advocate cooperation and mutual support, but also encourage competition. We need to formulate technological and economic policies to encourage the advanced and spur those that lag behind, and promote technological improvement.

With regard to the assembly and processing of and software development for consumer electronics and microcomputers for which demand is great, we need to allow the traditional division of labor to be broken down, and make the most of the technological advantages some enterprises possess in order to carry out cross-industry product development, production, and application services on the basis of the needs of the market. Government agencies of the electronics industry need to release economic and technological information, formulate technical standards and specifications, and use economic levers such as prices and taxes in order to provide guidance and restraint over poorly planned and redundant projects. If decentralization, redundancy, and disorder appear, we should not simply use administrative measures to intervene; on the contrary, we need to consciously make use of the law of value, market regulation, and competition. We should organize assessments, focus on supporting high-quality and brand name products, and encourage mergers and acquisitions so that superior enterprises prosper and inferior ones fall by the wayside.

In short, competition is a strong force driving the development of research and production. It can break blockades and monopolies, attract more human, material, and financial resources to the development of electronics, stimulate people's dynamism and creativity, and induce organizations and individuals to contribute more to the application, development, and innovation of electronic technology so that the entire electronics industry develops and improves.

II. EMANCIPATE OUR MINDS, QUICKEN OUR PACE, AND MAKE ECONOMIC RESTRUCTURING IN THE ELECTRONICS INDUSTRY A SUCCESS

Since the Third Plenary Session of the Eleventh Central Committee of the CPC, many experimental and explorative initiatives have been undertaken in the electronics industry with initial success. We have granted enterprises more autonomy in their operations and management and launched pilot projects to implement the system, whereby factory directors assume full responsibility and the contract system of compensation for science and technology. We have developed economic consortiums and specialized collaboration. We have also introduced many kinds of economic contract and responsibility systems in enterprises, and carried out preliminary reforms of the distribution system. All this has played a major role in the invigoration of enterprises and the development of production. However, enterprises cannot fully exercise the additional autonomy granted to them, and many enterprises, especially large- and medium-sized ones directly under the Ministry of Electronics Industry, have yet to be invigorated. The fact that government and business responsibilities have not yet been separated and departmental and regional barriers still exist hinders development of the productive forces in the electronics industry. Successfully carrying out thorough and systematic economic restructuring in the electronics industry is thus our central task.

The main ideas for economic restructuring in the electronics industry are to streamline administration, delegate power, and grant more autonomy to enterprises in order to end excessive, stifling control over them and increase their vitality; decentralize enterprises; develop consortiums; organize specialized production; ensure that no enterprise, big or small, is all inclusive; remove barriers between enterprises and define their ownership; reform the administration functions of government agencies of the electronics industry; separate government administration from enterprise management; and strengthen supervision of the industry. We plan to implement these ideas in rudimentary form in 2 years' time. The general schedule is that this year we will focus on granting more autonomy to enterprises, decentralizing them, developing economic consortiums and specialized collaboration, and creating and developing tertiary industry services for enterprises and users. Next year, we will focus on adjusting and streamlining government administrative agencies, replacing profit remittances with tax payments for all enterprises, and gradually separating government administration from enterprise management so that the Ministry of Electronics Industry can shift its function to supervision of the industry.

A. Grant more autonomy to enterprises

Strengthening enterprises' vitality, especially that of large- and medium-sized, state-owned enterprises, is the central link of our entire economic restructuring, which takes cities as its focus. Therefore, our economic restructuring should begin with streamlining administration, delegating power, and granting more autonomy to enterprises in order to first revitalize them. However, delegating power and granting more autonomy are easier said than done. At present, enterprises still do not exercise autonomy that has been granted to them in government documents. There are many reasons for this, but are mainly as follows: first, the responsible authorities have not really delegated the power; second, reforms have not been carried out in some areas, so there is still too much red tape; and third, some enterprises have not sufficiently emancipated their minds, so they are either not bold or capable enough to exercise the power they have received. To change this situation, we need to make granting more autonomy to enterprises a central link in economic restructuring of the electronics industry. The general requirements are as follows: we need to ensure the power that should be delegated to enterprises is done; we cannot permit the situation in which power is delegated on papers, while things continue to function in the same manner. In areas where related reforms have not been carried out, we need to help coordinate efforts, remove obstacles, and eliminate obstructions. At the same time as we grant enterprises more autonomy, we need to change our leadership system, management philosophy, and ways of doing business accordingly. We need to implement a system whereby factory directors assume full responsibility, and create an effective division of labor between the Party and the government. Enterprise leaders need to draw on collective wisdom, make sound business decisions, ensure workers' congresses fully play their role, and exercise power subject to worker oversight, so that they can genuinely shape the destiny of their enterprises.

B. Decentralize enterprises and develop economic consortiums

To fundamentally eliminate the lack of separation between government administration and enterprise management, excessive control over enterprises, and departmental and regional barriers, we have decided to decentralize enterprises directly under the Ministry of Electronics Industry. We suggest that governments of provinces, autonomous regions, and municipalities directly under the central government do the same. Because the conditions of enterprises and their localities vary, they should be decentralized in batches—the easy ones first and the tough ones last. Enterprises should be set loose when conditions are ripe and should not be subject to one-size-fits-all treatment.

When we decentralize enterprises, we have to be clear what this involves. As we use the term now, it does not mean the same as it did in the past. In the past, decentralization merely involved a change in what government agencies supervise enterprises; but now it means, in principle, government agencies will no longer directly operate and manage enterprises. Instead, enterprises will have autonomy over their operations and management. It also means government administration and enterprise management will be separated, so that enterprises become truly independent economic entities and socialist commodity producers and operators that run their own operations, take responsibility for their own profits and losses, and independently engage in production and operations based in central cities. Of course, central cities also need to separate government administration from enterprise management, streamline administration, and delegate power to prevent new departmental and regional barriers from arising.

Delegating power and granting more autonomy to enterprises will greatly stimulate horizontal relations between electronics enterprises and institutions, removal of departmental and regional barriers, development of diversified forms of technological and economic cooperation, and launch of joint undertakings in the electronics field. Our past experience indicates that when setting up economic consortiums, we should bear the following points in mind:

1. Members of a consortium should have inherent technological and economic relations with each other, and consortiums must be beneficial for developing the productive forces and improving economic performance.
2. The principles of mutual need, voluntary participation, equality, and mutual benefit need to be adhered to. The leading bodies should provide guidance and encourage the formation of consortiums, but they should not force any enterprise to join against its will.
3. Consortiums should be enterprises, not administrative agencies.
4. Consortiums, large or small, should not be all inclusive. They should engage in specialized production.
5. Consortiums should not be confined to a single fixed model; they may assume different forms. They can be consortiums based in central cities with large enterprises as their backbone, regional specialized consortiums, or trans-regional or trans-sector consortiums based on the products they produce. They can be bound by either close or loose ties. An enterprise may be permitted to join several consortiums at the same time as long as this gives it vitality.

The main work we need to do this year concerning consortiums is that we need to review the experience of well-run specialized and regional electronics consortiums in order to learn from their experience and strengthen and improve them. We need to rectify and adjust badly run consortiums lacking the necessary internal relations between their members and those whose members have joined involuntarily. Some consortiums are administrative companies and should transform themselves into enterprises on the basis of the principle of separating government administration from enterprise management. In big cities where there are many enterprises directly under the Ministry of Electronics Industry, we should further reorganize these enterprises and encourage them to form consortiums in order to make new progress. We will continue our success in operating specialized processing centers in the fields of forging and casting, die, injection molding, and electroplating, as well as measuring and testing centers and ensure that they engage in socialized and specialized mass production.

C. Reform the distribution system in enterprises

In order to revitalize enterprises and fully arouse the enthusiasm, initiative, and creativity of employees, we must abolish the faulty egalitarian distribution system, whereby everyone eats from the same big pot. The State Council has issued a notice concerning salary reform in state-owned industrial enterprises, which links employee salaries with their enterprises' economic performance as of 1985. Specifically, employee payrolls will vary within a stipulated range based on the enterprises' performance relative to economic and technological indices such as the profits and taxes they pay to the government. Salary levels in different enterprises will vary in accordance with variations in their economic performance. Enterprises need to distribute salaries and bonuses in accordance with the principle of more pay for more work, while differentiating between physical and mental labor and between skilled and unskilled labor. To successfully implement salary reform, we must soundly establish all kinds of economic contract, responsibility systems, and job responsibility systems, and successfully do the basic work of compiling original records, setting production quotas, and doing economic accounting so as to link employee remuneration to work performance.

D. Successfully reform the pricing, production, supply, and marketing systems

As enterprises gain more autonomy, the function of price in regulating production and management activities becomes increasingly significant. We should consciously apply the law of value and the principle of exchange at equal value to systematically reform the pricing system for electronic products. First, we need to lower the overall level of prices for electronic products and gradually bring them closer to those prevailing in international markets. As prices for raw and semi-finished materials rise, we must work hard to cut costs. Second, we need to establish internal rational parity and differential pricing systems, and ensure all types of enterprises have similar levels of profit distribution. In addition, we need to reform the pricing management system and gradually establish flexible systems for decision making, oversight and control, and information feedback relating to prices.

In reforming the planning system, we need to cut mandatory planning considerably, increase guidance planning, and expand the scope of control by market forces to an appropriate degree. With regard to the supply of materials and product marketing, we need to reduce the number of materials and products under state monopoly, reduce intermediate links, and further lift controls. We need to use a variety of operational methods, actively participate in market economic activities, strive to open up markets, and provide better services for enterprises and users.

E. Reform the systems for managing science and technology and the education system

The main orientation for reforming the system for managing electronic science and technology is as follows.

1. Scientific research needs to be oriented toward production and application and closely linked with production. Research institutes engaged in product development need to do everything possible to enter into economic and technological cooperation or form consortiums with corresponding enterprises.
2. We need to further institute the contract system of compensation for science and technology, vigorously develop the market for electronic technology, and spur the transformation of electronic technology into commodities. All research institutes, except for a small number engaged in basic research, need to gradually turn into technology-based businesses that generate their own income and are responsible for their profits and losses instead of depending on the government for their operating expenses.
3. Research institutes should implement a research project contract system and a system whereby their directors assume full responsibility, and reward outstanding contributors generously.

The objective of reform of the education system in the electronics industry should be to accelerate the training of scientific, technical, and managerial personnel in the electronics field through many channels, at many levels, and by various means, and integrate formal universities with on-the-job training schools in enterprises and institutions. A pilot contract system for admitting students who have predetermined employers will be implemented in universities so that universities will not have to find jobs for those students when they graduate. Universities should gear themselves to the needs of society and help invigorate the electronics industry.

F. Adjust and reform government functional bodies within the electronics industry

In the course of separating government administration from enterprise management and streamlining administration, the Ministry of Electronics Industry, supervisory bureaus, and government supervisory agencies of the electronics industry in provinces, autonomous regions, and municipalities directly under the central government and their functions, need to undergo corresponding adjustment and reform.

1. The existing double-tiered supervision system of the Ministry of Electronics Industry will be reformed. In the past, because the electronics industry was large, produced a wide variety of products, and used complicated technology, we practiced the double-tiered supervision system based on products produced at the level of the ministry and those produced at the level of supervisory bureaus and China National Electronic Devices Industry Corporation. This system played a role in strengthening the supervision of branches of the electronics industry, but it is no longer suited to the new situation in which we are separating government administration from enterprise management, streamlining administration, delegating power, and decentralizing enterprises. The ministry has therefore decided to restructure double-tiered supervision and centralize it at the ministerial level only. Because it will take a while to grant more autonomy to enterprises and decentralize them, it will also take some time to make adjustments in the ministry and its supervisory bureaus. During this transition period, all departments need to continue exercising their functions and all employees need to carry out their duties to ensure smooth progress in reform, production, and development.

2. Government supervisory agencies of the electronics industry at all levels will no longer be responsible for enterprise production and

operations. They need to make a gradual transition to exercising supervision of the industry at different levels on the basis of the eight economic supervision functions specified for the government in the decision of the CPC Central Committee on economic restructuring. They need to shift from their former practice of managing the day-to-day work of enterprises to assuming responsibility for carrying out investigations and studies; undertaking comprehensive analyses, overall planning, organization, and coordination; formulating principles, policies, and economic laws and regulations; and providing macro guidance and oversight. The Ministry of Electronics Industry, a functional department of the State Council, will be in charge of the electronics industry nationwide. Because the electronics industry is an emerging industry, we suggest that the governments of provinces, autonomous regions, and municipalities directly under the central government set up departments and bureaus of the electronics industry or similar agencies with responsibility for their local electronics industries.

3. We will improve the work style of government agencies in accordance with the principles of serving the people and of simplification, uniformity, and efficiency. In conformity with the requirement of "being open-minded in delegating power and providing attentive services," employees of all government departments in charge of the electronics industry must firmly adopt the mentality of wholeheartedly providing services for research and production, serving primary-level bodies and enterprises, and serving the people. In this new situation, they need to strive to improve their quality. Through reform, they need to thoroughly overcome longstanding bureaucratic abuses such as organizational overlap, overstaffing, vague demarcation of functions, ducking responsibility, and petty disputes, in order to significantly improve their work efficiency.

G. Strengthen the organization and leadership of reform efforts

Correct guiding ideology is essential for ensuring smooth progress in economic restructuring in the electronics industry. First, we need to emancipate our minds. We need to arm our minds with the new thinking and ideology of integrating the basic tenets of Marxism with Chinese realities as set forth in the decision of the CPC Central Committee on economic restructuring. We need to genuinely break free from the shackles of "Left" ideology, break down stereotypes, acquire a correct understanding of the new situation, study new developments and creatively explore new ways of invigorating the electronics industry. Second, we need to seek truth from facts. We need to use reform measures to address practical problems facing the development of the electronics industry in order to meet the objective requirements for accelerating development. Third, we need to actively engage in practice. We need to respect science, pay attention to investigations and studies, successfully implement pilot projects, and review experience and explore laws from the standpoint of actual practice. Fourth, we need to take solid steps. We need to avoid formalism in our reform efforts and not seek prestige. We need to strive for accelerated and steady progress in our reform. We need to take one step at a time and make changes only after correctly assessing the situation. When we are not sure, we should implement pilot projects first. We need to do solid work and seek practical results.

III. FURTHER OPEN TO THE OUTSIDE WORLD AND ACCELERATE THE IMPORT OF FOREIGN CAPITAL AND ADVANCED TECHNOLOGY

Opening to the outside world is an important strategic decision for accelerating our country's four modernizations. At present, electronic technology is developing rapidly. It would be inefficient and expensive to start from scratch and replace the backward technology of our country's electronics industry with advanced technology all by ourselves. We must take the path of importation, assimilation, development, and innovation and develop new technology and new products from a higher starting point. This will enable us to avoid wasting human, material, and financial resources repeating the work others have done developing technologies and solving problems. It will enable us to directly make use of foreign scientific and technological results, skip certain development stages, and achieve rapid technological and economic development from a higher starting point. In recent years the electronics industry has actively imported technology in accordance with the principles of invigorating the domestic economy and opening to the outside world. This has promoted technological progress and enabled many enterprises to make the transition from backward production modes to modern production, demonstrating that importing technology is an effective shortcut for narrowing the gap between China and foreign countries. There is now some disorder in the importation of complete sets of electronic equipment and the production and assembly of components, but this is an unavoidable problem in our forward progress. In general, the electronics industry needs to open wider. On this issue, we need to be strategically minded, stand on higher ground, be more farsighted, and continue to emancipate our minds.

A. Further ease policies

In order to initiate a new phase in importing technology and using foreign capital in the electronics industry, we need to adopt flexible methods and use multiple channels in order to continue to expand the integration of trade with industry and technology and increase compensation trade, while also seeking to establish more joint ventures and increase cooperative production. We need to create a better environment and conditions for Sino-foreign joint ventures. We need to use our domestic market as a bargaining chip for importing more advanced technology in accordance with the principles of equality and mutual benefit and of opening portions of our market to the outside world in return for foreign technology. However, we will open portions of our market only if we can import advanced technology and equipment we really need. In importing technology, we need to make full use of the enthusiasm of all departments, regions, enterprises and institutions by allowing them to independently import technology whenever possible to meet their actual needs. They may also establish factories and open information offices abroad.

B. Import technology from a higher starting point

In recent years, production line downstream assembly technology imported by the electronics industry has taken up a considerable share of the industry's technological imports. Many of the imported projects use only elementary technology, but our imports of basic and advanced technologies are weak. In the future, we need to strive to avoid redundant imports of low technology; our imports need to gradually extend forward from downstream processing in accordance with planning, and we need to import a greater proportion of basic and new advanced technologies that give us a higher starting point. We need to overcome the emphasis on importing hardware to the neglect of software and importing components to the neglect of basic technology, and the tendency to neglect the importation of talent. We need to stress importing product design technology, application development technology and modern production technology. While we build our production capacity, we need to establish experimental and development bases. We need to integrate the import of product technology and equipment with the introduction of managerial technology and talent, explore avenues for recruiting talent and create a situation in which we can import talent.

C. Give priority to assimilating and absorbing imported technology and stress development and innovation

Importing is a means, not an end. We need to concentrate our technological capabilities on assimilating imported technology in order to spread its use and achieve greater returns on investment. In addition, we need to integrate development based on imports with becoming self-reliant, do our best to use imported technology as a basis for our own innovations, and make our country more self-reliant. There are some kinds of basic technology, new technology and new products that foreign countries will not transfer to us; therefore, we need to organize research to tackle key projects so we can develop and produce them on our own. We have a large electronics research force. The electronics industry nationwide has over 120 research centers with tens of thousands of researchers, and they ought to be able to achieve something in research on key problems and develop more next-generation electronic products to win honor for the industry and the motherland.

D. Make use of special economic zones and open coastal cities as windows and springboards to promote the large-scale import and export of electronic technology and products

1. We must do a better job in introducing foreign technology and establishing lateral ties between the coastal region and the interior. We need to make full use of the favorable conditions of special

economic zones and open coastal cities to introduce foreign advanced technology and scientific managerial expertise, collect economic information worldwide, accelerate development of the electronics industry in the coastal region, and spread the technology and information in the interior. Moreover, we need to promote economic consortiums and technological cooperation in order to make full use of the advantages of enterprises in the interior and so they can support development of the industry in the coastal region.

2. We need to successfully establish lateral ties between the coastal region and the interior and export more electronic products. We need to place these products on the international market through special economic zones and open coastal cities and increase their export. The key to initiating a new phase in the export of electronic products is to update and upgrade them more quickly, improve their quality and technological level, bring them closer to international standards and lower their cost to make them more competitive. At the same time we need to implement reforms to formulate policies on price subsidies for export products and the proportion of foreign exchange exporters can retain, in order to increase enterprises' enthusiasm for exporting products.

IV. CONSCIENTIOUSLY FORMULATE THE SEVENTH FIVE-YEAR PROGRAM FOR THE ELECTRONICS INDUSTRY

Copies of the draft outline for the Seventh-Five Year Program were printed and distributed at a national working meeting of heads of departments and bureaus of the electronics industry last year, but the situation has changed somewhat over the past year. There are four guidelines I want to discuss.

A. Give equal emphasis to speed, level, and efficiency

Our preliminary estimates place the gross output value of the electronics industry at 60 billion yuan in 1990, six times the 1980 figure (an annual increase of 20.1%). We need to improve economic performance and ensure both production and performance increase in step. The development trend of the electronics industry over the past two years suggests that by 2000 its annual output value could be more than eight times its value in 1980, but it will be difficult for the technological level to reach the level developed countries will reach around 1990. With regard to development and technological upgrading of the electronics industry during the Seventh Five-Year Program period, we must focus on building a foundation and raising our level and strive to improve research methods and increase our capacity for developing new products and raise the level of our production technology. On the basis of a new foundation and technological level, we will stress speed and performance, increase our capacity for sustained development, and achieve long-term steady growth.

B. Focus on priorities, concentrate investment in certain areas, and raise funds in various ways and through multiple channels

During the Seventh Five-Year Program period, government investment in capital construction in the electronics industry will be limited, but there are many problems to solve. Therefore, we must focus on priorities and strive for balanced development. We will make integrated circuits, computers, communications equipment and software our priorities, and concentrate on making breakthroughs in certain appropriate new technologies in these fields while developing related complementary products such as electronic materials, technical equipment, measuring instruments, components, and devices. In order to achieve comprehensive and balanced development, we will give a leading position to electronic capital goods, and accelerate their development, while continuing to significantly increase production of consumer electronics. We need to concentrate our funds on certain areas and keep the focus of investment on the technological upgrading of old enterprises. In principle we will not launch new projects. We need to rid ourselves of the mentality of depending on the government for help and implant the mentality of developing production by relying on reform, government policy, and science and technology. We will raise funds through multiple channels and in various ways such as joint development, investment, and production with end-users in other industries. We will also actively develop Sino-foreign cooperation and attract foreign capital.

C. Make overall plans and maintain overall balance

We need to take the overall situation as our point of departure. We need to make overall plans for research and production; basic industries and products and whole systems; the coastal region, the interior and the hinterland; and military and civilian products. In the spirit of reform, we need to coordinate the distribution of our productive forces with ongoing efforts to reorganize enterprises, establish consortiums, plan comprehensive regional development, and promote socialized and specialized mass production. When formulating a regional electronics industry plan, we need to consider local conditions, make full use of our advantages and take care not to develop self-sufficient systems in disregard of objective conditions. We will organize enterprises and institutions to formulate development plans in accordance with the overall plan for the electronics industry, and complete the preparations for development, upgrading and importation projects as soon as possible.

D. Emphasize training talent

The electronics industry is an emerging technology- and knowledge-intensive industry. Both the development speed and technological level of the electronics industry as well as the breadth and depth of the application of electronic technology depend on the number and quality of skilled personnel. Future competition in R&D, production and application will inevitably become competition for talent. Leaders at all levels must promote talent training from a strategic perspective and generously invest in intellectual development. We need to send more students abroad for further studies in order to train a number of high-level technical personnel. We need to run institutions of higher learning effectively and expand training of mid-level technological and management personnel. We need to offer excellent training programs of various kinds to improve the professional skills and general knowledge of employees in the workplace and make on-the-job training an important channel for developing new talent. We need to emphasize improving the professional knowledge of our present technological and management personnel and help them constantly update their knowledge and improve their skills.

V. PROMOTE RESEARCH AND PRODUCTION AND CONTINUE TO DEVELOP THE PRESENT EXCELLENT SITUATION

Over the past year, the electronics industry has made major progress. However, we must remain clearheaded about our achievements and be aware of our shortcomings and deficiencies. For example, our output value and profits increased by a large margin, but a portion of our profits was obtained through the assembly of ready-to-assemble kits and is attributable to the import and export price differential; and our foundation is weak. In particular, we should be aware that in terms of variety, quantity, and technological level, our country's electronic products fall far short of the needs of the four modernizations and the masses, and they have a long way to go before they reach world advanced levels. In 1985, the last year of the Sixth Five-Year Program period, we need to both accomplish all the tasks for the year and make sound preparations for greater progress during the Seventh Five-Year Program period, so our task is difficult.

According to the plan, the gross output value of the electronics industry will be 24 billion yuan in 1985, an increase of 18% over last year in real terms, which is higher than the 8% projected increase for gross industrial output value nationwide. The output of major products will be as follows: 10.5 million TV sets, an increase of 14.5% over last year (of which 3 million are color TV sets, up 200%); 6 million tape recorders, an increase of 6.2%; 40,000 microcomputers, an increase of 12.5%; 340 small and medium-sized computers, up 10%; and 52.858 million integrated circuits, an increase of 46.7%. The output of other products will also increase considerably. The plan estimates profits and taxes for the year of 3.4 billion yuan. We have also planned 5215 R&D pilot projects for the year. On the one hand, in formulating plans for this year's research and production, we have decided to strive to increase production and accelerate R&D pilot projects in order to meet the urgent needs for electronic products in economic and national defense development and the consumer economy. On the other hand, our plans leave open the possibility that the production of many products will be subject to guidance planning and regulation by market forces. We will do all we can to exceed all our planned targets. To do so, we need to emphasize the following aspects of our work.

First, we need to improve product quality. As the electronics market expands and the demand for some electronic products outstrips supply, we need to increase the production of high-quality and brand name products and vigorously develop new products, paying particular attention to ensuring product quality and never allowing shoddy products to find their way onto to the market.

Second, we need to continue to comprehensively overhaul and turn around enterprises. Twenty percent of all electronics enterprises have not passed overhaul certification, and the bulk of them are losing money. All competent authorities need to exercise more effective guidance to help these enterprises complete their overhaul this year and turn around enterprises operating in the red. We need to change the content of the overhaul and the acceptance criteria in accordance with the new spirit of reform and focus the overhaul on the different problems enterprises have, especially core problems. We need to emphasize regular inspection and assessment and no longer deploy inspection and acceptance teams. Enterprises that have been certified need to further improve their operations and management on the basis of the reform, introduce scientific management methods in a planned and systematic way, and move in the direction of modern management.

Third, we need to conscientiously implement development and technological upgrading projects during the Sixth Five-Year Program period so that more of them will come into operation and produce practical results as early as possible. It is particularly important to successfully implement key national capital construction projects and the 550 key national technological upgrading projects. If we complete this aspect of our work well, we will reap enormous economic rewards.

We need to learn to concern ourselves with important matters, understand the whole picture, and manage our own industry. The five points mentioned above are major issues affecting the overall development of the electronics industry. We need to handle them effectively not only to continue to maintain and develop the excellent situation in 1985, but also to lay a solid foundation for development in the Seventh Five-Year Program period. Economic restructuring is deepening, and the new technological revolution centered on microelectronic technology has attracted great attention from the government. All this will surely stimulate the constant development of our national economy. In this new situation, employees in the electronics industry shoulder an arduous yet glorious historic mission. We must conscientiously implement the guiding principles of the Third Plenary Session of the Twelfth CPC Central Committee and work tirelessly to initiate a new phase in the electronics industry and accomplish the general tasks and objectives set forth at the Party's Twelfth National Congress.

APPENDIX A. BASIC STRATEGY AND MEASURES FOR ACCELERATING THE DEVELOPMENT OF OUR COUNTRY'S ELECTRONICS INDUSTRY[*]

January 24, 1985

On the basis of the trends in the world's new technological revolution and the development of electronic technology, as well as our country's actual conditions, and in order to embrace this revolution, accelerate the development of our country's electronics industry, and achieve the objectives of "octupling the industry's gross output value and getting 10 years ahead of the rest of the national economy,"[1] we have formulated the following development strategy and measures after much deliberation and discussion.

I. NEW CHARACTERISTICS OF DEVELOPMENT OF THE GLOBAL ELECTRONICS INDUSTRY AND THE SEVERE CHALLENGES OUR COUNTRY'S ELECTRONICS INDUSTRY IS FACING

Since the 1970s, Western countries have been mired in economic stagnation and their traditional industries have regressed, but their electronics industries have maintained a fast pace of development. The electronics industries in the US, Japan, the UK, France, and the Federal Republic of Germany grew at an annual average rate of 13.8% from 1970 to 1979. The output of electronic products in capitalist countries totaled approximately $363 billion in 1983, and this is expected to reach $686 billion in 1987, an increase of more than 88% since 1983. It is particularly

---

[*]Report by the leading Party group of the Ministry of Electronics Industry to the Secretariat of the CPC Central Committee. Drafted under the direction of Jiang Zemin, the report was designated for study at a national working meeting of heads of departments and bureaus of the electronics industry in 1985.

[1]"Octuple the gross output value and get 10 years ahead of the rest of the national economy" means by 2000, the 1980 gross output value of China's electronics industry should be octupled and major products and production technologies should reach the level advanced industrialized countries will have reached around 1990, with certain technologies reaching the world's advanced level prevailing at that time. The latter objective is 10 years more ambitious than the objective the government set for the national economy as a whole of reaching the level those countries reached around 1980.

noteworthy that the development of the modern global electronics industry exhibits the following new characteristics.

1. New breakthroughs in electronic science and technology are continuously being made; product price/performance ratios have increased considerably, and market competition is becoming fiercer. The speed of product updating and upgrading and differences in product price/performance ratios are important factors in beating the competition.

2. The emergence of the electronics industry as an R&D industry is becoming more prominent by the day as R&D and knowledge development capabilities are key to the electronics industry's development. Everyone in the industry depends on drastically increasing investment in R&D and knowledge development in order to beat the competition based on the strength of advanced technology.

3. Intensive and specialized mass production is impelling some enterprises to downsize and disperse. The integration of large and small enterprises raises the levels of automated production and labor productivity considerably and improves response capabilities greatly.

4. The modern electronics industry has developed into a high-tech, multifaceted industry based on microelectronics. Production of knowledge-based products is expanding rapidly, accounting for an ever-larger proportion of the output value of the electronics industry, whose main characteristic is the rapid development of the software and information services industries.

5. Modern electronic science and technology are permeating further into every area of society, raising the productive forces to a new level, and are becoming a trailblazer of the new technological revolution. Electronic technology is being extensively applied with a speed and on a scale never witnessed before. Development of the electronics industry is not only an important factor in the current economic recovery of Western countries, but will also exert a more profound influence on future economic and social development. Developed countries and many developing countries are making their own electronics industries the strategic focus of economic development in response to the new technological revolution, and are therefore investing in it heavily and making its development a priority.

Although our country's electronics industry has developed considerably over the past 35 years, it is still on a relatively small scale with a weak foundation and a low technological level, and it lags far behind the world's advanced level. These problems principally manifest themselves in the following ways:

1. China's electronics industry primarily focuses on manufacturing discrete components, whereas those of foreign countries have already entered a new phase based on microelectronic technology. Due to slow updating and upgrading and poor price/performance ratios, the industry lacks response capabilities and competitiveness.

2. Research and production methods are backward and unsuited to the demands of the electronics industry as an R&D industry, and research efficiency and labor productivity are low.

3. The electronics industry is badly structured and its capacity for comprehensive development and production is weak. In terms of technological structure, it is far from completing the shift to an industry based on microelectronic technology, and research is devoted too much to product models and too little to basic and mass production technology. In terms of product mix, software and information services are very underdeveloped and constitute only a very small proportion of total products; the percentage of electronic capital goods is also rather low and this area needs to be developed. Electronic components do not meet the needs for developing complete equipment. We still lack the capability to comprehensively develop systems engineering. Most enterprises, large or small, are all inclusive and have a low level of specialized production.

4. There is a lack of talent, and the available talent is not fully utilized. The specialization and hierarchical structures of the workforce are still fairly irrational. There is a severe shortage of senior researchers and economic management personnel, while there is disproportionate numbers of professionals and auxiliary personnel.

5. The development of the productive forces is hampered by antiquated management. Major problems include the management system beset by departmental and regional barriers, government administration not separated from enterprise management, our scattered strength, and the black economic vitality in enterprises. In addition, management

methods are backward and there is a lack of information and effective macro guidance and industry supervision.

6. There is a lack of funds, and this adversely affects the technological upgrading of existing enterprises and institutions, and the development of new technology and industries.

The current circumstances in which electronic technology is developing at lightning speed abroad and the new technological revolution is progressing vigorously worldwide, the onerous tasks we face of achieving the four modernizations and invigorating our economy present our country's electronics industry with two severe challenges. First, internationally, our technological level makes it difficult for us to compete with the world advanced level and close the gap with them. Especially as we open further to the outside world, the development of our national electronics industry will be subject to greater competitive pressure. Second, the country's four modernizations assign the industry the arduous tasks of providing modern electronic equipment for the development of the economy and national defense, and supplying the people with consumer electronics. Therefore, we must lay a solid foundation during the Seventh Five-Year Program period in order to satisfy the requirements for the national economy to develop in the ensuing 10 years. We need to seize the opportunities provided by the world's new technological revolution, rise to the challenges, and develop our country's electronics industry under the correct guidance of central leadership. To this end, we need to further correct our guiding business philosophy and formulate and adopt a suitable development strategy and appropriate measures.

II. OVERALL GUIDING BUSINESS PHILOSOPHY FOR DEVELOPING THE ELECTRONICS INDUSTRY

In macro guidance of the development of the electronics industry, we need to rid ourselves of the shackles of conventional thinking. In accordance with the line and principles adopted since the Third Plenary Session of the Eleventh CPC Central Committee, we need to correct our guiding business philosophy and seek a new development path to increase the inherent vitality of the industry. On the basis of a review of our experience and our present realities, we plan to introduce the following overall guiding business philosophy:

A. Develop the electronics industry on the basis of efficiency-oriented economic mechanisms

In developing the electronics industry, we need to follow the path of an efficiency-oriented economy, and emphasize quality and economic efficacy. We need to extend the scale of the economy and strive to increase the output value and growth rate under the guidance of efficiency-oriented economic mechanisms.

With regard to development principles, we will not emphasize the scale of ordinary production; rather, we will stress R&D capability, advanced production capability, and emerging industries in order to improve the vigor and vitality of the electronics industry.

With regard to product development, we need to stress breakthroughs in and mastery of basic technology, and improve our capacity for innovation and for updating and upgrading. We need to raise the price/performance ratios of our products and become more competitive in the market.

With regard to production technology and organization, we need to undertake specialized and intensive mass production while also emphasizing production technology and organization of a large variety of products in small lots.

B. Integrate research with production, taking into consideration the nature of the electronics industry as an R&D industry

The productivity indicators of the modern electronics industry are primarily its scientific and technological capability, R&D capability, and intellectual resources. At present, the degree of separation between research and production in our electronics industry is unsuitable for a high-tech industry. Our leadership work for the electronics industry should devote more attention to R&D and rely on advances in science and technology to invigorate the industry so that it competes on the basis of technology. We need to restructure the industry by closely integrating research with production and increase the value added to products by raising technological levels.

C. Stress knowledge development, taking into consideration the nature of the electronics industry as a knowledge- and technology-intensive industry

The electronics industry is not a labor-intensive industry, and its development depends mainly on tapping and utilizing intellectual resources and on the amount of knowledge and information its personnel possess. We need to focus on knowledge development to strengthen the electronics industry workforce and improve its expertise through various kinds of training and education.

D. Create a new management system that induces employees to boldly forge ahead

Abundant talent makes an industry flourish. However, our existing level of knowledge development is low. In addition, we still do not fully utilize the intellectual resources we have already developed and have not converted them into productive forces because of departmental restrictions on the flow of talent, rigid management, and remuneration systems. We plan to deal with the issue of talent by learning to use methods to stimulate people to boldly forge ahead and to create a new management system that respects knowledge, nurtures talent, and encourages everyone to tap their full potential.

E. Effectively implement the opening up policy, break out of isolation, and enter the international market

To develop the electronics industry, we need to overcome the closed-door mentality, orient ourselves toward the world, and participate in competition in the international market. We need to purchase raw and semifinished materials and components from abroad and use them to dramatically increase exports. We need to vigorously expand economic and technological exchanges and cooperation with foreign partners, import more technology, and accelerate the development process.

When restructuring the industry, we have to balance relationships between central and local governments, between departments, and between enterprises in an open-minded way. We need to gradually remove departmental and regional barriers, strengthen horizontal relations, put an end to the closed system under which all enterprises large or small are all inclusive, and promote specialized mass collaboration.

F. Eradicate egalitarianism in accordance with the principle of selecting the superior and culling the inferior

Under government planning guidance, we will implement the principle of selecting the superior throughout the course of production and development, including the areas of capital construction investment, supplying raw and semifinished materials and fuel, and approving production facilities. By doing so, we will eradicate egalitarianism and create a competitive environment and conditions that encourage the advanced and spur the laggards, thereby accelerating the development of the electronics industry.

III. BASIC STRATEGY FOR DEVELOPING THE ELECTRONICS INDUSTRY

The government's draft investment plan for the electronics industry in the Seventh Five-Year Program period falls far short of the industry's requirements. Due to this limited investment, we must concentrate on key areas and accomplish some tasks while setting others aside. Therefore, the basic strategy we plan to adopt is to pursue limited objectives; focus on key areas; concentrate on breakthroughs in microelectronic and microcomputer technologies; establish a microelectronic foundation for our country in the Seventh Five-Year Program period; accelerate the shift of development priorities such as military electronics, electronic computers, communications equipment, and other electronic capital equipment onto a foundation of microelectronics; and achieve comprehensive, balanced development of the electronics industry on a new structural foundation.

We are making the following specific arrangements for developing the microelectronics and microcomputer industries in line with this development strategy.

To develop microelectronics, we will give high priority to the industrialized production of medium- and low-grade large-scale integrated circuits in the short term and work hard to broaden their range of applications in order to create the conditions for a virtuous cycle of production and application. At the same time, we will energetically carry out R&D on high-grade, large-scale integrated circuits and very-large-scale integrated circuits. In the Seventh Five-Year Program period, we will establish microelectronics research institutes and production bases capable of producing 400 million circuits annually, thus creating the conditions for the electronics industry to take off in the 1990s.

Microelectronic technology is a technology for processing miniature material structures. It needs a series of unique micron- and submicron-scale micromachining equipment, automated design, inspection and test equipment, and ultrapure fine-structure materials. We still need to emphasize these related key links in order to develop the microelectronics industry.

To develop the microcomputer industry, we need to become oriented toward users, focus on upgrading traditional industries, vigorously develop all kinds of application systems, and achieve balanced development of host computers, peripherals, and software. By 1990, we will acquire an annual industrialized production capability of 2 million microcomputers, consisting of 200,000 microcomputer systems, 500,000 single-board computers, 1 million smart computers, and 300,000 control computers. We also need to establish a peripherals industry with an annual production capacity of over 1 million units to coordinate with the development of microcomputers.

IV. EMBRACING THE WORLD'S NEW TECHNOLOGICAL REVOLUTION AND BASIC MEASURES FOR ACCELERATING THE DEVELOPMENT OF THE ELECTRONICS INDUSTRY

A. Adopt a phased product development strategy to maintain relatively stable development of the electronics industry

Electronic technology is developing rapidly, and we must avoid indiscriminately acquiring all advanced technologies and instead adopt a phased development policy. In the course of developing the industry, we may skip some stages developed countries have gone through, and thus start from an achievable stage of relatively advanced technology that can meet the demand of most users with products of a fairly high level and that can maintain relatively stable development of production. We will temporarily defer domestic development of products for which we have a special need and permit their importation.

B. Strive to import advanced technology to raise our scientific and technological level more quickly

We will make use of the favorable international situation to import advanced technology and equipment and accelerate development. We need to assign a large number of scientists and engineers and invest heavily in the assimilation and absorption of imported technology, and then develop our own on this basis so that we begin from a higher starting point.

We need to take full advantage of the favorable conditions in open cities and special economic zones and take a variety of steps such as integrating trade with technology and industry, and supporting joint ventures and cooperative production to accelerate the pace of absorbing foreign investment and importing technology.

We need to actively explore ways of investing in and setting up factories or entering into Chinese–foreign joint ventures abroad and use the method of progressively putting down roots and gradually expanding our activities to directly import foreign advanced technology.

To accelerate R&D, we need to have overseas offices engage in sporadic, minor purchases of special components, electronic materials, and instruments and equipment in order to reduce the number of intermediate links and meet urgent needs.

C. Adjust the industrial structure to improve our competitiveness and response capability

We need to adjust the industrial structure on the basis of product grading. We need to organize production in accordance with the requirements of systems engineering and markets and on the basis of intrinsic relationships concerning manufacturing techniques and product technologies in order to raise overall efficiency and increase economic vitality.

We need to work hard to develop the information services industry, strengthen intermediary links between manufacturers and users, and promote industrial production by extending product usage. We need to actively develop markets; establish systems of product marketing, maintenance services, technical consultation, software supply, and staff training; become better equipped to contract for systems engineering projects; and strive to meet user and market demands.

We need to integrate the equipment and components industries more closely on the basis of the characteristics of the microelectronics industry and gradually unify production technology for equipment with that for microelectronic circuits, with the exception of widely used components.

D. Upgrade research and production systems and modernize research and production methods

We need to concentrate funds on key areas to upgrade technology. We need to build model enterprises (workshops) and research institutes (laboratories) and set up a number of major factories and institutes with advanced technology in order to establish models of modern research and production methods in a planned way. We need to spread the application of computers in aiding design, manufacturing, testing, and management; widen the use of automated electronic equipment and automated analysis and testing equipment; and strive to improve R&D efficiency and labor productivity.

E. Raise development funds through a variety of channels

In addition to making good use of state budget allocations, we need to strive to borrow money any way possible. We need to improve our managerial and administrative expertise and have the courage to gradually make use of loans from foreign sources. Given that regions and departments are very enthusiastic about developing the electronics industry, we need to formulate an overall plan; encourage joint investment by central and local governments, different departments, and different regions; accumulate as much funds as possible through multiple channels; and use them effectively.

F. Use the regulatory role of pricing policies to promote production and stimulate distribution

We need to use the law of value to set higher prices for good quality products, pursue quick turnover with a small profit margin, and steer the electronics industry onto the path of intensive development. We need to adopt a correct marketing strategy, shorten the growth phase of a product's sales curve, and reach the maturity phase more quickly. We need to implement a floating price policy, encourage competition, and gradually bring our product prices closer to international levels.

G. Vigorously develop expertise and train personnel

We need to update the knowledge of our existing scientists, engineers, and management personnel more quickly. We will establish universities that use periodicals as their main teaching resource and colleges that rely on local closed-circuit TV programs to help employees constantly acquire new knowledge and technology. We will send suitable personnel abroad for further studies, quickly cultivate a variety of urgently needed highly qualified scientists and engineers, intelligent and pragmatic managerial and administrative personnel, and sales persons who are well versed in technology, economics, law, and market development. In addition, we need to focus on producing high-level technical, economic, and management personnel.

Energetically reform the management system for the electronics industry and gradually implement comprehensive industry-wide supervision, with the goal of separating government administration from enterprise management and invigorating the economy.

V. SPECIAL POLICIES AND MEASURES

In addition to adopting an appropriate overall guiding business philosophy, development strategy, and policies for the electronics industry, we suggest that the government should formulate and implement a number of special policies and measures that take into consideration the characteristics of the electronics industry as an emerging industry using new technologies.

A. Place the electronics industry on a strategic footing and formulate corresponding investment policies

Since the existing scale and level of our country's electronics industry fall far short of meeting the requirements of the four modernizations, we must accelerate its development to avoid the occurrence of errors. According to estimates, the electronics industry will require approximately 10 billion yuan of capital construction investment during the Seventh Five-Year

Program period in order for it to offer a suitable foundation for the national economy to take off after 1990. We should therefore give the same strategic weight to the electronics industry as we do to energy and transportation, increase investment in the industry to the point where the proportion of its investment in the country's total capital construction investment is raised from 1% to 3%, and make this a fixed investment policy.

B. Implement preferential banking and tax policies to support the electronics industry

To invigorate the industry, we should provide low-interest, discounted-interest, or interest-free loans for major or key projects in line with the method of supporting superior performers.

We need to reduce or exempt import tariffs on key equipment, raw and semi-finished materials, and components needed to develop major projects on a case-by-case basis. To encourage exports, we need to reduce or exempt taxes or provide government subsidies for newly introduced export products.

On the basis of actual conditions, we need to speed up depreciation of fixed assets in certain electronics enterprises and institutions and return all their depreciation costs in order to accelerate technological progress.

C. Formulate reasonable policies concerning electronic equipment for different stages to provide appropriate protection to domestically produced electronic products

On the basis of the actual needs of our country's economic development, and the technological level and production capability of electronic products that can be produced domestically, we need to formulate policies concerning electronic equipment for a specified period. Within the prescribed time, all domestically produced electronic products whose performance, quality, and quantity basically meet the requirements for use should be put into wide use in accordance with our equipment policy, so that domestic enterprises have the time and opportunity to further improve their quality and steadily develop production. Imports of the same types of foreign electronic products should be strictly limited or restricted through the imposition of high import tariffs. During the protection period, we should strive to achieve the objective of meeting general international standards. In general, this protection will end when the specified period expires. In addition, we need to organize the importation in a planned fashion of technologies and products we cannot provide for the time being to meet the needs for developing the electronics industry and expanding the use of electronic products. Every year, we will promulgate a list of the electronic technologies, products, components, raw and semi-finished materials, equipment, and instruments for which special import permits are given, and implement the policy of reducing or exempting import tariffs on them. Import of goods and materials not on the list will be subject to tariffs in accordance with regulations.

APPENDIX B. IDEAS FOR THE REFORM OF THE ELECTRONICS INDUSTRY'S MANAGEMENT SYSTEM*

January 24, 1985

After the Third Plenary Session of the Twelfth CPC Central Committee, the Ministry of Electronics Industry established a leading group for the reform of the electronics industry's management system. On the basis of a thorough study of the decision of the CPC Central Committee on economic restructuring, investigations and studies in localities and enterprises, and opinions solicited from a wide range of sources, we hereby present our main ideas for reform in light of the new situation.

I. MAIN IDEAS FOR REFORM

The main purposes and tasks of this reform are to streamline administration, delegate power, and grant more autonomy to enterprises in order to end excessive, stifling control over them and increase their vitality; decentralize enterprises; develop consortiums; organize specialized production; ensure that no enterprise, big or small, is all inclusive; remove barriers between enterprises and define their ownership; reform the administration functions of government agencies of the electronics industry; separate government administration from enterprise management; and strengthen supervision of the entire industry. These measures should result in an accelerated development of the electronics industry; assist in completing the general tasks and reaching the overall objectives of "building a foundation, raising our level, improving quality, pursuing profits, octupling the gross output value, and getting 10 years ahead of the rest of the national economy"[1] on time or

---

*Plan for the reform of the management system of the electronics industry submitted by the Leading Party Group of the Ministry of Electronics Industry to the Secretariat of the CPC Central Committee. It was written under the direction of Jiang Zemin, and designated for study at a national working meeting of heads of departments and bureaus of the electronics industry in 1985.

[1]This is a summary of the electronics industry's development tasks for the foreseeable future made at a national working meeting of heads of departments and bureaus of the electronics industry. "Octuple the gross output value and get 10 years ahead of the rest of the national economy" means by 2000, the 1980 gross output value of China's electronics industry should be octupled and major products and production technologies should reach the level advanced industrialized countries will have reached around 1990, with certain technologies reaching the world's advanced level prevailing at that time. The latter objective is 10 years more ambitious than the objective the government set for the national economy as a whole of reaching the level those countries reached around 1980.

ahead of schedule; better serve the four modernizations and social activities; and help the entire national economy achieve the strategic target of quadrupling China's 1980 GNP by 2000.

The orientation for the reform of the management system of the electronics industry is as follows: The Ministry of Electronics Industry and the governments of all provinces, autonomous regions, and municipalities directly under the central government need to decentralize all of their subordinate electronics enterprises in order to break down departmental and regional barriers and develop various types of consortiums based on inherent technological and economic relations between enterprises. On the basis of the requirement to separate government administration from enterprise management, government departments at all levels in charge of the electronics industry need to streamline their agencies and clarify the division of labor. They should also shift from supervising enterprises to supervising the industry, and from directly managing enterprise operations to administering principles and policies, making overall plans, achieving overall balance in the industry, organizing and coordinating activities, exercising oversight, and providing services. In addition, diverse types of tertiary industries and industrial organizations should be established to help enterprises develop production and invigorate the economy, and they should become a bridge and bond linking enterprises and the government.

II. PLAN FOR IMPLEMENTING REFORM

A. Streamline administration, delegate power, and grant more autonomy to enterprises

Increasing the vitality of enterprises is the central link in the entire reform of the management system of the electronics industry. This reform takes streamlining administration and delegating power as the breakthrough point, and it delegates decision-making power over production and operations to enterprises. It is particularly important to grant more autonomy to large and medium-sized enterprises and fully unleash their inherent drive. In streamlining administration and delegating power, we first need to implement the Provisional Regulations of the State Council on granting more autonomy to state-run industrial enterprises. In order to implement these regulations, the Ministry of Electronics Industry considered the actual conditions of electronics industry enterprises directly under it and formulated nine supplementary regulations to help invigorate them. In order to prevent research institutes from receiving equal treatment from the state regardless of their performance and to promote the integration of research with production, the ministry is carrying out pilot projects to grant more autonomy to research institutes under its jurisdiction and implementing a contract system for paying for their research expenses. Due to a lack of related reform measures, this work has not been fully carried out in some institutes and further guidance is required. In the future, enterprises will be granted more autonomy in the following areas:

1. Enterprises will be given a certain amount of authority to approve capital construction and technological upgrading and improvement projects.
2. The enterprise fixed asset depreciation rate will rise, and enterprises will retain all proceeds therefrom to carry out technological upgrading.
3. The total payroll of enterprises will be allowed to fluctuate in proportion to their profits.
4. Enterprises will be given certain import and export rights and will have decision-making power over the use of foreign exchange they earn in accordance with regulations.
5. Enterprises will be allowed to retain a certain proportion of their sales revenue for development and trial production of new products.
6. Enterprises will also be allowed to purchase goods and materials and dispose of overstocked and expired goods and materials of their own accord.
7. Enterprises may use their surplus capacity to provide processing services, retain all income therefrom, and distribute a portion of it as incentives.
8. Enterprises affiliated to the ministry will be allowed to implement local government regulations that grant them more autonomy and allow them to increase benefits paid to their cadres and workers.

In order to ensure enterprises can truly exercise autonomy, it is necessary to effectively implement reforms of the systems for managing production, supply, and sales, as well as human, financial, and material resources. Specific measures need to be formulated to ensure that all reforms proceed in concert. In delegating power over ministerial enterprises in different localities, it is necessary to consider the extent to which reforms have been developed in the provinces, autonomous regions, and municipalities and the characteristics and current conditions of each enterprise. We cannot rigidly apply the same pattern across the board.

B. Decentralize enterprises and establish different types of consortiums

The Ministry of Electronics Industry will decentralize all its enterprises. In principle, it should transfer them to large and medium-sized cities. Enterprises outside of large or medium-sized cities in the hinterlands should be transferred to the provinces they are in or to large and medium-sized cities nearby.

Enterprises should be decentralized in groups in connection with the formation of consortiums. Consortiums need to be established on the basis of voluntary participation and mutual benefit at the urging of leaders, and they need to be based in large and medium-sized cities with large enterprises at their core. The organization of consortiums can be either tight or loose. An enterprise may join several consortiums, but it must take one as primary. Consortiums must depend on the inherent technological and economic connections between their members to hold them together and must not become administrative companies. Existing consortiums that lack internal connections and are not well run need to be dissolved and reconstituted.

1. We should establish economic consortiums in large and medium-sized cities with large enterprises at their core. This is the main structure for consortiums. After enterprises directly under the Ministry of Electronics Industry are decentralized, they need to break down barriers between sectors and forms of ownership, and actively establish consortiums with local electronics enterprises.
2. We should develop consortiums that span a number of cities, provinces, autonomous regions, and municipalities. They can either take the form of cooperative complementary enterprises that produce related products, groupings of hinterland and coastal enterprises, or groups of enterprises in the same field and industry. Enterprises in the same field and industry should not be allowed to become nationwide monopolies, so that competition is preserved and competitors spur each other.

3. We should establish comprehensive regional companies based at electronics industry bases.

4. We should develop consortiums of enterprises, research institutes, and universities for the purpose of developing products.

Consortiums should determine where they are registered based on their situation. When consortiums are composed of enterprises in the same large and medium-sized cities, they should register there. If they are composed of enterprises in different cities in the same province or autonomous region, they should register in the city where their major factories or companies are located. If they span a number of provinces, autonomous regions, and municipalities, they should register in the one where their major companies are located. However, when a consortium is registered somewhere, this does not subordinate it to the local government, though it has to pay taxes and fees there. Government agencies will no longer direct production and operations.

Because most of the enterprises directly under the Ministry of Electronics Industry are situated in the hinterlands and are responsible for producing a variety of military products, policy issues concerning decentralization and the establishment of consortiums need to be solved to make it easier for companies to develop and accomplish military tasks.

First, these enterprises produce military products under contract subject to a mandatory plan and to economic and administrative measures. Because military products are highly technical, not produced in large quantities and therefore unprofitable, it is suggested that the government adopt special policies to support these enterprises and implement prices according to the economic batch quantity formula. Relevant departments should bear the economic responsibility for maintaining essential production lines to make products for which there are few orders. Enterprises need to not only meet military needs, but also vigorously develop civilian products.

Second, after enterprises in the hinterlands that operate at a loss or on very narrow margins are decentralized, they will find it hard to operate independently, so it is suggested that their taxes be reduced by an appropriate amount during the Seventh Five-Year Plan period to allow them to recover and gradually improve.

Finally, the government needs to make funding available for hinterland enterprises that have to undergo mergers, change product lines or relocate, and pick up the pace of their restructuring while decentralizing them and allowing them to establish consortiums.

C. Separate government administration from enterprise management and supervise the industry well

In the process of decentralizing enterprises and developing consortiums, it is necessary to specify the powers and responsibilities as well as the division of labor for electronics government agencies at all levels so that they properly carry out their function of supervising the economy.

First, with regard to principles, policies, programs, and plans, the Ministry of Electronics Industry will focus on formulating development principles, programs, plans, policies, and regulations for the entire industry, and it will solicit the opinion of local governments in doing so. Local governments at all levels will be responsible for formulating local development programs, policies, and regulations in line with general industry requirements.

Second, with regard to the inspection and oversight of the implementation of policies, regulations, programs, and plans, the Ministry of Electronics Industry will be responsible for only the general orientation and major issues of principle, and local governments are expected to do the bulk of specific inspection and oversight work.

Third, the Ministry of Electronics Industry will be responsible for the appointment and removal of the principal leaders of only a few major enterprises, and local governments at all levels will be responsible for the appointment and removal of the principal leaders of other enterprises.

Fourth, government agencies of the electronics industry at all levels should provide good services to enterprises to guide and help them to invigorate the economy through supervision of the industry. City governments need to fully perform the functions of their cities to provide the best possible social services to factories and create a favorable environment for developing the economy in accordance with the requirements of the decision of the CPC Central Committee on economic restructuring.

After government administration is separated from enterprise management, the Ministry of Electronics Industry, which is a functional department of the State Council, will adjust and streamline its supervisory departments accordingly. It will scrap its existing double-tiered supervisory system by transferring the industry supervision function exercised by industry supervisory bureaus and China National Electronic Devices Industry Corporation to the ministry. It is suggested that provinces, autonomous regions, and municipalities, as well as cities where electronics industry enterprises are highly concentrated establish a department or bureau of the electronics industry or a similar body as a functional department of their government.

The Ministry of Electronics Industry should exercise its industry supervision function nationwide. Government agencies of the electronics industry of provinces, autonomous regions, and municipalities should likewise supervise the electronics industry in their localities.

The specific tasks of industry supervision are as follows:

1. To formulate strategies, specific principles, policies, laws, and regulations for developing the electronics industry
2. To organize the formulation of long- and medium-term plans for the electronics industry and annual plans for the industry from bottom to top
3. To organize and coordinate the production of military electronics, major electronic systems engineering equipment, and needed materials and components
4. To organize and coordinate efforts to solve difficult technological problems in major research projects and the development of major new products
5. To organize the drafting, revision, examination, and approval of technical policies and standards as well as the certification, oversight, and inspection of product quality
6. To organize surveys of domestic and foreign electronics markets and collect, collate, and release relevant economic and technological information
7. To organize major technological exchanges and imports, and other important foreign economic and technological activities
8. To establish education programs to train all types of personnel
9. To review and exchange experiences
10. To guide the work of organizations in the electronics industry

These tasks indicate that the content and scope of industry supervision will be different from its current form, and supervisory methods will also be reformed on the basis of the principle of exercising effective supervision of important matters while lifting control over lesser ones.

In order to effectively carry out supervision of the industry, it is suggested that the State Planning Commission and the State Economic Commission devolve the requisite authority and regulatory means to the Ministry of Electronics Industry. In particular:

1. New electronics factories should register with the Administration of Industry and Commerce after they have received approval of the Ministry of Electronics Industry or the electronics industry authority responsible for their province, autonomous region, or municipality.
2. New capital construction projects and major technological upgrading projects should be subject to the unified planning of the Ministry of Electronics Industry.
3. The Ministry of Electronics Industry should apply to the government for investment and loan quotas for capital construction projects and major technological upgrading projects as well as for funds for primary R&D projects and allocate them in accordance with development plans. Government funds for exploratory research on military electronic equipment and electronic components should also be subject to the supervision of the Ministry of Electronics Industry.
4. The Ministry of Electronics Industry should participate in determining the adjustment tax rate for electronics enterprises, what electronic products will be taxed and the tax rates for them, and interest rates on loans used for different purposes in the electronics industry.
5. The Ministry of Electronics Industry should have the authority to set prices for electronic products, except for a few key electronic products whose prices should be set by the State Administration of Commodity Prices.
6. The Ministry of Electronics Industry should participate in setting the rate of fixed asset depreciation within the electronics industry, determining fixed assets classifications and calculating their depreciable life.
7. Limited protectionist policies should be adopted for the import and export of products and technology imports. In order to promote the development of the electronics industry, policies should be lenient for areas that help the industry develop, and there need to be necessary restrictions for areas that hinder its development.

8. After the Ministry of Electronics Industry takes charge of the supervision of the whole industry, it should cultivate lateral relations between manufacturers and users and ensure the former provide good services to the latter. It is suggested that the user and operations departments refrain from manufacturing electronic products to allow better products to be developed and the best of them selected for use.

III. REFORM PROGRESS AND MEASURES

It is planned that the above suggestions for reform will be basically implemented within two years.

In 1985, on the foundation of formulating reform plans and granting more autonomy to enterprises, the Ministry of Electronics Industry will decentralize its enterprises in groups and encourage them to develop different forms of consortiums in light of their particular situations. In addition, great effort will go into establishing tertiary industries to serve these enterprises, for example, commercial entities in the areas of systems engineering, information, technical consulting, R&D, trade sales, product accessories, materials supply, and life services, making it possible for some departments and personnel of the ministry to gradually transfer to jobs directly serving enterprises.

In 1986, all types of consortiums of electronics enterprises will improve, consolidate, and further develop. All these enterprises will shift from remitting their profits to the state to paying taxes. Supervisory departments of the Ministry of Electronics Industry will be streamlined and adjusted, and its tertiary industries will begin to operate independently. By the end of the year, reform of the economic management system will be basically complete, and the Ministry of Electronics Industry and the industry's local government agencies will gradually shift to industry supervision.

In order to ensure smooth progress of reform, the following measures will be adopted:

1. Improve understanding and strengthen leadership. With a full understanding of the necessity and urgency of reform, the Ministry of Electronics Industry has established a leading group for the reform of the management system of the electronics industry and assigned principal ministry leaders to personally take charge of the work in order to change the old, slow way of doing things. Leaders at all levels need to shift their main efforts to reform, immerse themselves in reality, promptly identify and resolve problems, undertake sound ideological and political work, and guide the reform forward smoothly. All cadres at or above the department and bureau chief level in the ministry, supervisory bureaus, and China National Electronic Devices Industry Corporation, and all cadres at or above the section chief level in government agencies of the electronics industry in all provinces, autonomous regions, and municipalities must personally take charge of enterprise reform.

2. Actively explore and formulate specific reform plans. To meet the above requirements of reform of the management system of the electronics industry, within the near future, the Ministry of Electronics Industry will research and formulate the following specific reform plans in line with the overall plan.

   i. Supplementary regulations to grant more autonomy to enterprises

   ii. Plans for reforming planning, production, financial affairs, prices, supply of materials and goods, product marketing, cadres and personnel, and wages

   iii. Plans for streamlining the ministry's organs and adjusting its institutions

   iv. Specific plans for the reform of industry supervisory bureaus and China National Electronic Devices Industry Corporation

   v. Guidelines for the production of military electronic equipment and products and for the management of research

   vi. Division of responsibility between central and local government supervisory agencies of the electronics industry

3. Make prompt arrangements and provide careful guidance. A national working meeting of heads of bureaus and departments of the electronics industry was held in January 1985 to study and plan the reform of the management system of the electronics industry. In order to gain a better understanding of the situation, the Ministry of Electronics Industry will send investigative teams to solicit opinions in all localities in the first half of this year. The ministry has decided to carry out pilot reforms in Jiangsu Province, Beijing, Nanjing, and Chengdu in order to gain experience to guide the entire reform.

4. Promote people who have the courage to reform. It is essential to identify and boldly promote people who are well-versed in modern economics and technology, have an innovative spirit, boldly create, and are able to usher in a new period of development. Young cadres who have been held in reserve should be placed in the forefront of the reform to permit them to put their talent to good use and grow to maturity by facing challenges in the course of reform. Moreover, it is important to kindle the enthusiasm of both cadres and workers so that the reforms are based on widespread popular support.

Several Issues Concerning Shifting the Focus of Services in the Electronics Industry and Reforming Its Management System*

February 4, 1985

This national working meeting of heads of departments and bureaus of the electronics industry has had a spirit of reform, clear central ideas, and focused topics. Taking the overall interests of the country's economic development and the electronics industry as their starting point and giving consideration to local conditions, participants conducted thorough discussions and studies closely centered on important issues such as accelerating the pace of reform, making the "two shifts,"[1] and the Seventh Five-Year Program, thereby unifying our thinking, clarifying our orientation, and fortifying our confidence. During our discussions, we arrived at the consensus that we should be aware of the current excellent situation, but even more realize our shortcomings, guard against arrogance and rashness, and keep our heads clear. In short, this meeting has accomplished a lot and been a complete success.

Some comrades raised questions during our discussions. I would now like to address these issues.

---

*Speech at the conclusion of a national working meeting of heads of departments and bureaus of the electronics industry.

[1]The two shifts are: during the period of the Seventh Five-Year Plan for National Economic and Social Development, the focus of the electronics and information industries' services will shift to the national economy, the four modernizations, and all social activities, and the development path of the electronics industry will shift to one based on microelectronic technology and dominated by computers and communications equipment.

I. EXPANDING THE SCOPE OF SERVICES AND OPENING UP THE MARKET FOR ELECTRONIC PRODUCTS

You have expressed misgivings about how to implement the development strategy approved by the State Council for our country's electronics and information industries, which at the level of the guiding principles expressly requires that the focus of service in the two industries be shifted to the national economy, the four modernizations, and all social activities. Comrades representing some provinces and municipalities directly under the central government have said that they have difficulty opening up markets because they are dominated by other provinces and municipalities with well-developed electronics industries and brand name products. Here are some ideas for your consideration. At present, the scope of the electronics industry's services is broad; therefore, we should not only pay attention to the actual market, but more importantly, study the potential market. Many enterprises are scrambling to manufacture readily marketable products, such as color TV sets, video recorders, radio/tape recorders, picture tubes, and integrated circuits, but it is impossible to produce them everywhere in the country. The scope of our services is wide, so backward regions need not follow the footsteps of developed regions. If they use their heads and make an effort, there are many areas they could open up. Truly competent entrepreneurs are ones who turn potential markets into real markets.

To develop products seemingly not in great demand, but that hold great market potential, we must successfully carry out market forecasting. Market forecasting should include forecasting of both scientific and technological trends and economic results. We should realize that scientific and technological results also constitute a market. We need to not only supply stand-alone equipment and products, but more importantly, actively contract for systems engineering projects in electronics and provide a full spectrum of services ranging from designing, manufacturing, and supplying equipment, to installing and testing it and putting it into operation. We have the capability and necessary conditions to do this. Every enterprise should also strive to develop its own brand name products through competition. Enterprises without such products may enter into joint operations or form consortiums with those that have them to increase horizontal ties so that the enterprises can grow by expanding the production of brand name products.

In short, we must change the situation wherein enterprises arrange production only when they have tasks assigned to them by government authorities. The service field can be opened wider only by making manufacturing enterprises market and R&D oriented.

II. ENSURING THE PRODUCTION OF MILITARY PRODUCTS AND FINDING CIVILIAN APPLICATIONS FOR MILITARY TECHNOLOGY

Since this issue arose at this meeting, some comrades asked for clarification as to how to do this. As for ensuring the production of military products, I wish to make some points clear.

First, the importance of defense production will not diminish in the least due to the current economic restructuring. At present, electronic technology is used in aircraft, tanks, and missiles, and the electronics industry is of particular importance to the war industry.

Second, war will not break out anytime soon, so military production work does not need to be so prodigious; however, research on new military products is arduous, and we need to constantly update and upgrade these products.

Third, military production tasks, including research, are mandatory and we must ensure they are accomplished. At the same time, we must strengthen planning, coordination, and auxiliary work for the production of military products, and cooperation between enterprises and the army must not be arbitrarily interrupted. After enterprises responsible for producing military products are decentralized, their military tasks go with them wherever they go. If it is necessary for them to shift from military to civilian production, they must receive the approval of the Ministry of Electronics Industry to do so.

Fourth, R&D on and trial production of military products require substantial investment, and these products have a long production cycle, high costs, and small-scale production. Thus, we should formulate appropriate policies to ensure procedures are in accordance with economic laws.

On the issue of finding civilian applications for military technology, I also wish to make some points clear.

First, we need to strictly adhere to the guiding principle that the focus of service in the electronics industry should be shifted to the national economy, the four modernizations, and all social activities.

Second, we need to become adept at finding civilian applications for military technology.

Third, research work cannot be focused solely on military products, but also needs to develop technology for civilian products. We need to tap our full potential, produce more with less investment, and invigorate enterprises.

In short, ensuring the production of military products and finding civilian applications for military technology are two aspects of an integral whole and cannot be viewed in a one-sided manner.

III. DECENTRALIZING ENTERPRISES

Many comrades mentioned they want to know the specific steps for decentralizing enterprises and more detailed and specific procedures for managing them afterwards. This is understandable. The decision to decentralize enterprises was a major step that breaks new ground, so we need to clarify it in the course of implementation. This decentralization differs from previous ones. Though we use the same term, it has different connotations and implications. What we are doing now is delegating power to enterprises and making them reliant on central cities so they can give free rein to their own vitality. Both central and local governments should work hard for this common goal. We have decided to decentralize all enterprises currently under the Ministry of Electronics Industry, and we absolutely will not hold onto the best and let go of only the worst. However, to progress steadily, we should carry out pilot projects first and then decentralize enterprises in groups. The specific avenue for doing this will depend on the results of our explorations.

All enterprises, both central and provincial, will be decentralized. Some enterprises express concern that after they are decentralized, first, their supply lines will be cut off, thus affecting normal production; second, the new oversight authorities might subject them to greater, more stifling control; and third, assets and human resources might be transferred. The central authorities are very clear on this matter. When enterprises are decentralized, they will not acquire a new master; rather, central and local governments will work together to invigorate them and prevent their economic activities from being disrupted in any way.

To avoid the situations enterprises are concerned about from occurring, we need to complete the following work successfully:

First, work out detailed procedures based on investigations, studies, and pilot projects to decentralize enterprises in an orderly and step-by-step manner.

Second, clarify the functions of the Ministry of Electronics Industry and government supervisory agencies of the electronics industry of provinces, autonomous regions, and municipalities.

Third, decentralize enterprises at the same pace as and in coordination with reforms in their planning, financial affairs, personnel, goods and materials, and sales.

Fourth, ensure that all supervisory bureaus of the electronics industry under the ministry and China National Electronic Devices Industry Corporation complete all preparatory work, and that they each hold meetings with enterprises' leading cadres to unify everyone's thinking and understanding, take full responsibility for handling the decentralization of enterprises, and never stop till the work is done.

Fifth, ensure higher level governments intervene if decentralization is not handled properly.

In short, everyone needs to dispel all misgivings, work hard together, subordinate themselves to the whole, and invigorate enterprises.

IV. SETTING UP AGENCIES

This meeting has proposed that provinces, autonomous regions, and municipalities set up departments and bureaus or corresponding agencies within their governments to take charge of their local electronics industry. In the course of discussions, comrades from many provinces, autonomous regions, and municipalities requested more detailed regulations in this regard. I would like to provide some explanations here.

First, the Ministry of Electronics Industry is an agency under the State Council, and it provides guidance in the area of the electronics industry for local governments, but it cannot set mandatory rules for how local governments set up agencies; agencies need to be set up by local Party committees and governments themselves.

Second, the size of the electronics industry varies in different provinces, autonomous regions, and municipalities; therefore, it is unsuitable to set up the same kinds of supervisory agencies for the electronics industry everywhere. For instance, we cannot require Tibet and Xinjiang to have the same kind of supervisory agencies as coastal provinces and municipalities.

Therefore, the one-size-fits-all method is not a sound method. Instead, measures should be tailored to local conditions.

At present, the setup of local supervisory agencies of the electronics industry varies greatly. Due to staffing limits imposed by institutional reform, many local governments have turned their departments and bureaus of the electronics industry into companies, which in reality still perform government functions, Moreover, in some localities there are still too many agencies in charge of managing the industry. All this runs counter to the guiding principles for ongoing economic restructuring. Accordingly, we have amended the relevant document to read, "In light of the fact that the electronics industry is an emerging industry, all provinces, autonomous regions, and municipalities directly under the central government should create corresponding government supervisory agencies. It is improper for them to substitute administrative companies for government supervisory agencies. It is therefore proposed provinces and municipalities with a relatively developed electronics industry set up departments and bureaus to specifically exercise oversight of their local electronics industry." I believe these modifications are quite practical.

V. THE SEVENTH FIVE-YEAR PROGRAM FOR THE ELECTRONICS INDUSTRY

Everyone at this meeting has spoken freely, and all projects for provinces, autonomous regions, and municipalities have been announced. This has never been done before and everyone is pleased. However, a few issues arose during discussions. Some provinces, autonomous regions, and municipalities want to manufacture readily marketable products, especially color TV sets and tape recorders, but these projects have not been included in the Seventh Five-Year Program. In my view, we need to adapt measures to local conditions, provide positive guidance, and advocate consideration of the overall situation. We have announced all projects at this meeting in order to guide provinces, autonomous regions, and municipalities in formulating their own plans. From now on, the ministry will release information to government agencies of the electronics industry of provinces, autonomous regions, and municipalities at regular or irregular intervals to keep them informed of the situation across the country and facilitate decision making. All projects funded by state loans will then be awarded on the basis of public bidding, and those with unsuccessful bids will be excluded from government plans. If the government cannot provide enough funding for projects with great market demand, we may allow those with sufficient funds to launch such projects. Furthermore, the targets set in the Seventh Five-Year Program are subject to change during its implementation. We need to be aware that some of our output value comes from assembling imported components our foundation is weak; it will be difficult to ensure current output value if we run out of foreign exchange. So we need to allow some leeway when formulating plans. More importantly, we need to remain self-reliant and become able to produce products domestically. This is the only way we can sustain rapid growth in our output value. To achieve the objectives in the Seventh Five-Year Program, we must work even harder and never underestimate problems.

This year is the final year of the Sixth Five-Year Program period, and also a crucial year for preparing for the Seventh Five-Year Program period. Our guiding principle will shift to serving the national economy, the four modernizations, and all social activities. This shift will bring about major changes in the economic management system and industrial structure. To be successful in this stage, we need to first, be firmly confident; second, unify our thinking; third, boldly explore new phenomena and carry out reform; and fourth, intensify investigations and studies and carry out co-ordination work effectively. It is inevitable that we will make a few detours and encounter some complications in the course of this transition, but we must strive to avert significant detours and disturbances.

I want to point out that we should not just look at the difficulties in reform and development, but also recognize the many favorable conditions. The Party and the government's high regard for the electronics industry; the policy of reform and opening up; the guidance provided in the decision of the CPC Central Committee on economic restructuring; the large number of young and middle-aged leading cadres with a pioneering spirit who are more revolutionary, younger, better educated, and more professionally competent; and enterprises that have improved themselves through rectification and used technological upgrading and imports to improve their production methods—all these are the conditions and foundation for our continued progress. To sum up, though our tasks are formidable, the future is bright. We need to have a heightened sense of responsibility and urgency, intensify investigations and studies, take measures suited to local conditions, and work effectively.

Conscientiously Study and Solve Problems Facing the Development of Our Country's Electronics Industry*

June 1, 1985

I. STRENGTHEN MACRO-CONTROL OVER THE DEVELOPMENT OF THE ELECTRONICS INDUSTRY TO ELIMINATE EXCESSIVE DISPERSION

At present, there is excessive dispersion in the development of our country's electronics industry. Departments and regions make independent policy decisions, and there is a lack of centralized control of macro guidance. They all want to produce picture tubes, integrated circuits, computers, and video recorders. This disperses our limited funds and ends up accomplishing little. For example, five or six factories across the country want to produce video recorders, but total annual output is only 100,000 units. From the perspective of economies of scale, concentrating funds on building one factory produces much better results than building several all at once. In addition, when funds are spread thin they earn poor returns, making it hard for factories to survive. The problem of dispersion also plagues integrated circuits; 20–30 factories nationwide produced little more than 40 million integrated circuits last year. R&D work for integrated circuits is also considerably diffuse.

The government should tighten centralized macro-control over high-tech industries such as the electronics industry. We need to undertake mass production under overall government planning in developing our capability to produce major products for which there is strong demand, such as picture tubes, integrated circuits, video recorders, computers, and switchboards, and select enterprises to produce them through public bidding.

---

*Excerpt from a report to the State Council following an inspection tour to Japan by a delegation led by Jiang Zemin.

II. ADJUST THE STRUCTURE OF OUR SCIENTIFIC AND TECHNOLOGICAL WORK TO IMPROVE R&D ON PRODUCTION TECHNOLOGY AND SPECIAL PRODUCTION EQUIPMENT

R&D on production technology and special production equipment is a weak link in the development of our electronics industry. This is the main reason why we have difficulty translating research results into actual commodities. The transition from research to production is hampered by a lack of R&D on production technology and special production equipment, although we are gradually making up for this lack in the production process. To solve this problem, we need to start by adjusting the structure of our scientific and technological work, transfer significant technological assets to strengthen work on production technology, and make the electronics industry better able to provide itself with technology. We first of all need to assimilate and absorb all kinds of production technology imported in recent years and take this as a starting point for developing our own technology through innovation in order to gradually gain independence. I suggest that we begin by producing products with large production volumes suitable for each industry sector and gradually establish a number of R&D centers for production technology.

III. ENSURE R&D STAFF ARE QUALIFIED AND HAVE STATE-OF-THE-ART EQUIPMENT

In reforming the research system, we should pay special attention to R&D on products and accelerate the conversion of research results into the productive forces on the basis of our country's actual conditions. At present, many research institutes are overstaffed, and some lack the technological level research institutes require. Therefore, research institutes should be adjusted. Those without the requisite technological level should become production enterprises, while those with higher technological levels should gradually reduce their staff size so that they have qualified staff and state-of-the-art equipment. We need to concentrate our funds on establishing or upgrading a number of well-equipped research institutes according to development priorities and make them more dynamic so that they truly serve as pioneers.

IV. PAY CLOSE ATTENTION TO THE TREND TOWARD VERTICAL AND HORIZONTAL INTEGRATION IN THE INDUSTRIAL STRUCTURE, WITH DUE CONSIDERATION OF FEATURES OF THE MICROELECTRONICS INDUSTRY

Our country has formulated a development strategy for shifting the focus of the electronics industry to microelectronic technology. In this process, we need to pay attention to structural development trends in the microelectronics industry and not stick to traditional ways of thinking, such as mechanically severing the horizontal and vertical integration of sectors and fields that microelectronic technology has given rise to. In order to accelerate the shift to microelectronic technology, I suggest that pilot projects for vertical integration of the computer industry be carried out so that we can gain new development experience.

V. ACKNOWLEDGE THAT MARKET DISTRIBUTION IS AN IMPORTANT ASPECT OF THE INDUSTRY AND DO IT WELL

We have put far too little effort into market distribution work. The market is a big school. If we want to make use of its mechanisms, we must study hard. Research, production, and market distribution all fall within the scope of industrial activities. Our industrial sector devotes its greatest attention to production, less to research, and far too little to market distribution work. If we want to develop a commodity economy and achieve better economic results from industrial activities, we need to give the same attention to market distribution work as we do to research and production. We need to set up teams responsible for sales, technical maintenance services, contracted project design, and staff training, and study the market, master information, and revitalize industrial activities. We need to transfer a group of technically proficient, energetic engineers and technicians to enrich market distribution work.

VI. LEARN FROM EXPERIENCE AND SUCCESSFULLY INTRODUCE FOREIGN TECHNOLOGY

In recent years, there have been many duplicate technology imports in our country's electronics industry. Moreover, we make many technology purchases from the same foreign company, which leaves us open to exploitation. We should conscientiously learn from this experience and formulate a unified policy for importing foreign technology. Departments and regions should act in a coordinated manner in their foreign dealings. We should try our best to avoid duplicate imports of technology. We need to promptly organize all our resources to assimilate and absorb imported technology and do everything possible to meet the requirements of expanding production through its use. In addition, we should end our current practice of mainly importing complete sets of production equipment. In projects for which we already have a certain technological foundation, we can gradually shift our focus to primarily importing software technology, while organizing our resources to produce complete sets of specialist equipment on our own.

VII. LEARN FROM FOREIGN EXPERIENCE OF ORGANIZING INDUSTRIAL ACTIVITIES, AND CONSCIENTIOUSLY STUDY AND SOLVE PROBLEMS CONCERNING ECONOMIC RESTRUCTURING OF THE ELECTRONICS INDUSTRY

All sectors and fields of the electronics industry are closely and organically integrated with each other. In carrying out economic restructuring, in addition to decentralizing enterprises and encouraging them to organize their economic activities in central cities, we also need to conscientiously study the laws of vertical and horizontal integration between sectors and fields. Enterprises need to be incorporated into both the network of economic activities in the cities where they are located and the network of economic activities in the sectors and fields of their industry, and to become dependent on both the cities where they are located and the sectors and fields of their industry. They need to become relatively independent economic entities that are closely and organically linked to each other. Finally, we need to organize resources to further study these issues in order to promote smooth progress in economic restructuring.

Development Strategy Issues in Our Country's Electronics Industry*

June 5, 1985

The electronics industry is an emerging high-tech industry that plays a vital role in the new technological revolution and modernization drive. To accelerate the development and vitalization of the electronics industry, we must formulate and adopt appropriate development strategies, policies, and measures in light of our country's national conditions. In December 1984, the State Council endorsed and issued the Report on the Development Strategy of Our Country's Electronics and Information Industries prepared by the Leading Group of the State Council for Vitalizing the Electronics Industry. In January 1985, leading comrades of the Secretariat of the CPC Central Committee and the State Council issued important directives on energizing our country's electronics industry, including the directive to "emphasize application to promote development, and emphasize competition to further improvement." These directives and the Report on the Development Strategy of Our Country's Electronics and Information Industries, a programmatic document for developing the electronics industry, are a comprehensive distillation of the comments and suggestions made by economic, scientific, and technological authorities and experts and scholars in various fields during discussions on the world's new technological revolution and relevant policies. They review the basic domestic and foreign experience in developing the electronics industry, and point the way for our country to energize its electronics industry. They are therefore of great practical significance and far-reaching strategic importance.

---

*Originally published in the *China Machinery and Electronics Industries Yearbook* 1985.

I. DEVELOPMENT TRENDS OF ELECTRONICS INDUSTRIES ABROAD AND THE CURRENT CONDITION OF OUR COUNTRY'S ELECTRONICS INDUSTRY

There is a phenomenon in the contemporary world economy that has captured people's attention. Since the beginning of the 1970s, although traditional industries in Western countries have been mired in decline and their economies have stagnated, their electronics industries have burst onto the scene, maintained rapid development, and been full of vitality. Between 1970 and 1979, the electronics industries of the US, Japan, the UK, France, and the Federal Republic of Germany had an average annual growth rate of 13.8%. In 1984, the gross value of the world's electronic products reached $450.9 billion, an increase of nearly 20% over 1983, and it is predicted gross value will top $510 billion in 1985, up about 15% for the year.

The following aspects of the sustained rapid development trend in foreign electronics industries deserve our attention.

1. New breakthroughs are constantly being made in electronic science and technology, and the field is developing rapidly. In particular, microprocessing devices, which were developed in 1971 on the foundation of large-scale integrated circuits, have brought about a fundamental change for the better in microelectronic technology and its applications, and this technology has become the technological foundation for the rapid development of the modern electronics industry. The comprehensive development of microelectronic, computer, fiber-optic digital communications, satellite communications, and software technologies has made the field of IT the most active and influential emerging high technology in the new technological revolution and an important resource indispensable for economic and social modernization. Many countries have made IT a development priority. Facts show that the modern electronics industry is driven by R&D and based on microelectronic technology, and that competition in the electronics industry is mainly competition in electronic technology.

2. The rapid development of electronic technology accelerates the updating and upgrading of electronic products and the technology and equipment for manufacturing them, and considerably increases productivity,

price/performance ratios, and economic performance. A prominent characteristic of foreign electronics enterprises is that they closely integrate research with production, place research directly in the service of updating and upgrading products and modernizing means of production, quickly translate scientific and technological advances into commodities, and at the same time engage in intensive, specialized, and automated production. This helps enterprises develop into dispersed, small businesses more capable of adapting to change. The main purpose for doing this is to accelerate product updates and upgrades, improve price/performance ratios, and maintain competitiveness in the market.

3. Electronic science and technology permeate every aspect of society, are becoming widely applied at an unprecedented speed, and have become important pillars of the modern productive forces. Development of the electronics industry has not only become a major factor underlying the upgrading of traditional products and economic recovery in Western countries, but more importantly it has opened up a broad avenue for high-speed, high-efficiency, and high-value production in human society, and the industry has exerted and will continue to exert a profound influence over future social development. Developed countries and many developing ones focus strongly on developing and energizing their electronics industries and supporting them as a strategic development priority.

4. The rapid development of electronic science and technology and the constant expansion of their area of application have engendered significant changes in the structure of the electronics industry. The most important changes are while manufacturing continues to grow, the software and information services industries have developed rapidly, and the value of knowledge-based products and technical services claims an ever-increasing share of the electronics industry output value. It is predicted that it will not be long before the output value of the software industry and the information services industry will each catch up with and overtake that of the hardware manufacturing industry. This development illustrates that the wider application of electronic technology and the development of the electronics industry depend to a large extent on the support of the software and information services industries and that it is very difficult to estimate the economic value of these two emerging industries.

5. In developing their electronics industries, all countries stress developing intellectual resources and bringing together talent. Specialized personnel account for over 40% of the employees in electronics industries in countries such as the US and Japan. Silicon Valley in the US is thriving because it has an excellent natural environment and superb economic conditions, but the most important reason is that it has drawn together strong talent in science and technology. This shows that competition in electronic products and technology is, in the final analysis, competition in talent. The electronics industry is a technology- and knowledge-intensive industry, and talent is the key to its development and vitalization.

Our country's electronics industry is an emerging industrial sector established after the founding of New China. It has developed considerably over the past 35 years. According to statistics for 1984, its gross output value reached 21.446 billion Yuan, an increase of 56.8% over 1983, and its profits totaled 2.65 billion Yuan, up by 51.5%. This shows that the electronics industry is developing rapidly and that its economic performance has improved significantly. In particular, the use of technological imports and upgrading has led to a marked improvement in levels of product and production technology in recent years. Electronic technology and particularly computers are applied in more and more areas, making a contribution to modernization. However, in terms of scale, technology, and production capability, our electronics industry falls far short of the needs of modernization and is far behind the international advanced level, as principally manifested in the following ways.

1. The electronics industry has a weak foundation and a low level of product technology. The electronics industries of industrialized developed countries have already entered a new phase based on microelectronics; whereas in our country, the electronics industry has not formed a microelectronics industry system and is basically at the stage of mainly producing discrete devices. At present, our country's integrated circuit technology is at the primary or intermediate stage of large-scale integrated circuits, and we need to depend on imports for a considerable proportion of key components for many kinds of equipment. Our weak technological foundation, slow updating and upgrading of products, and poor product price/performance ratios make us uncompetitive.

For example, in the areas of integrated circuits and computers, which are representative of the industry as a whole, we lag about 10–15 years behind the foreign advanced level.

2. Our methods of research and production are backward and productivity is low. Foreign electronics industries universally use advanced technology and modern methods such as computer-aided design, manufacturing, and testing in research and production. They have strong R&D capabilities and high productivity, whereas we are still in the stage of carrying out trials of these new technologies and beginning to apply them in production. Our research and testing methods are backward, and most of our enterprises use obsolete equipment and have difficulty engaging in intensive, specialized, and automated mass production, which leads to low productivity, high costs, and poor quality.

3. Our industrial structure is irrational, and software and information services remain weak links. Our technological structure has not yet completed the shift to a foundation of microelectronic technology and neglects R&D on mass production technologies. As for the product mix, we emphasize hardware manufacturing too much while neglecting the development and production of knowledge-based products and software, and our information services industry is underdeveloped. The proportion of capital goods is too small. Our electronic components (including electronic materials) are inadequate for the requirements of equipment development. Our comprehensive R&D capabilities in systems engineering remain too weak. In terms of structure, enterprises, whether large or small, are all-inclusive, and they have a low level of specialization.

4. Many problems in our management system shackle development of the productive forces. Prominent problems are departmental and regional barriers, dispersed resources, lack of separation between government administration and enterprise management, lack of enterprise vitality, and low quality of management. All this hinders development of the productive forces.

5. There is a shortage of talent and insufficient funding. At present, engineers and technicians account for only about 10% of the workforce in our country's electronics industry, and economic management personnel are even more scarce. In addition, due to limited government finances, government investment in the electronics industry is

disproportionately small, which directly affects the launching of new projects, R&D, technological upgrading, and the widespread use of electronic technology, and considerably restricts the vitalization of the electronics industry.

The booming new technological revolution, the rapid development of electronic technology, and our country's urgent need to apply electronic technology in every field in its modernization drive all pose severe challenges to our electronics industry. Nevertheless, opening to the outside world presents us with the opportunity to learn from and selectively and directly use foreign achievements in electronic technology and thus accelerate our technological progress. Given the challenges and opportunities, formulating and implementing corresponding development strategies and measures and providing more effective macro guidance is a truly urgent task.

II. GUIDING IDEOLOGY AND STRATEGIC OBJECTIVES

Our country's electronics industry shoulders a heavy and arduous burden in our effort to carry out modernization, revitalize China's economy, and attain the grand objective of quadrupling our 1980 gross industrial and agricultural output value by 2000. The main tasks are to provide advanced electronic technology and equipment and complete technical services for the upgrading of traditional industries in all sectors of the economy; develop and supply IT and electronic equipment systems needed to establish high-speed, accurate, and free-flowing information systems in our country; provide next-generation military electronic equipment for national defense modernization; provide electronic equipment and tools for science and technology, culture, education, health, broadcasting, publicity, and office use; supply a greater variety and larger numbers of consumer electronics with better functions and quality to improve people's material and cultural standard of living; and increase exports of electronic products to earn more foreign exchange for the country. In brief, the fundamental tasks of the electronics industry are to provide services for establishing modern material and technological bases for our country's socialist modernization, elevate the productive forces to a new level, ensure the quadrupling of gross industrial and agricultural output value, and help the people attain a level of moderate prosperity. To this end, the development rate and technological level of the electronics industry should be ahead of the rest of the national economy by an appropriate amount.

1. The general ideology guiding the development of the electronics industry is to gear it to the needs of application; advocate and encourage competition; emphasize application to promote development; emphasize competition to further improvement; provide services for the national economy, the four modernizations, and all social activities; and strive to achieve the general tasks and objectives as defined at the Party's Twelfth National Congress.

    We need to balance the following relationships in our practical work.

    i. The relationship between the application of electronic technology and the manufacturing of electronic equipment. We need to continue to give application greater weight, make it our objective, and use it to promote manufacturing. We need to stress development of applied technology and open up more areas of application. We especially need to emphasize software development and the establishment and development of the information services industry.

    ii. The relationship between emerging and traditional industries. The electronics industry is an emerging industry and needs to continue to provide services for technological upgrading and the development of traditional industries, supply them with larger quantities of modern electronic equipment to accelerate their technological progress so that they develop production on a new technological basis, and improve their economic performance and help the national economy take off. The electronics industry should play a leading role in the new technological revolution. We should therefore ensure emerging and traditional industries are closely integrated, support and reinforce each other, and progress together.

    iii. The relationship between military and civilian products. We need to continue to ensure the production of military products and find civilian applications for military technology. We need to ensure that all the industry's military tasks are accomplished, and put more scientific and technological effort and production capability into serving economic development and social activities. This will enable us to better meet the needs of modernization, fully tap the electronics industry's potential, invigorate enterprises and research institutes, and develop the electronics industry more rapidly.

iv. The relationship between planning guidance and competition. We need to advocate and encourage competition within the framework of overall planning, and provide more effective guidance as competition grows. In the new situation where all sectors of the economy, all industries and professions, and all regions are becoming increasingly enthusiastic about developing and applying electronic technology, we need to correctly balance centralization and decentralization. Basic electronic products that are capital and technology intensive and have long production cycles, such as integrated circuits and key basic components, must be subject to unified national planning. We must make overall plans for the human and material resources needed to produce them just as we did in developing the atomic and hydrogen bombs and artificial satellites in the old days, and avoid pell-mell development and the waste of human and material resources. However, we need to lift controls on the application of electronic technology and the production of general electronic products, break blockades and monopolies, and give full play to everyone's initiative. We need to overcome the mindset of overemphasizing stability out of fear of disorder. Instead of reining in enthusiasm for developing electronics, we must facilitate and guide it. We need to use all types of economic means and adopt appropriate technological and economic policies to arouse initiative and creativity, support the superior, and let the inferior fall by the wayside so that the entire electronics industry develops and improves through competition.

2. The strategic objective of our country's electronics industry is to octuple its 1980 gross output value and get 10 years ahead of the rest of the national economy by 2000 in order to ensure that the country's GNP quadruples by then. At that time, the gross output value of the electronics industry should reach 80 billion Yuan, eight times the 1980 figure (an average annual increase of 10.9%), the industry's proportion of the country's gross industrial and agricultural output value should be raised from its 1980 level of 1.4% to about 3%;

this basically conforms to the development of the entire national economy. The level of major products and production technologies should reach the level advanced industrialized countries will have reached around 1990. This objective is 10 years more ambitious than the objective the government set for the national economy as a whole of reaching the level those countries reached around 1980.

Our country's electronics industry achieved its output targets for the last year of the Sixth Five-Year Program period in 1983, 2 years ahead of schedule. In 1984, output value and profits were both twice the 1980 figures. However, we should be aware that our foundation is very weak, and a significant proportion of output value is achieved by assembling imported components; we cannot let this continue for long. We must make every effort to improve our ability to produce components domestically. We should not overemphasize speed; sound growth is based on good performance. It is crucial we continue to build infrastructure during the Seventh Five-Year Program period in order to create conditions for greater development during the ensuing 10 years.

During the Seventh Five-Year Program period, the development objective of our country's electronics industry (including the information industry) is to make the following two shifts;

1. We will shift the focus of the electronics and information industries' services to the national economy, the four modernizations, and all social activities. We need to address the needs of users; serve them; integrate manufacturing, operations, and services; vigorously spread the application of electronic technology; and open up more new markets in order to promote the commercial production of electronic products, maximize economic and social benefits, accelerate capital accumulation, and provide conditions under which the electronics and information industries can develop on their own.

2. The development of the electronics industry needs to shift to a foundation of microelectronic technology and emphasize computers and communications equipment. We need to develop next-generation basic components to improve the foundation for the entire electronics industry. We need to accelerate development of new electronic products needed for military equipment and technology and equipment

needed for civilian production. In addition, we will considerably increase production of consumer electronics. In 1990, our major products and production technologies will reach the level developed countries reached around 1980, and the four major technological fields—integrated circuits, computers, communications, and software—will approach advanced foreign levels. The quantity, variety, and quality of electronic products will increase considerably. We will develop the capability to mass produce these products to basically meet the needs of all industries and sectors.

In brief, the short- and medium-term objectives of our country's electronics industry can be summed up in these words, "building a foundation, raising our level, improving quality, pursuing profits, octupling the gross output value, and getting 10 years ahead of the rest of the national economy." Development of the electronics industry over the past 2 years makes it nearly certain that by 2000 we will increase the 1980 output value eightfold, and perhaps even more if everything goes smoothly. However, it will be difficult and take a lot of effort to get 10 years ahead of the rest of the national economy and narrow the gap between us and the world's advanced level. To do so, in addition to upholding correct guiding ideology, we must also adopt corresponding specific policies and measures in our practical work.

III. PRINCIPLES, POLICIES, AND MEASURES TO BE ADOPTED

We will adopt the following specific principles and policies and important measures in accordance with the guiding ideology and strategic objectives for developing our country's electronics industry.

A. Carry out publicity and education work to popularize electronic technology

Our country is modernizing on a foundation of backward science and technology. Some cadres and members of the general public lack an adequate understanding of the importance of electronic technology in modernization, and this is an obstacle to the widespread use of electronic technology.

We hope newspapers, periodicals, radio and TV stations, and other publicity and education departments work hard to explain the important position and role of science and technology in modernization as well as the results of using electronic technology, and popularize knowledge about electronic technology using various means and through a number of channels in order to promote its development and wider application in all fields.

B. Emphasize priority items that give impetus to other areas

Development priorities in the electronics and information industries are integrated circuits, computers, communications, and software. We will select some key products and technologies and concentrate our efforts on breakthroughs in them in order to drive balanced development of other products.

We will concentrate our efforts on breakthroughs in microelectronic technology to lay a foundation for our country's microelectronics industry. In the near term, we will focus on developing small- and medium-scale and low-grade, large-scale integrated circuits, stressing the development of technology for industrialized mass production of them so that annual production reaches 400 million circuits in 1990 and their performance and price approximate those prevailing on the international market then. Further, we will strive to build a capability to produce micron-size, high-grade, and large-scale integrated circuits and conduct R&D on 1–2 μ very-large-scale integrated circuits. To do this, we need to concentrate our limited financial and technological resources, use our existing foundation, develop research and production bases, and upgrade our technology in order to create a microelectronics industry system.

In the area of computers, we will focus on developing microcomputers, while also producing small, medium-sized, and large computers and industrial control computers. We will implement the principle of being application oriented, actively develop all types of application systems, vigorously develop application software, and balance the development of host computers with that of peripherals, software, and technical services. Our 1990 annual production of microcomputers will reach 200,000 units and we will try to spread the use of computers to more than 80% of large enterprises, institutions of higher learning, and key research and design institutes.

In the area of communications equipment, we will focus on developing and producing electronic program controlled telephone exchanges, and fiber-optic digital microwave communications and satellite communications. We will establish industrial production lines for that purpose and promote the balanced development of channels, switches and terminals to create conditions for the future development of our country's communications.

We will emphasize and strengthen R&D on and the widespread application of software, formulate policies and measures to protect copyrighted software and transferred technology, and promote software engineering and commercialization in order to drive development of the entire software industry.

With the focus on the above four development priorities, we will also develop auxiliary products such as electronic materials, technological equipment, and testing instruments, as well as electronic components, radio and TV broadcasting equipment, and home appliances in order to drive research and production in the entire electronics industry.

C. Implement the principles of importation, assimilation, development, and innovation and become more self-reliant

First, further loosen control over the electronics industry's foreign economic and technological exchanges. We will adopt flexible means and use multiple channels to import advanced and appropriate technologies, and equipment and managerial expertise, so we can skip certain development stages and achieve rapid technological and economic development from a relatively high starting point. Also, we need to strengthen overall planning and policy guidance in order to keep from doing our import work blindly and avoid importing products that are unnecessary or redundant.

Second, do all we can to raise the starting point for imported technology. The starting point can be either end or semifinished products; our imports need to gradually extend from downstream processes up the chain, and we need to increase the proportion of new, high-level technology, and basic technology. We need to make a point of importing and mastering product design technology, mass production technology, and software technology, and make breakthroughs in the areas of attracting foreign capital and talent.

Third, ensure we assimilate and absorb imported technology, stress development and innovation, and integrate technology and equipment imports with self-reliance. We need to concentrate our technological efforts on assimilating major imported projects and key imported technology and achieve returns on our investment. On this basis, we will carry out R&D and innovation, develop the ability to produce what we need domestically more quickly, and become more self-reliant.

Fourth, make full use of special economic zones and open coastal cities as windows and springboards to promote large volume importation and exportation of electronic technology and products. We need to successfully introduce foreign technology and establish lateral ties between the coastal region and the interior. Open areas should provide information for the electronics industries in the interior and transfer technology and managerial expertise to them. The interior should provide technological and economic support for the electronics industries in open coastal cities and promote lateral ties with the coastal region in order to place more domestic electronic products on the international market. We need to adopt corresponding policies and measures to encourage and support the export of electronic products.

D. Carry out technological upgrading in a planned and focused manner, and raise the level of our R&D and industrialized mass production technology

In accordance with our development priorities, we will concentrate financial and material resources on the technological upgrading of existing enterprises and research institutes, and integrate this work with technology imports. During the Seventh Five-Year Program period, we will use technology imports and technological upgrading to basically modernize research and production methods in the four development priority areas so that they will develop their industrialized mass production capability on the basis of new technology, shorten the R&D cycle, and improve productivity. To this end, we must orient science and technology toward production and application, and ensure that production and application rely on science and technology. We also need to greatly intensify research, improve R&D infrastructure, and closely integrate research and production. We need to spread the application of computer-assisted design, manufacturing, testing, and management, use automated electronic machinery and equipment, and automated analytical and testing equipment, and at the same time institute modern managerial methods.

E. Vigorously restructure the industry, guided by the principle of being application oriented

Concerning the technological structure, we will develop microelectronic technology, promote the production of microelectronic products, and at the same time actively develop modern manufacturing technology. Concerning the product mix, we will develop both electronic capital goods and consumer electronics. In order to meet the urgent needs of all industries and trades to make technological progress, we should accord top priority to the production of electronic capital goods and give them a dominant position. In addition, in order to make the market flourish and meet the people's daily needs, we will continue to greatly increase the production of consumer electronics. We need to focus on microelectronic components, successfully develop and produce basic products, and become more self-sufficient in producing components, and raw and semi-finished materials needed for equipment. We need to actively develop and produce software and other knowledge-based products. With regard to the industrial structure, while continuing to develop hardware manufacturing, we need to expand the information services industry and significantly increase our ability to comprehensively develop and build electronic systems engineering projects.

F. Emphasize intellectual development and strengthen talent training

Talent is the most fundamental factor in energizing the electronics industry. We need to provide the necessary funding for institutions of higher learning, specialized secondary schools, secondary technical training schools, and especially TV universities and correspondence schools, so that they can develop their electronics and information departments. We need to popularize electronic knowledge, beginning with primary school students. As we spread the application of electronic technology, we need to develop electronic technology training throughout society. We need to strengthen the technical training of employees in the electronics industry and update their knowledge. We need to further implement the policy on intellectuals, tap the potential of our current talent, gradually change the personnel structure in the electronics industry to make the division of high, medium, and primary levels more reasonable, and accelerate the cultivation of high-level scientific and technological, operational, and management personnel.

G. Actively yet prudently work on reform and accelerate the development of the electronics industry

In accordance with the decision of the CPC Central Committee on economic restructuring and the principle of being unshakable, starting cautiously and ensuring victory, the main ideas for economic restructuring in the electronics industry are to streamline administration, delegate power, and grant more autonomy to enterprises in order to end excessive, stifling control over them and increase their vitality; decentralize enterprises; develop consortiums; organize specialized production; ensure that no enterprise, big or small, is all inclusive; remove barriers between enterprises and define their ownership; reform the administration functions of government agencies of the electronics industry; separate government administration from enterprise management; and strengthen supervision of the industry. We plan to achieve these objectives in rudimentary form in 2 years' time. In 1985, we will focus on granting more autonomy to enterprises, decentralizing them, developing economic consortiums and specialized collaboration, creating high-tech tertiary industry services for enterprises and users, and genuinely invigorating enterprises, especially large- and medium-sized ones. In 1986, we will focus on adjusting and streamlining government administrative agencies, and gradually separating government administration from enterprise management so that the Ministry of Electronics Industry can shift its function to supervision of the industry, and strengthen overall planning and macro guidance. In order to ensure smooth progress in reform, we need to implement the decision of the CPC Central Committee on economic restructuring in both our guiding ideology and practical action. We need to be firm and steadfast, emancipate our minds, and boldly innovate while seeking truth from facts, emphasize investigations and studies, act prudently, take solid yet careful steps, and strive to achieve practical results.

H. The government will adopt a number of special policies and measures necessary to support the vitalization of the electronics industry

Our country's electronics industry is an emerging industry with a weak foundation. To accelerate its development, the government has adopted and will continue to implement a number of necessary policies and measures to support it.

1. Special funds (including foreign exchange) will be established for developing key state projects vital to the electronics and information industries. These funds should be used to support enterprises, institutions, universities, and colleges selected on the basis of public bidding and fund raising and that have significant technological advantages and sound economic performances in order to develop new projects, conduct R&D on new technology, and produce new products.

2. We will implement preferential and appropriately protectionist policies to support the development of key products. All sectors and enterprises that develop and produce these products in accordance with government regulations will be entitled to low-interest loans, tax reductions or exemptions, special depreciation consideration, and other preferential treatment subject to government approval. In addition, we will enact economic legislation and implement an appropriately protectionist policy to support the development and application of advanced and appropriate domestic electronic technologies and products, and restrict and eliminate the production of backward products.

3. Special policies will be implemented for the small number of leading enterprises and institutions undertaking key state projects, and they will be given considerable decision-making power over operations subject to government examination and approval. For example, these enterprises and institutions may exercise control over a certain amount of foreign exchange, maintain separate bank accounts, and enter into foreign contracts independently. They may also independently set prices on their exports, raise or lower the prices of goods sold domestically, and lower prices freely. However, these enterprises must be responsible to the government and attain their economic and technological objectives within the prescribed time.

4. We will establish an incentive fund to energize the electronics industry. Proceeds from the fund should be awarded to organizations, collectives,

and individuals who make outstanding contributions to developing and applying electronic technology.

5. We will formulate reasonable policies concerning electronic equipment for different stages to maintain relatively stable production of electronic products. Electronic technology and products develop rapidly, so it is inadvisable to indiscriminately acquire all the most advanced electronic equipment and technology for purchase or application. Rather, we need to formulate equipment policies for certain periods to meet the actual needs of every industry and sector in accordance with the scientific and technological development and application situation in our country. Within a prescribed time, all domestically produced electronic products whose performance, quality, and quantity basically meet the requirements for use should be put into wide use in accordance with our equipment policy, so that domestic electronics enterprises have the time and opportunity to steadily develop production and further improve their technology and quality. Imports of the same types of foreign electronic products should be strictly limited or restricted through the imposition of high tariffs. This will both meet the demand for products and help the electronics industry develop in a steady and sound manner.

6. In order to accelerate the spread and application of electronic products, the government may adopt economic means such as soft loans to support the development of electronic products and services that are worth spreading and using.

To accelerate the vitalization of our country's electronics industry, the State Council established the Leading Group for Vitalizing the Electronics Industry in September 1984 in order to strengthen the unified leadership, organization, and coordination of our country's electronics and information industries. Thereafter, the government formulated a strategy for developing these industries, pointed out the direction for development of our electronics industry, and worked out the main principles, policies, and measures. All this shows that our country's electronics industry is on the path of vitalization. With the solicitude and under the leadership of the Party Central Committee and State Council, our country's electronics industry will develop in a more rapid and healthy manner and play a bigger role in socialist modernization.

New Characteristics in the Development of the World's Electronic Information Industry and Strategy Issues Concerning the Development of China's Electronic Information Industry*

May 26, 1989

In the 1980s, the world's electronic information industry developed rapidly and with great momentum. The industry's output value in 1988 reached $587.5 billion, and its annual output value is predicted to exceed $1 trillion by the mid-1990s. This would make it one of the largest industries in the world, surpassing many traditional industries. The massive development and widespread application of electronic information technology is ushering the world into the era of a so-called information economy, and electronics has already become the most important indicator of the productive forces of post-industrialized developed countries.

Electronic information technology is an effective multiplier of our country's economy as well as the new technology that is the most permeative and widely applicable. By giving more strategic prominence to promoting the widespread application of electronic information technology and making full use of its multiplier effect on the economy, we can increase the efficiency of the national economy, reduce resource consumption, and exploit our existing sizable iron and steel, coal, electricity and petroleum resources to multiply our GNP several fold.

The output value of China's electronic information industry in 1988 was 59.5 billion yuan, an increase of 39% over the previous year. This could be considered a very high rate of growth; however, compared to the growth of the world's electronic information industry, the gap is widening, which

*Originally published in the *Journal of Shanghai Jiao Tong University*, No. 6, 1989.

is a truly serious situation. In the current circumstances of massive constraints on national capital investment, we must thoroughly examine the issue of how to develop China's electronic information industry. We need to study both our own situation and the international situation, with particular emphasis on the new characteristics in the development of the world's electronic information industry. We need to draw lessons from the experiences of both developed and developing countries, look for development opportunities and explore new development strategies, in order to meet the requirements the four modernizations place on electronic information technology.

I. NEW CHARACTERISTICS IN THE DEVELOPMENT OF THE WORLD'S ELECTRONIC INFORMATION INDUSTRY

The development of the world's electronic information industry exhibits many new characteristics. Studying these characteristics will assist us in finding new opportunities, deliberating new strategies and exploring new paths for development.

1. The foundation of world's electronic information industry is the development of integrated circuit technology, but the industry has fully completed the transition to microelectronics. In 1988, total world sales of integrated circuits exceeded $33.7 billion. The distinction between equipment and components, established through several generations of electronic technology based upon discrete components, is becoming increasingly blurred. Hundreds of thousands, and even millions, of components can now fit on a microchip. Equipment technology is fusing with component technology to put whole systems on single chips, thus greatly improving the price/performance ratios, quality and reliability of products, and also significantly reducing energy consumption and product size; thereby creating a brand new generation of microelectronic products. Changes in the technology system have led to changes in the organizational structure of production. Because integrated circuits are not end products, their value added far exceeds the profits they generate. To boost their competitiveness, companies in the international electronic information industry are gradually merging the integrated circuit industry with the equipment manufacturing

industry to vertically integrate their organizational structures of production. Companies that formerly specialized in integrated circuits, such as Texas Instruments in the US, are making use of their superior integrated circuit technology to branch out in the direction of electronic equipment. Companies that did not produce integrated circuits and whose main business was equipment manufacturing have started to merge with integrated circuit companies or have built their own integrated circuit plants. The wide use of application-specific integrated circuits (ASIC) in recent years has further promoted vertical integration of the electronic information industry. This demonstrates that the organizational structure of production must adapt to requirements imposed by the development of the productive forces. The organizational structure of production in our country's electronic information industry still rests on a foundation of discrete components. This kind of structure makes it difficult to harmonize the interests of integrated circuit enterprises and equipment manufacturing enterprises, and thus hinders the smooth development of the integrated circuit industry.

2. Technological upgrading is accelerating and product lifecycles are shortening. The world's electronic information industry is entering a new era of rapid development and is increasingly driven by R&D. The widespread use of automation in design and manufacturing and of flexible manufacturing systems (FMS) has greatly reduced the time between product research and mass production.

The lifecycles for some products have become as short as 2 to 3 years. Semiconductor memory is a good case in point. The process of developing 4 K memory from laboratory research to marketing peak took 5 years. The same process for 16 K products took 3 years, 64 K 2 years, and 3 years for 256 K and 1 M memory. The production output of 1 M memory chips is expected to exceed that of 256 K memory chips this year and 4 M memory chips will go into industrial production by 1990. Japan's NTT Communications was the first to develop a 16 M memory chip, which has nearly 40 million components on an 8.9 × 16.6 mm microchip, and a linewidth of 0.7 μm. It is predicted that 64 M memory will be successfully developed by the mid-1990s, with each unit containing more than 100 million components. This situation already makes it difficult for us to use long product lifecycles to catch up. However, it also holds forth the potential for skipping some development stages. This is how the Republic of Korea developed its electronic information industry. It did not begin to manufacture integrated circuits until 1977, 16 years after the US and 11 years after Japan, but it now mass-produces very-large-scale integrated circuits (VLSI) such as 64 K, 256 K, and 1 M semiconductor memory for export to the US, and it plans to begin manufacturing 4 M memory this year. South Korea skipped the large-scale integrated circuit (LSI) phase and entered the VLSI phase directly, taking only 12 years to achieve what took the Americans 28 years and the Japanese 23 years.

3. Digitization and intelligentization techniques are new mega-trends in technological development, and technology combining audio, optical and electronic features is in the ascendancy. Microelectronic integrated circuit technology and digitization technology are complementary, and they are the two wheels that drive modern electronic technology. Electronic technology is now developing from analog to digital in all areas, and all kinds of electronic equipment such as communications equipment, radar and navigation instruments (not to mention computers) have all become digitized or employ digital technology. Digital technology is already being put to use in consumer electronics. For example, digital television sets, cassette recorders and radios are already on the market. The entire communications system is moving toward an integrated services digital network (ISDN), which incorporates telephone, telex, fax, data and television. On the basis of digitization, computer technology is being integrated into various types of electronic equipment, enabling it to develop in the direction of intelligentization and automation. The new field of artificial intelligence is engendering ever-greater breakthroughs and a new generation of electronic technology. Optical fiber is rapidly replacing conductor cable as the major means of communication. As of 1986 the US had installed more than 98,000 kilometers of long-distance fiber-optic communications lines. Britain will replace half of its telecommunications facilities with fiber-optics by 1990. The Federal Republic of Germany plans to install 800,000 km of fiber-optic communications lines within the next 5 years. High fidelity digital optical discs are in industrialized production and rapidly gaining in popularity.

4. Software has become an industry of considerable size, with an average growth of over 20% per year. US software sales reached $20.9 billion

in 1988, accounting for 36.4% of the $57.436 billion of total computer sales in the US that year, and software is expected to account for 41.3% of US computer sales this year. Predictions are that software sales will gradually surpass computer hardware sales by the mid-1990s. More and more independent software factories and stores have appeared in recent years. The software industry is a knowledge industry and therefore produces knowledge. People engaged in software production need not only a higher education and a thorough knowledge of software technology, but also specialized knowledge of the subject of the application. Almost 2 million people work in the US software industry, and even more are needed. The software industry requires low investment, and China is relatively rich in intellectual resources, so we should consider focusing more on developing the software industry as an important area for our entry into the international market.

5. The emphasis of the electronic information industry in developed countries is shifting toward the production of high-tech products, of which big-ticket electronic products account for an ever-increasing proportion. In 1988, the structure of the US electronic information industry was: big-ticket electronic products 68%, consumer products 11.5%, and components 20.5%, with the computer industry accounting for 55.5% of big-ticket electronic products. The Japanese electronic information industry began with the development of electronic consumer products, but during the 1980s the percentage of big-ticket electronic products increased rapidly, far surpassing consumer electronics, therefore causing a major shift in the emphasis and structure of the Japanese electronic information industry toward high-tech products. In 1988, the industry's structure consisted of: big-ticket electronic products 62%, consumer products 14% and components 24%, with the computer industry accounting for 73.9% of big-ticket electronic products. This shift of emphasis toward the production of high-tech products shows that the use of electronic information technology has already extensively permeated all areas of the national economy and military applications, and that the extent of the economy's informationization is growing daily. In 1988, purchases of electronic equipment by the US government reached $12.6 billion and US military purchases amounted to $47.9 billion. Thus, changes in the industrial structure have triggered

changes in the technological structure. In the US electronic information industry, the percentage of medium- and low-tech products has decreased. Since the value of the Japanese yen rose, Japan has further restructured its industry by reducing its manufacturing of medium- and low-tech products or by shifting such manufacturing to foreign countries. This creates an excellent opportunity for China to export medium- and low-tech electronic products.

6. The development trend in the electronic information industry is toward both competition and coalition between enterprises. High-tech development demands huge capital investment, a burden that is difficult for a single company to bear alone. Consequently, many companies have adopted methods of association such as alliances, joint ventures and mergers to accomplish projects or goals. For example, Texas Instruments, Motorola, NSC, Intel, AMD, IBM, DEC, and Hewlett Packard in the US formed the Sematech consortium to develop advanced semiconductor manufacturing technology. The group's first objective is to develop 0.35-μm microelectronic technology before 1992, and create a foundation for maintaining its world leadership in semiconductor technology by 1995. Philips of the Netherlands and Siemens of the Federal Republic of Germany jointly formed the Megabit Memory Project to develop and manufacture 1 M and 4 M memory. CGE of France and the telecommunications division of ITT in the US have jointly formed Alcatel, which is now the world's second largest telecommunications equipment manufacturing corporation after AT&T. France's Bull, America's Honeywell and Japan's NEC have united to form Honeywell Bull, in order to jointly develop and produce distributive-processing computers. These types of consortia and mergers improve investment and competitive capability, and they have created a new paradigm in industrial development that will further accelerate the development of electronic information technology. China's electronic information industry can learn a lot from their successful experience, and gradually progress from the present state of dispersed, redundant and small-scale production in the direction of cooperation, intensive operations and economies of scale.

7. The development of the electronic information industry has given birth to and fostered information services. The US information processing services industry comprised 2150 companies in 1987, with an output value of $22 billion and over 270,000 workers. In the same year, the

output value of information processing services in Japan, the Federal Republic of Germany, Britain and France reached a total of more than $6.8 billion. The global output value of computer services (program and design services, choice of computer systems, computer/communications interfaces, system and network management, and computer system education and training) reached $21.8 billion, and the global output value of database services was $2.7 billion. Furthermore, it is predicted that the information services industry will develop on an even larger scale; this development is an important indicator of the informationization of an economy. Information has become a modern economic resource to which we need to give our full attention.

II. STRATEGY ISSUES CONCERNING THE DEVELOPMENT OF CHINA'S ELECTRONIC INFORMATION INDUSTRY

New characteristics in the development of the world's electronic information industry not only give us insights, but also offer us excellent opportunities. The current international situation opens up the possibility for us to build an environment for peaceful development in which our country can deepen reform and open wider to the outside world. This creates favorable conditions for developing China's electronic information industry; however, many difficulties and problems still exist, so we should thoroughly consider the development strategy we adopt.

A. Problems confronting China's electronic information industry

Investment in China's electronic information industry is insufficient, and funding for both production and scientific research falls short of what is required for a high-tech industry. Spending on capital construction and scientific research each accounts for only about 1% of the annual gross output value of the electronic information industry, which is far lower than in foreign countries and is considered to be below the threshold for high-tech industries (some developed countries believe that only an industry whose research investment equals about 10% of its total sales volume can be said to be high-tech). As a result of inadequate funding, China's high-tech development faces considerable challenges and the gap between us and the world's advanced level continues to expand.

China's electronic information industry is essentially a domestically oriented industry. Its annual export volume accounts for only about 10% of its annual gross output value. The amount of foreign exchange the industry earns through exports does not even equal the amount the government supplies for production, so it still requires government foreign-exchange support and its ability to compete internationally is very weak.

Our country's electronic information industry primarily produces electronic consumer products and is still in the initial stage of development. The four modernizations rely mainly on imports for high-tech capital goods, and total imports of electronic equipment for the whole country amounted to more than $3.5 billion in 1987.

The rapid growth of China's electronic information industry in recent years has been achieved on the basis of technology imports worth over $1.6 billion during the Sixth Five-Year Plan period. However, due to the rapid development of electronic technology, this policy of relying on imports for development is untenable in the long term. To maintain a fast pace of development, we must adhere to the principles of importation, assimilation, development and innovation, use imports to promote development and innovation, and accelerate the process of becoming self-reliant.

Due to problems in the economic system, China's electronic information industry suffers greatly from decentralization and redundancy, and has not yet moved in the direction of intensive operations. Consequently, many products are manufactured under conditions below the threshold for economies of scale.

The phenomena of inequity in social distribution and shortsightedness in recent years have seriously hindered our technological progress and development as well as affected the stability of our scientific workforce.

B. Strategic choices confronting China

We face the following choices in development strategy issues.

1. Import substitution vs. export orientation

Import substitution and export orientation are two different strategies. They involve different trade policies, investment orientations, degrees of openness, and tariff and exchange rate policies. From an international point of view, relying solely on import substitution usually results in foreign exchange difficulties that necessitate a shift to export orientation. The electronic information industries of Brazil and India originally overemphasized import substitution, neither with much success, and the two countries now focus more on export orientation. Asia's four little dragons quickly shifted to export orientation after a period of import substitution, with very good results. With regard to China's situation, we should adopt a mixed strategy of combining an appropriate amount of import substitution with the active promotion of export orientation. We need to domestically produce medium- and low-tech goods such as electronic consumer products and work hard to promote their export. However, we should also permit the import the high-tech products we currently do not have the technology to produce but which are needed to prevent the national economy from being encumbered. By adopting an effective export orientation strategy, we can overcome the severe problem of a shortage of foreign exchange and create favorable conditions for increasing technology imports.

2. Orienting toward a domestic vs. an international market

Under the conditions of opening up, we should unite our domestic and international markets. Successfully entering the international market will enable us to control the domestic market better, and controlling and developing the domestic market well will similarly provide strong support for our entry into the international market. Opening up the international market to promote domestic development has already become the principal paradox in our country's electronic information industry today. If China does not accelerate its movement into the international market, the development and technological progress of its electronic industry will inevitably decelerate, and the gap between China's technological level and the advanced international level will widen. We cannot afford to assume the domestic market is so large that we need only continue to adopt a domestically oriented strategy. In fact, in some areas, our domestic market is not very big; for example in China's computer market, sales volume is only a little more than 4 billion yuan. Only by drawing on the international market can we get the boost to make large-scale production possible.

3. High technology vs. medium and low technology

At present, our country's electronic information industry has primarily a medium- and low-tech structure. We should focus on developing high technology; however, our current financial strength and scientific and technological levels limit us to making progress in only a few areas. For a certain period of time, China should primarily develop medium and low technology and make breakthroughs in these areas that lay a foundation for high-tech development. Yet we cannot view these two orientations as being in opposition. In fact, some medium- and low-tech products also contain high technology. For example, the technologies necessary to create magnetic drums and heads for video recorders and digital recording technology all contain high technology.

4. Independent R&D vs. importing technology

Other countries will not simply sell us genuine high technology. We must rely on our own efforts, put self-reliance first and give technology imports a secondary role. To do this, we must consider the country's long-term interests; balance basic, applied and development research effectively; and strive to coordinate and connect these research areas. From an overall perspective, for a number of years to come, our R&D work will largely involve following in others' footsteps, using advanced science and technology from other countries as a reference, and integrating inventions and innovations with China's actual conditions. Other backward countries have successfully used this approach to invigorate their economies. Under the conditions of opening up, it is inconceivable for a country to establish a new industry without any imported technology. We should to try to create better conditions for cooperation and exchanges with all developed countries, on the basis of equality and mutual benefit. We also need to absorb and assimilate foreign technology and use it as a foundation to develop our own technology.

5. Intensive operations vs. dispersed and redundant operations

The problem of departmental and regional barriers in our country's electronic information industry is far from being solved, and is leading to high levels of dispersion and redundancy within the industry. There are currently more than 30 factories producing integrated circuits in China, but only one of them has attained annual output of more than 10 million chips. The production of color television sets, video cassette recorders, and program controlled switchboards is so widely dispersed that no one has reached an economy of scale. Funds are limited and widely distributed, which makes it hard to improve the situation. Therefore, we should resolutely take the path of intensive operations, and adopt economic, administrative and legal means to cure the chronic disease of dispersed and redundant operations.

6. Traditional industries vs. new industries

Although China's traditional industries already operate on a significant scale, they still need to develop further. However, primarily depending on the continued expansion of traditional industries is not the most effective way to achieve economic growth. The principal problems now are low thermal efficiency in the national economy and the over-consumption of energy and raw materials. Energy consumption per unit of GNP is three to five times that of developed countries. We should make improving efficiency and reducing energy consumption key goals in China's economic development strategy. To achieve these goals, we must rely on the support of new technology and emerging industries. Although the country continues to face many difficulties, it is still possible to give strategic priority to developing the electronic information industry by adjusting industrial policies.

C. The strategy of combining import substitution with an export orientation

We should now adopt a strategy of combining an appropriate level of import substitution with actively promoting an export orientation, and take effective measures to expand exports and actively carry out import substitution.

Based on this development strategy and given that the country cannot provide enough funds at the moment, we should try to do less, and resolve to set aside some projects in order to concentrate our efforts on several key areas, and then increase funding in these areas, create a good situation, compete on the international market and use competition to promote development.

1. Vigorously expand exports of electronic consumer products

We have already established a strong manufacturing base for electronic consumer products and related components. Developed countries are now adjusting their industrial structures, and we need to seize the opportunity this presents to significantly expand exports and achieve success in international competition. There is a vast global market for electronic consumer products. In developed countries alone the market is worth more than $60 billion. Asia's four little dragons are currently trying to take Japan's place and capture the international market. This situation provides an opportunity for us but even more of a challenge.

2. Stimulate the export of hardware and software through the export of computer systems

China's electronic information industry is still concentrated on hardware processing and manufacturing, and many people are not fully aware that systems, software, and related services are important aspects of the industry. In the current global electronics market, hardware prices are constantly decreasing, while systems and software prices are increasing. This is because systems design and software production require high-tech staff. In the area of big-ticket electronic products, it is difficult to enter the international market by selling only hardware and prospects for succeeding this way are slim. China has a strong science and technology workforce that far outnumbers and is far more qualified and experienced in systems engineering than some other countries; this gives us a great advantage. In exporting big-ticket electronic products, we need to develop several standard systems and contract special systems engineering projects, and this will stimulate the export of equipment, software and related services. In exporting systems, we should produce hardware we are able to make, and buy the rest. By making use of international resources, we can put together whole systems for export and obtain more value added. To this end, we need to strengthen our systems engineering contract capability and applied software development capability, as well as maintenance and repair services and staff-training capability. This will enable China's electronic information industry to gradually move from hardware processing and manufacturing to become a multifaceted industry.

3. Strive to expand the export of original equipment manufacturing (OEM) products

OEM is a good way to enter the international market. It is very difficult to enter the market at first, but we could start by producing auxiliary products, parts, client systems and whole equipment for foreign companies for export, putting their trademarks on them, and thus entering their international sales channels. In this way we can improve our own capabilities with others' help and gradually bring China's product quality up to international standards. Some parts in high-tech products are not high-tech. There are many types of such products and they are needed in large quantities, and we could explore the possibility of manufacturing them for foreign companies. The trade volume in this field is huge, but we have, in the past, neglected to explore such possibilities.

4. Expand exports of discrete components

Companies in developed countries are no longer willing to produce discrete components because profits for them are decreasing, and many of them are currently attempting to transfer their production abroad. China should take advantage of this situation and seize the market.

China's electronic information industry has already established a relatively good foundation, and in particular, the military scientific research system has a very strong workforce of electronic information scientists and engineers who can play a bigger role by finding civilian applications for their military technology. We should make full use of our own advantages, and actively promote import substitution while vigorously expanding exports. We should give prominence to domestic production in a planned and progressive manner, and adopt measures to gradually upgrade our products until they have the same quality and price as the best imported ones, and ensure their timely delivery.

Sources

1. IEEE Journal of Quantum Electronics January 1989.
2. IEEE Spectrum January 1989.
3. US industrial outlook. US Department of Commerce International Trade Administration; 1987.
4. Porat MU. The information economy. Washington, DC: US Department of Commerce; 1977.
5. Huang J, Huang JQ. Progress and disparity: achievements in the ten years of our country's reform and opening up, together with an international comparison. Chin. ed. Research Office of the State Council; 1988.
6. A tentative analysis of china's information economy. Chin. ed. Center for Technological Development Research of the State Science and Technology Commission and the China Academy of Electronics and Information Technology; 1986.
7. Informationization: A historic mission. Chin. ed. Beijing: Publishing House of Electronics Industry; 1987.
8. Forester T. The microelectronics revolution. The MIT Press; 1984.

9. Forester T. The information technology revolution. The MIT Press; 1985.
10. Mackintosh I. Sunrise Europe: the dynamics of information technology. Basil Blackwell; 1986.
11. Ohmae K. Triad power: the coming shape of global competition. Collier Macmillan Publishers; 1985.

Computerize Financial Management*

June 1, 1993

The first thing that needs to be done to create a satellite financial communications network is to further unify our understanding, because at present people do not sufficiently realize the importance and urgency of this project. I believe this is due to our being in the midst of a transition from an old to a new economic system. During this transition period, it is not surprising if we fall behind in some areas, problems arise or our management is somewhat chaotic. This is because old ways of doing things are gradually losing their effectiveness and new mechanisms are not fully in place. When problems arise, we need to promptly learn from these experiences and remember that the fundamental solution lies in picking up the pace of reform and steadfastly proceeding down the path of instituting a socialist market economy. We must do so resolutely and not waver when we encounter difficulties. There is no turning back. We need to assemble the necessary human, material and financial resources to accomplish large undertakings of broad economic significance. This is something we cannot do without at any time, but it is of particular importance now. Through deepening reform we can deal with this matter in a timely and effective manner. Computerization of finance is one of the important matters urgently needing attention.

Developed capitalist countries like the US, Japan, Germany, and others have already been using financial communications networks for a considerable time, and their use is compulsory. In these countries, the majority of consumers use bank credit cards, and it is difficult to get by without one. They can be used to pay for purchases wherever you shop. Your salary is not paid in cash because it is paid into your credit card account. If you need cash, you can get it from an ATM using your credit card. In short, in developed capitalist countries, people rely on credit cards and financial communications networks for almost everything including clothing, food,

---

*Excerpt from remarks made when inspecting the China National Clearing Center at the People's Bank of China.

shelter and transportation. I think that if all of us from top to bottom realize the necessity, importance, and urgency of creating a satellite financial communications network, it should not be hard to find the funds to pay for it. There is no better way to spend the money we have than this, and even if we had less to spend, we should still spend it on this. Leading comrades in the Party Central Committee, the State Council, the banking sector, and all localities and departments need to achieve consensus on this. If everyone from top to bottom acts in concert, jointly supports the effort and works hard, it will not be too difficult to build this network, and progress can accelerate. I believe we are able to accomplish this, given the strength of our electronics, communications and national defense industries nationwide.

I believe that after we genuinely institute computerized banking, its functions will become apparent and it will begin to play a significant role.

First, transactions involving large sums of money are monitored and controlled by the central bank, and if a situation were to arise, the central bank would know about it immediately. Therefore, this way of doing things effectively monitors people engaged in dishonest practices and pursuit of their department's narrow interests. What should be centralized and unified must be centralized and unified. Every locality, department, and sector must accept unified central leadership and the macro guidance and control of the state. Financial activities must be guaranteed by disciplinary rules and the law; in fact, all economic activities must be so guaranteed. Of course, disciplinary rules and the law need to reflect and embody the requirements of the objective laws of economics and the market. Without a rigorous system of discipline and laws, economic and social development cannot proceed in an orderly and smooth manner.

All organizations, especially large ones, must conduct all their financial transactions through the financial communications network. They may not conduct transactions outside the network. People engaged in dishonest practices or pursuit of their department's narrow interests and those who have unauthorized departmental coffers naturally do not want others to know their secrets. This is perhaps the greatest obstacle we face in instituting computerized banking. However, these obstacles must be eliminated. We cannot tolerate misconduct.

Next, implementing computerized banking and limiting the circulation of cash will help to prevent and decrease corruption, which arises or increases when oversight of cash transactions is weak. Implementing computerized banking will greatly decrease pressure on the cash supply. None of the developed countries in the world have as much cash in circulation as we do. They put a limit on how much cash a person can withdraw from the bank at one time, and that limit is relatively low. Anyone who wants to withdraw more must inform the bank beforehand. This kind of oversight is very effective. The existence of corruption in our social activities is a serious problem, and we cannot treat it lightly or be indifferent to it. If we do not have a financial communications network and our oversight of cash transactions is weak, people can withdraw large quantities of money from the bank. People engaged in dishonest practices can then pass out cash-filled envelopes and attempt to obtain whatever they want through bribery. Therefore, the absence of a financial communications network creates conditions ripe for improprieties and corruption. The corrupt will not welcome this network. In order to deter and crack down on corruption, we must promptly build this kind of network, the faster the better. If this large project is completed effectively, tax evasion will also be relatively easy to deal with. You already monitor and control large accounts. If you can also monitor and control small accounts and strictly control the circulation of cash, this will play an important role in curbing and eliminating corruption. Of course, setting up a financial communications network must include technology to protect the privacy of account holders and transactions. This is something that is required by banking law and regulations.

The better our banking supervision is, the better our supervision over other economic activities will be. Supervision of different areas cannot be cut off from each other and carried out in isolation. No one can be allowed to set up a small fiefdom and run it in disregard of what is going on outside. We should implement modern matrix management with each matrix consisting of many departments and involving a high degree of interconnectivity. Why do we always end up with redundant construction in our production and development, repeatedly making every project, large or small, all inclusive, which seriously affects economic performance? In fact, this is closely related to the way of thinking and doing things in which departments and localities cut themselves off from each other and work in isolation, each creating its own system and going its own way. They only consider their own interests and never or rarely consider others' interests or the overall situation. This does not correspond with the requirements of modern scientific management and is not conducive to deepening reform and developing a socialist market economy. I hope, through reform, we can genuinely make revolutionary changes in our macromanagement; we simply cannot keep doing things the same old way. Regardless, we need to resolve to build a satellite financial communications network. You could say that this will be a revolutionary change we bring to financial management. Once we make up our minds, we will be able to overcome all difficulties and succeed. We need to fully mobilize and organize scientists and engineers to complete this project as fast as possible. Building this network is not just an issue concerning management or technology; more importantly, it benefits the stability and unity of our country and society and the sound, smooth development of the whole national economy. In sum, we have great hopes that banks will strengthen their oversight of cash transactions.

A single sector cannot implement computerized matrix management alone. To do so, we must make full use of the resources of all electronics and telecommunications sectors and get them working together. Because this kind of management involves a huge network, it requires large numbers of design, research and technical personnel, all of whom must work closely together. For a long time to come, the Ministry of Electronics Industry and the Ministry of Posts and Telecommunications will need to view the computerization of finance as an important and pressing task and do everything they can to organize their forces to promptly complete it. All departments and sectors must actively support and contribute to this effort. In short, we must make up our minds, work together, keep at it, and never give up in order to complete this great project.

Seizing Information Superiority Will Become a Focus in Warfare*

December 14, 1996

New and high technologies are currently developing very rapidly around the world. For example, IT based on microelectronic, computer, artificial intelligence, and communications technologies; areas of biotechnology such as genetic engineering; new materials technology such as composite and high-temperature materials; new energy technology; and space technology are all developing rapidly. Microelectronic technology, for example, in the short span of 20 plus years, has progressed from large-scale to very-large-scale, and then to ultra-large-scale integration and has now reached the stage of giga-scale integration. That means that hundreds of millions of components can be integrated on a silicon chip the size of a postage stamp (350 square millimeters). The fifth generation of computer systems has already been developed. Last month, Japan exhibited a computer in the US that can perform 600 billion calculations per second. It is presently the world's fastest computer.

The wide application of new and high technologies is profoundly changing the world, not only socially and economically, but also militarily, and is ushering in revolutionary changes in the military sphere. Weapons and equipment are becoming more computerized, intelligent, and integrated and are being combined into organic systems. This greatly enhances their long-range attack capability, gives them unprecedented attack accuracy, and exponentially increases their ability to inflict casualties. Forms and tactics of war have adopted new characteristics, and operations deep inside enemy territory and nonlinear operations may become the norm in high-tech warfare. We used to stress integrating land, sea, and air forces, but now we must integrate land, sea, air, and space forces. In particular, seizing information superiority or even information dominance will become a focus in warfare. Major changes and reforms are also

---

*Excerpt from a speech at an enlarged meeting of the Central Military Commission.

occurring in military organizations. Combat units are becoming highly integrated and tending to become smaller, lighter, and more versatile. The number of vertical levels in the command system has been reduced so that it can function more flexibly and efficiently. In response to this development trend, the major countries of the world are all accelerating efforts to modernize their armed forces, and entering a new phase of competition based on high-tech development. In light of this situation, it seems likely that some major countries and regions of the world may make new breakthroughs in the quality of their armed forces sometime around 2010.

The trend toward intense military development occurring in the world poses a tough challenge for us to improve our army's quality and military preparedness. After several years of deliberation following the Gulf War, we formulated a military strategy for the new period in early 1993, which takes winning local wars fought under modern technological conditions, especially high-tech conditions, as its foundation. Guided by this military strategy, we decided last year to shift the focus of army building from increasing quantity and scale to enhancing quality and efficiency, and from being manpower intensive to being science and technology intensive. All of this is absolutely correct.

Create a Set of Effective Mechanisms to Develop New and High Technologies and Industries That Use Them*

February 10, 1999

At present, science and technology are constantly changing and developing rapidly. When I was in college, advanced fields such as genetic engineering still did not exist. I studied electrical engineering, and there were only vacuum tubes then. Transistors were not invented until 1948, integrated circuits were invented in 1958, and the invention of large-scale and very-large-scale integrated circuits came later. When I was Minister of Electronics Industry, we were still developing 64K integrated circuits, although foreign countries had already developed 256K circuits; this was a huge gap. Thereafter, worldwide development of integrated circuits became more rapid, and a new generation emerged almost every 3 years. Science and technology have achieved astonishing progress over the 20th century, and the next century will bring even greater breakthroughs in the areas of physical science, information science, bioengineering, materials science, cosmology, and environmental science. We cannot close the gap in scientific and technological development between us and the rest of the world all at once. However, we will gradually catch up. We must have this ambition.

In developing new and high technologies and the industries using them, we need to not only do good R&D work, but also take care to build a complete set of effective mechanisms. If we want to develop a technology or product, we must consider the market for it. Without the impetus of market demand, it is very difficult to develop. Consider the development of integrated circuits. One major problem is that a few foreign companies have a huge share of our electronic products market. Integrated circuits in these electronic products find their way to China installed in

---

*Excerpt from a speech during an inspection tour in Beijing.

equipment we import. We do not have a market for the integrated circuits we produce, so there is no way to mass produce them.

I participated in the work of making China's first generator, which had a capacity of 6000 kW. We are now capable of manufacturing generators as large as 600,000 kW. The capacity of generators our country can produce is not small, and their technological level is also not low. However, in some places we still use foreign generators. Why? Because foreign companies sell them on credit, supplying the equipment to the buyer immediately and bearing the investment burden themselves. Hence, this involves the issue of capital operations. Large world famous corporations, such as General Motors of the United States and Siemens of Germany, not only engage in manufacturing but also put great effort into their stock market activities. In recent years, a stock market specially dedicated to high technology has appeared in America. It is different from ordinary stock markets in that it operates mainly through computer networks. High-tech support is necessary for economic development. An important reason for America's relatively good economic performance in recent years is that the country has achieved remarkable results in making use of new and high technologies to improve its industrial structure and product mix. America has attracted large numbers of talented people to its shores from all over the world. Chinese–American scientists engage in high-tech R&D in a number of large American companies. These phenomena raise important questions that deserve careful consideration and require thorough investigation.

Accelerate the Development of Our Country's Information and Network Technologies*

March 3, 2000

Rapid progress in science and technology around the world has led to great changes in our economic and social life. The present rapid development of information networks should command the close attention of cadres at all levels and the whole of society. Information networks developed considerably in the 1990s and forecasts predict that by the end of 2000, the Internet will connect more than a million networks of all kinds, 100 million host computers, and about 500 million users. The Internet is rapidly developing into an integrated, high-performance, intelligent system and is gradually becoming a worldwide network for exploiting and using information resources that permeates every aspect of social activities.

Rapid development of information networks has deeply impacted the spheres of politics, economics, military affairs, science and technology, as well as culture and society, and it has accelerated connections between national economies and the international economy and enabled them to influence each other more directly. These developments are prominently manifested in the vigorous growth of online media and education as well as e-commerce such as online banking, transactions, and marketing. A Credit Suisse research report states that in 1999, worldwide electronic trade reached $98 billion, and that e-commerce will double every year for the foreseeable future and surpass $1.2 trillion by 2003. All large companies throughout the world are focusing on e-commerce. According to the report, American companies invested more than $150 billion in developing e-commerce in 1999. The development of information networks has directly brought about revolutionary changes in military affairs and is dramatically raising the ability of armies to wage informationized and

---

*Excerpt from a speech at a meeting of the responsible Party members attending the Third Session of the Ninth NPC and the Third Session of the Ninth National Committee of the Chinese People's Political Consultative Conference (CPPCC).

network warfare, and the development of digitized troops has already become a focus of army building in developed countries. Information networks provide a more prompt channel for disseminating all kinds of ideas and cultures. Networks are an important means of spreading culture and a vehicle for carrying large quantities of information to all corners of society. Many developed countries, such as the US, the UK, Germany, and Japan, are investing large sums and drawing up plans to develop information networks.

We need to seize the opportunities presented by the development of information networks, accelerate the development of our country's information and network technologies, and actively apply them in economics, society, science and technology, national defense, education, culture, and law. At the same time, we also need to pay close attention to the serious challenges that building information networks entails. We can use these networks to assist reform and opening up and disseminate our ideas and culture. At present, there is every imaginable kind of information on the Internet, with good content intermingled with bad, which includes large amounts of reactionary, superstitious, and pornographic material. It can be said that information networks have already become a new arena of thought and culture and a new ideological and political battleground. Therefore, leading cadres in all localities and departments must intensify their study of the Internet and attach great importance to the online battle. Our Party building work and our ideological, political, organizational, publicity, and mass work all need to adapt to the characteristics of information networks; otherwise, it will be difficult to do them well. In sum, the basic policy concerning information networks is to actively develop them, strengthen supervision over them, seek their advantages while avoiding their disadvantages, use them for our own purposes, and strive for a position where we always hold the initiative in the global development of information networks.

Speech at the Opening Ceremony of the 16th World Computer Congress

August 21, 2000

Mr. Chairman, delegates, ladies, and gentlemen:

Today is the grand opening of the 16th World Computer Congress, sponsored by the International Federation for Information Processing. This cross-century distinguished gathering of personages in the global information field is where experts and entrepreneurs from many countries have convened to exchange academic ideas, exhibit technological achievements, and discuss development trends, which will exert a significant impact on the development of IT worldwide. On behalf of the Chinese government, I warmly salute and cordially welcome all of you to this congress.

The human race attained glittering scientific and technological achievements in the 20th century. From the creation of quantum theory and the theory of relativity, the discovery of the double-helix structure of DNA, and the birth of information science, to the assembly of a working draft of the human genome sequence, world science and technology have undergone a profound revolution and the productive forces have increased tremendously. One may anticipate that further scientific and technological developments in the 21st century—especially constant breakthroughs in IT and life sciences—will exert an ever more profound influence on political, economic, and cultural activities and production worldwide. Experts believe that in the early decades of this century, digitization will be the new force driving the development of IT, integrated circuits will develop to a new stage of integrated systems, the transmission capacity of dense wavelength division multiplexing systems will greatly increase, and the technology and capability of personal mobile telecommunications and the Internet will increase manifold. Therefore, we ought to have a profound understanding of the great power of IT and actively promote its development.

The earth's material resources are limited. For mankind to achieve sustained development, we must find new ways to exploit and utilize

257

resources. The development of IT enables the human race to uncover enormous information resources latent in the motion of matter and make greater use of them. Information resources have already achieved an importance at par with material resources, and that importance is increasing by the day. The fact that information can be transmitted rapidly and widely is turning the world into a borderless information space. Information crosses rivers and mountains effortlessly and spreads throughout the whole world. Developments in distance learning, telemedicine, e-commerce, email, and virtual reality have led to profound changes in the way we work, study, and live. Constant progress in knowledge innovation and technological innovation, and the integration of material with knowledge production of hardware with software manufacturing and of the traditional economy with information network technology will provide a powerful stimulus for economic and social development in the 21st century.

The present imbalance in the level of information networking between various countries deserves our attention. Developed countries have information technology superiority and ever-increasing information resources, making them information rich; whereas, information technology in developing countries lags far behind. Not only is their level of economic and social development low, but so is their degree of informationization. In today's world, the disparity between different countries' degrees of informationization is increasing, not shrinking. If this kind of situation does not change, the gap between north and south will become greater, and it will be difficult for the world economy to develop soundly. Therefore, developed countries have a duty to help developing countries accelerate their informationization by providing assistance in the areas of technology, capital, and human resources.

The rapid development of the Internet plays an important role in promoting world economic growth and strengthening contacts between people of different countries. However, we must also consider a number of disquieting Internet issues: there is a flood of antiscience, pseudoscience, and unhealthy and even outright harmful misinformation. Some people deliberately spread information contrary to facts in order to mislead others into a false understanding of the actual situation. People's privacy and corporate secrets are easily compromised, and hacker attacks can disrupt telecommunications and paralyze networks. To promote sound development of the Internet, we advocate adopting an international Internet treaty to bring countries together to work to strengthen supervision of information security in order for us to be able to fully enjoy the positive aspects of the Internet.

The Chinese government places a premium on developing the information industry and is now energetically informationizing the national economy and society. However, China is still a developing country and it faces the enormous task of informationization at a time when it has not yet completed the task of industrialization. Our strategy is, in the course of completing industrialization, to emphasize the use of IT to raise our level of industrialization; and in the course of carrying out informationization, to emphasize the application of IT to transform traditional industries, use informationization to drive industrialization, make the most of the advantages of a late start, and strive to skip stages in developing technology.

Faced with a new century and a new millennium, this congress should attempt to accurately forecast the role information technologies such as computers, communications, and television will play in human development in the new century so that IT can bring ever-greater prosperity to the human race.

Finally, I wish to congratulate this congress in advance on a resounding success! I wish all of you a pleasant stay in Beijing.

Thank you.

Strive to Accomplish the Two Historic Tasks of Mechanizing and Informationizing Our Army*

December 11, 2000

Since the beginning of the last century, the basic form of war has been mechanized warfare using the machine industry as a technological foundation. The two world wars are classic examples. The methods and means armies use to fight wars are currently taking on a brand new aspect, as the form of war shifts from mechanization to informationization, and weapons and equipment become more intelligent. Attack weapons now have accurate guidance systems and the ability to strike from a long distance and covertly penetrate defenses. All major battle platforms have information sensing, target detection, and guidance capabilities, as well as information attack and defense capabilities. Command and control are becoming more automated; weapons systems, battle platforms, and logistics support equipment from each branch of the military on the battlefield are combined into an organic whole through the use of the C^4ISR^1 system, and a multifaceted battlefield can be created whose dimensions span land, sea, air, space, and electromagnetic radiation. Electronic warfare, with the application of electronic equipment and computer networks as its primary component, has begun to play a major role in war. In addition to customary issues of sovereignty over territorial waters and airspace, there is now also the issue of sovereignty over information. In a high-tech war, an army cannot exercise sovereignty over its territorial waters and airspace without sovereignty over its information. Local high-tech wars since the Gulf War have shown that IT plays an extremely important role in modern warfare. Indeed, the main characteristic of high-tech war is informationization. Therefore, the new revolution in military affairs is in essence a

---

*Excerpt from a speech at an enlarged meeting of the Central Military Commission.

[1]C^4ISR stands for command, control, communications, computers, intelligence, surveillance, and reconnaissance.

revolution of informationization. Moreover, informationization is becoming a multiplier of an army's combat capability, and it is precisely because of this that developed countries are setting informationization as the main objective of army modernization in the new century. One can foresee that informatio-nized warfare will be the main form of war in the 21st century.

Our army is now going through a unique transition phase in which it has not yet completed mechanization, yet at the same time, it needs to strive toward informationization. Beginning in the early days of New China, Comrade Mao Zedong and other proletarian revolutionaries of the older generation began to mechanize the military, focusing on building up the navy, the air force, the Second Artillery Force, and the technical branches of the army. However, the military is still in the stage of semime-chanization due to restraints deriving from the country's level of economic and technological development; thus, informationization has barely begun. Over the past decade, great strides have been made in automating army command, infrastructure development for processing military information has been basically completed, and marked improvement has been made in conditions for safeguarding military information and in the command of key army units. Overall, however, the level of automation in the command system of our army is low and the ability to fight in an informationized war is weak. We must change this situation as quickly as possible.

It should be noted that our country's IT level is rather good. In many areas of IT, such as by computers, we have achieved world-class results. The Fifth Plenary Session of the Fifteenth CPC Central Committee decided to vigor-ously informationize the country's economy and society, and this will provide favorable conditions for informationizing our army. We must take advantage of this acceleration of informationization in the national economy and society to speed up informationization in the army, while intensifying mechanization efforts. If we wait until mechanization is completed before beginning infor-mationization work, we will waste a valuable opportunity and it will be impossible to catch up with the pace of the development of Western devel-oped countries' armies. Of course, if we were to forgo work on mechaniza-tion and shift our entire focus to informationization, it would be out of line with conditions in the country and our army and we might still be unable to achieve the goals for informationization. We need to concentrate on developing electronic launch control systems for weaponry, and automated command systems, which are the nerve center of the battlefield, while also working to informationize existing weapons and equipment, use informatio-nization to drive mechanization, make the most of the advantages of a late start, and skip stages in modernizing the army.

Promote Rapid and Sound Development of Our Country's Information Networks*

July 11, 2001

In today's world, rapid development of science and technology, particularly IT and network technology, has a profound effect on global political, economic, military, scientific and technological, cultural, and social affairs. This demands our close attention. The Fifth Plenary Session of the Fifteenth CPC Central Committee decided that the country must strongly promote informationization in the national economy and society, use informationization to drive industrialization, make the most of the advantages of a late start, and skip stages of development of the productive forces. This is a strategic measure that has implications for all aspects of our country's modernization.

I once said that, concerning information networking, our basic principles are to energetically develop it, strengthen its regulation, make the most of its advantages while avoiding its disadvantages, ensure it serves our purposes, and strive to maintain the initiative in its global development. We need to seize opportunities to accelerate the development of our country's IT and computer network technology and energetically work to increase their application in the economic, social, scientific and technological, educational, cultural, national defense, and legal spheres. However, we also need to pay close attention to the severe challenges information networking brings. Leading cadres in all localities and departments must intensify their study of information networking and pay close attention to the struggle taking place online. Our Party building work, and our ideological, political, organizational, publicity, and mass work should all adapt to the characteristics of information networking. We need to energetically promote the development of infrastructure for information networks, while also actively strengthening our supervision of them. If we

---

*Speech at a workshop on the legal system hosted by the CPC Central Committee.

do both of these things well, we will be able to develop information networking both rapidly and soundly in our country.

Our country's IT and information industries have developed rapidly in recent years, particularly computer information networks. The development of information networks provides not only a fresh stimulus to and support for our country's economic growth, but also new ways and means to enrich people's cultural lives and improve the work of the Party and government agencies.

However, we must recognize that the development of information networking also presents new problems for government and social administration. For example, with the development of information networking, online harmful information concerning superstition, pornography, and violence poses a danger to the mental and physical health of people, especially our youth. Illegal and criminal activities on the Internet are becoming more pronounced, and online illegal activities such as fraud are disrupting market order. Hostile forces are using information networks to engage in ideological infiltration and spread political rumors in an attempt to undermine the overall stability and unity of the country and confuse people. In addition, there are still many unsolved problems concerning how to safeguard our country's information security. If we ignore these problems, are not vigilant and fail to do more to solve them or strengthen regulation of information networks, serious consequences will inevitably ensue. Therefore, we must conduct further research and adopt practical and effective measures. In addition to strengthening the system of online security guarantees, we must also concentrate even more on using all legal means to effectively regulate information networks and promote their rapid and sound development.

First, we need to fully recognize the importance of guaranteeing and promoting the sound development of information networks in accordance with the law. Whether security guarantees and regulations concerning information networks are effective or not affects the country's economic, political and cultural development, as well as its interests and security. In the course of energetically informationizing our national economy and society, we must give high priority to the security of information networks. On the one hand, we need to actively support and promote information networking, while on the other, we need to increase standardization and manage networks in accordance with the law to ensure and promote the sound and orderly development of IT and information networks in our country.

Second, we need to strengthen and improve information network legislation. We have already done a lot of legislative work regarding information networks and enacted a number of laws and regulations, but generally they are still inadequate to meet the needs of promoting development and improving regulation in accordance with the law. We need to further strengthen our work in this regard. We need to enact not only prohibitive and administrative laws and regulations, but also laws and regulations that promote sound development of IT and the information industry and regulations that promote self-discipline among organizations whose work involves information networks. We need to enact sound laws and regulations concerning the system of online security guarantees and establish a robust administration system that effectively prevents the online transmission of harmful information. We need to establish legal norms for the use of information networks to make government affairs more transparent and widen channels for citizens to participate in and deliberate government affairs, and form an effective mechanism for using information networks to guide and encourage the whole of society to promote outstanding Chinese culture.

Third, we need to strengthen law enforcement and judicial proceedings relating to information networks. As information networking develops, the tasks of law enforcement and the judiciary relating to the information sphere are becoming greater. We must strive to improve the system of administrative law enforcement in this regard, improve law enforcement agencies, clarify responsibilities and ensure that decision making, administration and regulation all occur in accordance with the law. We need to strengthen judicial work relating to online activities, use judicial means to protect the lawful rights and interests of citizens, ensure our country's political and economic security, and guarantee and promote the sound and orderly development of information networks.

Fourth, we need to actively participate in the formulation of international regulations on information networks. Information networks are international, and therefore need to be not only standardized by Chinese law, but also regulated through international regulations. We must actively participate in the formulation of international treaties by relevant international organizations concerning information networks. In addition, we need to strengthen international exchanges and cooperation, work with other countries to combat and prevent hackers from threatening information and online security, and combat and prevent online fraud and other transnational online criminal activities.

Fifth, we need to intensify the training of information network super-visory personnel. Qualified personnel are ultimately essential whether for the development of IT and the information industry or for supervision of information networks. Information network supervision is a new field and cannot be done well without a pool of versatile personnel who have high political standards and strong professional skills, who are knowledge-able in information networks and the law and who have sound supervisory skills. We must give the training of these personnel a strategic position and adopt a variety of measures to speed up its progress.

Accelerate Our Country's Informationization*

August 25, 2001

Since the adoption of the reform and opening up policy, our country has attained great accomplishments in informationization, and the information industry has become an important pillar industry. We need to further understand the important role informationization plays in economic and social development from the general perspective of our country's modernization.

Materials, energy, and information are the three main resources of modern social development. The rapid development of IT makes information resources more important by the day. Economic development and social progress make the importance of information resources ever more apparent. The shortage of resources is an important issue that global economic development must face. In order to maintain sustained, sound, and rapid development of our country's economy, we must give an important strategic position to developing and utilizing information resources. If we vigorously develop and utilize them, we can effectively reduce the consumption of materials and energy per unit of gross national product (GNP). I once said that if we make full use of the multiplicative effect electronic information technology exercises on the economy, we can increase the efficiency of our national economy, decrease consumption, and use our already considerable steel, coal, electricity, and oil resources to better develop our economy. We should draw up a practical information resources strategy, adopt policies and measures, and promptly implement them.

Informationization is a technological innovation of profound revolutionary significance. The use of information intelligence tools can greatly increase the productive forces and lead to new advances. We should actively promote the integration of industrialization with informationization, use informationization to drive industrialization, and raise our country's industrialization to the level where information intelligence tools

---

*Foreword to the book *Explorations and Practice in China's Informationization*.

enjoy wide use. We should also use IT to arm industry and the national economy in order to increase our international competitiveness and make a quantum leap in our development.

To carry out informationization of our country, we must get the whole of society to work in concert and promptly create a sound framework of macrocontrol and supervision that meets the needs of informationization. We need to use macrocontrol and market allocation methods to break monopolies, encourage competition, promote extensive cooperation, and strive in concert in accordance with the requirement that informationization needs shared resources, interconnectedness, intercommunicability, and unified standards. We must eliminate the retrograde view that people can isolate themselves from the world and engage in small-scale, completely independent production.

We need to strengthen the management of information and network security and make full use of the Internet's positive functions. Rapid development of the Internet is key to promoting economic and social development and strengthening contacts between peoples in different countries. However, we must realize that a number of problems concerning it deserve our full attention; for example, the existence of antiscience, pseudo-science, and unhealthy and outright harmful misinformation, and hacker attacks that can disrupt communications and paralyze networks. Information and network security affects national security. In accordance with the principles of actively developing information, strengthening supervision over it, seeking its advantages while avoiding its disadvantages, and using it for our own purposes, we need to raise the level of R&D on information and network security, establish standards for information security, improve laws and regulations concerning information security and the system of oversight and law enforcement regulating it, and create an equitable, reasonable, and orderly market environment. We also need to actively promote the enactment of an international Internet treaty and work with the international community to strengthen management of information security.

In the course of informationizing the national economy and society, we must focus on raising people's knowledge of informationization and their ability to use it. We need to teach basic knowledge about information to all primary and secondary school students and carry out training of cadres and workers in the use of information. In short, we need to use informationization to greatly raise the scientific and cultural level of the whole nation.

I wrote these comments at the invitation of Comrade Hu Qili[1] as a foreword to his book *Explorations and Practice in China's Informationization*.

---

[1]Former Minister of Electronics Industry and Vice Chairman of the Ninth National Committee of the CPPCC.

Use Informationization to Drive Industrialization and Use Industrialization to Promote Informationization*

November 8, 2002

Achieving industrialization remains an arduous historic task in the course of our country's modernization. Informationization is an inevitable choice for accelerating our country's industrialization and modernization. We need to persevere in using informationization to drive industrialization and using industrialization to promote informationization, and take a new path of industrialization that has a high scientific and technological content, good economic returns, low resource consumption, and little environmental pollution, and makes full use of our advantages in human resources.

We need to optimize and upgrade the industrial structure so that new- and high-technology industries play a leading role, basic and manufacturing industries play a supporting role, and service industries develop comprehensively. We need to give high priority to the development of the information industry and apply IT in all economic and social spheres. We need to actively develop new- and high-technology industries that can achieve breakthroughs and provide a powerful stimulus to economic growth. We need to use new, high, advanced, and appropriate technologies to transform traditional industries and invigorate the equipment manufacturing industry. We need to continue to strengthen infrastructure. We need to accelerate development of the modern services sector and increase the proportion of tertiary industry in the national economy. We need to correctly balance the development of new- and high-technology industries with traditional industries, that of capital- and technology-intensive industries with labor-intensive industries, and that of the virtual and real economies.

---

*Excerpt from "Build a Moderately Prosperous Society in All Respects and Initiate a New Phase in Building Socialism with Chinese Characteristics," the political report to the Sixteenth National Congress of the CPC.

Informationize the Army*

December 27, 2002

I. DEVELOPMENT AND STRATEGIC IMPACT OF THE NEW WORLD REVOLUTION IN MILITARY AFFAIRS

I have always closely followed the new world revolution in military affairs. When the Gulf War broke out in 1991, I suggested that we study the characteristics of modern warfare during the conflict and recommended that the Headquarters of the PLA General Staff and the PLA Academy of Military Sciences both hold research conferences. I attended these conferences and expressed my opinions. At the time, I came to the conclusion that modern warfare was becoming high-tech and that a profound change was underway in world military affairs. At the beginning of 1993, after a period of observation, we formulated a military strategic principle for the new period that takes into account changes in the international situation and the national security situation following the Cold War. The principle defined the basis for future military preparedness as the ability to win local wars fought under modern technological conditions, especially high-tech conditions. In 1996 an enlarged meeting of the Central Military Commission comprehensively analyzed the new world revolution in military affairs based on a study of the entire army and called on it to respond to the challenges of this revolution with a spirit of reform and innovation. When the Kosovo War began in 1999 I was visiting the Italian city of Milan. After returning home, I presented my views on the conflict to an enlarged meeting of the Central Military Commission, at which I stated that the use of high technology was becoming an increasingly prominent feature of modern warfare. The Central Military Commission then convened a special session in 2001 after the Afghan War, to study the new world revolution in military affairs. Generally speaking, we were quick to catch on, prompt in our decisions and effective in the measures we took

---

*Excerpt from a speech at an enlarged meeting of the Central Military Commission.

in response to this revolution. From the very beginning we addressed this new revolution and responded to it from a strategic standpoint, resulting in the present sound state of our army.

I want to reemphasize this point at this meeting because the new world revolution in military affairs is now accelerating, and it demands our further attention. Beginning with the use of such primitive weapons as wooden clubs and rocks, the history of human warfare has undergone a number of major revolutions, from warfare using cold weapons, to warfare using explosive weapons, and thence to mechanized warfare. The current revolution in military affairs is the most far-reaching and profound in human history. In the nearly 30 years since the first signs of this revolution emerged, through to its actual start and development, its course progressed from quantitative to qualitative changes. The first stirrings of the current revolution appeared in the latter part of the Vietnam War with "smart bombs" and the world's first automated command system C^3I.[1] By the end of the 1970s, strong military powers such as the United States and the Soviet Union possessed a number of precision-guided weapons and had achieved the first stage in command automation. The new world revolution in military affairs truly began to emerge with local wars such as the Falklands War between the United Kingdom and Argentina. The Gulf War marked a turning point in this revolution, and constituted an embryonic form of modern high-tech warfare. Over the last decade or so, driven in particular by the conflicts in Kosovo and Afghanistan, the new world

---

[1] C^3I stands for command, control, communications and intelligence and was the name given to automated command systems during the 1960s and 1970s. When military equipment was modernized and automated in the 1950s, the control concept was introduced for military command and the C^2 (command and control) system was established. During the 1960s and 1970s, the role of communications and intelligence systems was perfected and they gradually became indispensable elements for automated command systems. They were integrated with the C^2 system to make the C^3 and C^3I systems. Afterward, the increasing importance of computer technology and rapid improvement in the ability to grasp the battlefield situation led to a constant expansion of the meaning of automated command systems to include the use of computers, surveillance and reconnaissance, resulting in creation of the C^4ISR system. As military informationization progresses, the C^4ISR system is becoming increasingly integrated with combat systems such as weapons platforms and munitions. The C^4ISR system is not only a logistics command and control system but will also gradually add a kill function to become the C^4KISR system with kill attack combat capabilities.

revolution in military affairs has entered a new stage of qualitative changes and is likely to become a profound revolution in military affairs that will sweep across the entire globe and affect all areas of military affairs.

Surveying the course of development of this revolution, one can clearly see that it is a product of the shift of human civilization from the industrial age to the information age and a reflection of the competition among countries for overall national strength in military affairs. Its emergence and development are a historical inevitability. During the Cold War, the arms race between the United States and the Soviet Union was a struggle for world dominance and it led to the rapid development of military technology and weapons and equipment. The contest among major countries, especially between the superpowers, to gain the strategic initiative became the direct force driving the new world revolution in military affairs. Rapid advances in science and technology, particularly in the field of new and high technologies—epitomized by IT—provided the technological conditions for this revolution and the abundant economic strength of the developed countries provided the material foundation for it. After the end of the Cold War, the United States strengthened its military power in order to achieve world dominance, and recent high-tech conflicts around the world have perpetuated this revolution.

Informationization is at the heart of the new revolution in military affairs. Human warfare is changing from mechanized to informationized warfare. All facets of the industrial-age army, including weapons and equipment, organizational structure, military theory, military training and methods for ensuring logistics support are undergoing a thorough transformation to meet the demands of informationization. The mechanized army of the industrial age is becoming an informationized army. Even greater breakthroughs can be expected around 2020 in a number of new technologies such as nanotechnology, biotechnology, new materials technology, new energy technology, masking technology and directed energy technology. In addition, new and even more efficient weapons should emerge, such as laser weapons, kinetic energy weapons, high-power microwave weapons and electromagnetic shock weapons, and they will form the new material and technical foundation for the revolution in military affairs and promote a higher level of development, ultimately resulting in the formation of a new military system.

The new revolution in military affairs built on a new material and technical foundation will inevitably lead to revolutionary changes in many areas such as army building and methods of warfare. Looking at the overall picture, four trends merit our attention.

First, informationized weapons and equipment are becoming a key determinant of an army's combat ability. All the equipment of the armies of the major countries of the world, whether the equipment of ground forces, navies or air forces, and whether combat equipment or logistics support equipment, is becoming informationized. All major battle platforms possess the capability to gather and process information, network horizontally, and use information offensively and defensively. Intelligent attack weapons can track and accurately hit a target after launching. Battle command has become automated through the C^4ISR system.[2] Weapons, equipment and technical means have been developed that can be used in electronic and network warfare and other information warfare. Informationization of equipment in the US army has already reached 50% in the ground forces and 70% in the navy and air force. Automation of the United States' command system is now progressing toward the Global Information Grid,[3] allowing the C^4ISR system to develop from only providing information support to providing decision-making support and forming a seamless information connection between sensors and gunners. In addition, the United States is now exploring ways of adding kill capability to the C^4ISR system to make it the C^4KISR system. It is estimated that by about 2020, all battlefield weapons and equipment in the US army will be informationized and that other developed countries will also reach a very high level of informationization. Judging from recent high-tech local wars, informationization has become incorporated into the entire

---

[2] Cf. note 1.

[3] The Global Information Grid is an information network that covers the whole earth and divides it into a grid. In essence, it is an integrated communications and computing environment that provides users with interconnected, interoperable and intercommunicable capabilities anytime and anyplace. This concept was first articulated by the US military in 1999 in order to make all types of information systems more interconnected and intercommunicable and meet the increasing demand for communications and information processing. The main content is to connect US army units around the globe by integrating all types of military communications and information systems; establish an information grid that connects the whole globe; fully support efforts to collect, process, store, disseminate, and transmit information; provide warfighters, commanders, policy makers, and support personnel with seamless information sharing and services in order to acquire information and policy-making superiority; and support network-centric warfare.

process of waging war and has permeated all aspects of it. Seeking information superiority has become a focus of warfare and seeking information dominance has become the key to controlling airspace, the sea and other battle arenas. In future informationized warfare, information capability will play a guiding role and the side that has the edge in information and is able to use it effectively for decision-making advantage will be better able to hold the strategic and battlefield initiative.

Second, noncontact and nonlinear operations are becoming an important means of waging war. Informationized weapons and equipment can move over an enemy's defensive barrier and natural geographical screen to directly and accurately attack a deep target from medium- and long-range distances. In this kind of noncontact operation, the strategy is not to break through at one point and then penetrate into enemy territory as in the past, but to launch deep attacks from the very beginning. The boundary between the front and the rear of the battlefield is becoming more vague, and strategy, operations and tactics are beginning to fuse into a single whole. The attacking army no longer concentrates on reducing enemy manpower, but instead carries out targeted strikes against the enemy's detection and warning, command and control, and air defense systems in order to paralyze its entire combat system, and destroy its combat potential and the national will to achieve strategic objectives. Even if the defending army has a large mechanized force, if it lacks similar medium- and long-range noncontact attack and defense means, it will be unable to strike back. During the Gulf War, the million-strong Iraqi army struggled to form the Great Saddam Belt, but the multinational force took only 38 days of air warfare to completely destroy Iraq's air defense, command, and rear supply systems, followed by four days of ground war to defeat the Iraqi army. During the Kosovo War, it took NATO forces only 78 days of air warfare to rout the Federal Republic of Yugoslavia. During the Afghan War, the US army used advanced battlefield sensing technologies and capabilities to conduct super-long-range large-scale attacks and accurately hit small, scattered and hidden forces and cave targets of the Taliban and al-Qaeda, quickly devastating their defensive capabilities. The US military has clearly made comprehensive, penetrative, and accurate warfare its basic approach to war and is energetically working to develop all types of precision-guided munitions, and working particularly hard to develop low-cost munitions guided by the Global Positioning System and install them in large numbers. According to reports, during the

Gulf War only 8% of munitions used by the US army were precision guided, with the figure rising to 35% in Kosovo and reaching 60% in Afghanistan. The armies of other major countries are also working hard to develop precision-guided weapons and gradually moving toward noncontact and nonlinear methods of warfare.

Third, combat between systems is becoming the basic feature of combat on the battlefield. Using IT, combat platforms, weapons systems, reconnaissance and command and control systems, and logistics support systems, each branch of the army can be integrated into a unified combat system. Informationized warfare is no longer a battle between individual combat units; rather, it has become a battle between systems based on the integration of combat units and elements, as well as different branches of the army fighting together as a joint force. During the Kosovo War, the most advanced aircraft of the Yugoslav army had barely taken off before NATO forces began to track them using their detection system, and then shot them down after only a few minutes. This shows that without an informationized combat system, it is difficult for even the most advanced weapons and equipment in the world to function effectively. The US military gives high priority to improving combat systems. It views integration as a basic means of optimizing the structure and combat strength of the army and emphasizes a high level of integration among the various combat units and elements. The armies of other major countries are following the United States' lead and building unified combat systems that meet the requirements for integration.

Fourth, space is becoming the new strategic high ground in international military competition. Space is an increasingly important combat arena and it can have a decisive impact on the course and outcome of war. Statistics show that the United States used more than 70 satellites during the Gulf War and over 50 satellites during the wars in Kosovo and Afghanistan, providing comprehensive information support and guarantees for air, sea and ground assault systems. Space has become the new strategic high ground and the race for military superiority in space has begun. Major military powers such as the United States and Russia are working hard to develop military aeronautic and aerospace technologies and weapons systems for combat in space, strengthen their capability to fight a war in space, integrate their air and space military forces, and develop space-based offensive and defensive capabilities. According to the predictions of military experts, future noncontact warfare will most likely have aerospace systems at its core; effective space-based strategic global reconnaissance and attack systems will be established to guide the combat platforms of the ground forces, navy, and air force in executing accurate long-distance attacks; space-based weapons systems will be used to directly attack ground, sea and air targets; and anti-satellite weapons and combat spacecraft will be used to interfere with, damage and destroy the enemy's space-based systems, seize dominance of space and limit the enemy's freedom to maneuver in space. The main objective of the United States in withdrawing from the Anti-Ballistic Missile Treaty and actively developing anti-missile systems was to build a space-based offensive and defensive system. The US military has set the goal of developing an air and space force and is currently setting up an aeronautics and aerospace expeditionary force. In June 2001, Russia established an independent aerospace force, and Europe plans to set up its own satellite navigation system, Galileo, in the next 5 years to free itself from the restrictions imposed by the United States. Competition in military affairs, centering on space, among the major countries of the world is likely to change the pattern of international military struggles.

The occurrence and rapid development of the new world revolution in military affairs has had a profound and far-reaching effect on international strategy. The United States is carrying out a new revolution in military affairs in an attempt to gain absolute military superiority both offensively and defensively and further consolidate its position as a military superpower, thus exacerbating the imbalance in international strategic strength. In terms of technology and equipment, the United States military has not only created a generation gap between itself and the armies of developing countries, but also enlarged the gap between itself and the other great powers.

With respect to China, the challenges arising from the new revolution in military affairs are an important manifestation of the pressure we still face from the economic and scientific superiority of developed countries, and this military pressure is in essence the complement of political pressure. The new revolution in military affairs is likely to further widen the gap in military strength between China and the major countries of the world as well as increase the potential danger to China's military security. Efforts to improve our military preparedness and modernize the army thus face a formidable task.

We must fully understand the nature of the new revolution in military affairs, have a correct grasp of its development trends, take its strategic impact fully into account, and prepare ourselves in our thinking and our work for its challenges.

II. ACTIVELY PROMOTING A DISTINCTIVELY CHINESE REVOLUTION IN MILITARY AFFAIRS

The new world revolution in military affairs presents us with severe challenges as well as historic opportunities. Due to the decadence of feudal political rule in modern Chinese history, old China lost opportunities to revolutionize its military affairs and therefore lagged behind other countries in military development. This is an important reason why China was backward and suffered attack for so long in its modern history. Since the founding of New China, our country has made great strides in modernizing national defense and the army; however we are still only half way through industrial mechanization. The next 20 years will be a period of important strategic opportunities for China's development and the modernization of national defense and the army. If we allow these opportunities to slip through our fingers in the next one or two decades, we could possibly lose out for a long time to come. We must have a sense of urgency based on the knowledge that time waits for no one and energetically promote a distinctively Chinese revolution in military affairs, accelerate the transformation of the army from semi-mechanized to informationized, and comprehensively raise its deterrence capabilities and actual combat capabilities in order to provide a firm and effective guarantee for national security and unity, as well as for building a moderately prosperous society in all respects.

A. The military strategic principle for the new period

The military strategic principle for the new period formulated by the Central Military Commission in 1993 correctly assessed the changes in the situation in international strategy and in our country's security environment after the end of the Cold War and correctly evaluated the development trends in the new world revolution in military affairs emerging at that time. This principle plays an important guiding role for future preparedness and the modernization efforts of our army.

Profound changes have taken place in the last decade in global strategy and in the form of warfare. In particular, many serious conflicts and issues have emerged as our military preparedness has intensified, and we need to further understand and address them from a strategic standpoint.

First is the issue of the basis for military preparedness. The evolution of warfare is an extremely complex social and historical process, and our understanding of it is also a continually deepening process. Looking back, experience has shown that 10 years ago we were completely correct when we defined the form of contemporary warfare as high-tech warfare and shifted the basis for future military preparedness from responding to local wars under ordinary conditions to winning local wars fought under modern technological conditions, especially high-tech conditions. In essence, this was a shift from preparing to respond to an industrial age war to preparing for an information age war and the beginning of an advance in modernization of the army from mechanization to informationization. You could say this was a revolutionary shift. It is precisely because of this shift that a series of adjustments and changes have been made to modernize our army.

Since then, we have focused more on studying the form of contemporary warfare. In 1998 we realized the core of high-tech warfare was informationization and that human warfare was entering an informationized stage. In 1999 I clearly stated that informationized warfare was gradually replacing industrial age mechanized warfare and that it would become the basic form of warfare in the future. In 2000, I again stressed that informationized warfare would become the main form of war in the 21st century. After considering the issue for more than 5 years, we have gained a fairly mature understanding of the emerging form of informationized warfare. It is certain that future warfare will have a very high degree of informationization. We need to closely follow this issue and plan to improve military preparedness and the modernization of the army from a higher starting point.[4]

Second is the issue of the basic approach and principles for strategic guidance. The military strategic principle in the new period, which is entirely correct, is a systematic summary of the long-term experiences of

---

[4]On June 22, 2004, Jiang Zemin stated at an enlarged meeting of the Central Military Commission: In essence, high-tech warfare is informationized warfare, and it will become the basic form of war in the 21st century. We must clearly define the basis for our military preparedness as winning local wars fought under informationized conditions. All members of the army must adapt to the shift in the basis for their military preparedness, deepen the distinctively Chinese revolution in military affairs, and attain the strategic objectives of informationizing the army and winning informationized wars.

our army in combat and army building and provides scientific thinking and principles for strategic guidance. Our strategic approach is active defense; this is not only in line with the nature of China as a socialist country, but will also help us in our foreign relations work and international political struggles. By active defense we mean offensive defense, including attacking the enemy on the battlefield and launching a strategic attack. We need to adhere to these basic ideas for a long time to come. At the same time, we need to carry out more thorough research on the issues of approaches and principles for strategic guidance.

An example is the issue of how to contain a war and how to win it. How to contain a war, delay its outbreak or curb its escalation to avoid or reduce the destruction of war through strategic deterrence is an issue attracting increasing attention from the international community. Strategic deterrence has become an important component of today's global military rivalry. Nuclear powers such as the United States, Russia, the United Kingdom, and France have all made nuclear weapons the core of their strategic deterrence power. The United States introduced the new tripartite deterrence strategy this year, which includes nuclear and nonnuclear attack systems, active and passive defense systems, and national defense infrastructure. The core idea of this strategy is to make strategic deterrence tools practical. Tools available for strategic deterrence will expand along with advances in military technology. We need to stay grounded in what we have now while keeping an eye on future developments in order to gradually develop a strategic deterrence system with multiple deterrence tools working in synchronization.

Another example is the issue of joint operations and cooperation between different branches of the army. Joint operations are a major form of modern warfare. As informationization progresses, joint operations are constantly attaining higher levels of development and will eventually result in troops from all branches of the army working as an integral whole. Because our army is a composite military force made up of various branches with the land army as its mainstay, in the past combat and training primarily emphasized supporting and assisting each other. There were very few joint operations and exercises, and our joint operation theory was far from adequate. In 1993, we were still emphasizing the approach of cooperation between branches, and it now appears that we need to greatly intensify our study of joint operations between branches in order to promote improvement in our theories and actual experience.

Third is the issue of innovation in our army's military theory. Military practice gives rise to military theory, which in turn guides military practice. Only by understanding military practice from the high vantage point of military theory can we ensure that it proceeds in the right direction. During the long years of revolutionary war, the key to our army's ability to use inferior equipment to defeat an enemy with superior equipment was that, through military practice, we formed a complete set of unique theories of army building and combat, particularly, a flexible strategy, and tactics. In future informationized warfare, a great many unfamiliar factors will confront us. The new revolution in military affairs is promoting a complete transformation of the army and fundamental changes in the way wars are fought. The breadth and depth of this revolution will be unprecedented, and we must actively push ahead with innovation in military theory. Changes in the international and domestic situations, as well as the development of a socialist market economy, present many new problems in army building and military preparedness. Innovating our military theory, particularly our thinking on warfare, is a major issue facing the entire army. Guided by Mao Zedong's military thinking and Deng Xiaoping's thinking on army building in the new period, we have been constantly exploring solutions in recent years to issues such as what kind of army to build, how to build it, what kind of wars it will fight in the future, and how to fight them, and we have reached important theoretical conclusions. As our practice constantly develops, so too must our theory. In relation to these two interrelated and fundamental issues, including the issue I have often raised of researching a people's war under high-tech conditions, we need to embrace democracy and pool the wisdom of the entire army in order to intensify our research and continuously enrich and develop our military theory.

B. Development strategy for the modernization of national defense and the army

Modernization of national defense and the army is a dynamic concept. When we spoke of modernization of national defense and the army in the 1950s, we meant mechanization. However, since the 1990s, informationization has been the defining characteristic of this concept. Replacing mechanized warfare with informationized warfare is already inevitable.

A mechanized army without extensive information capabilities will lag behind in the development of warfare. We have already set forth a three-step strategic approach for modernizing national defense and the army in the new century, and made it clear that modernization includes the two historic tasks of mechanization and informationization. Now, we can further note that the objectives set out in the three-step strategic approach are to gradually informationize national defense and the army during the first 50 years of this century. We need to correctly balance mechanization and informationization, with mechanization as the foundation and informationization as the main orientation, and with informationization driving mechanization and mechanization promoting informationization, in order to accelerate informationization of the army. This is an inevitable necessity for us to be able to respond to the challenges of the new world revolution in military affairs, as well as an objective requirement for safeguarding the security, unity and continued development of the strategic interests of the country. In the first two decades of this century we must lay the foundation and the first decade will be crucial for attaining this objective. We must diligently study the successful experience of developed countries in modernizing their armies, make full use of domestic and international strategic resources, make sure we carry out the first two steps well, and strive to basically complete the mechanization of the army and make major progress in its informationization within 20 years. Thereafter, over the ensuing 30 years of development, we should be able to complete the strategic task of informationizing the army. When I speak of mechanizing the army I do not mean mechanization in the traditional sense, but mechanization closely tied to informationization. We need to formulate a long-range plan for national defense development and army building in line with this general strategic objective and develop a complementary plan for modernizing the various branches of the army.

To reach the objective of informationizing the army, we must take the path of skipping stages of development. We do not need to complete the process of army mechanization before starting informationization, as the developed countries did. Instead we need to strive to combine mechanization and informationization. We have decided to take a new path to industrialization, with informationization driving industrialization and industrialization promoting informationization. The rapid informationization of the whole of society has created excellent conditions for the army to accelerate completion of the two historic tasks of mechanization and informationization. We must mechanize and informationize from a high starting point, which we are entirely capable of doing, and balance improvements in the firepower, mobility and information capabilities of the army. This requires us to skip some stages in the process of mechanization and informationization. In addition, we must absorb the lessons developed countries learned from their mistakes in mechanizing and informationizing in order to avoid detours whenever possible. Skipping development stages means getting away from the development model of passively following the course developed countries have taken in an attempt to finally catch up with them. Therefore, in terms of development strategy, we can never be satisfied with using existing mature technologies. We must always keep our eye on development trends in science and technology as well as in informationized warfare, have a futuristic outlook, pay close attention to major emerging technologies, increase prospective research on cutting-edge military technology and new-concept weapons technology, have a high regard for technological innovation, and strive to produce strategic, foresighted and key technologies and equipment for which China holds the intellectual property rights in order to give the Chinese army the killer edge in an informationized war.

Mechanizing and informationizing the army require investment, but our financial resources do not allow us to simply spend as we wish. Therefore, we must further concentrate resources, identify priorities, and make breakthroughs in some areas to promote overall progress. Although the United States has great financial resources, it began the transformation of its military with a small number of units and proceeded one step at a time. Americans believe a reformed and streamlined army with key technological capabilities has great strategic influence. This viewpoint is worth noting. We are a developing country and no matter how much we increase military spending we will never be able to spend what the United States does. It is more important that we concentrate our resources on developing a combat capability that can have a strategic impact. For some time to come we need to give high priority to developing Resolving Emergency Mobile Combat Forces (REMCF) and mechanize and informationize this unit before the rest of the army so that it can act as the army's strategic fist.

Modernization of the army requires us to pay close attention to practical threats as well as to meet future challenges. In all military development work we need to continue to put military combat preparedness first.

Looking ahead, safeguarding national security will impose ever-heightened demands on the strategic capabilities of the army as the country's strategic interests expand. All the work of improving the country's military preparedness is consistent with the long-term objectives of improving strategic capabilities and developing an informationized army; therefore, we must make improving the country's military preparedness a part of all our efforts to reform, innovate and modernize the army.

C. Adjustment and reform of organization and staffing in the army

The development of high-tech weapons and equipment and the evolution of warfare inexorably require that we adjust and reform the traditional organization and staffing of the army. We have made conspicuous progress in this regard, but various deep-seated conflicts and problems remain fundamentally unresolved, and further adjustments and reforms are necessary. We must carefully study the general characteristics and rules for organizing and staffing a modern army, thoroughly study and fully discuss the issues, and listen to opinions from all sides in determining how to improve the army's ability to fight an informationized war, taking actual conditions in the country and army as our starting point. We need to make solid and thoughtful preparations, actively yet prudently carry out adjustment and reform of the army's organization and staffing, and improve related policies and institutions. We need to do this as promptly as possible while ensuring troop stability.

We need to continue on the distinctively Chinese path of having fewer but better troops. In response to the new revolution in military affairs, reducing numbers, improving quality and developing a streamlined and efficient standing army are the common choices of the armies of the major countries. Since the Gulf War, we have increasingly emphasized quality development against the backdrop of this revolution, and streamlined the scale of the army during both the Eighth and Ninth Five-Year Plan periods. The size of our army dropped to under 3 million during the Eighth Five-Year Plan period, and by another half a million during the Ninth Five-Year Plan period. Although our army is now down to 2.5 million personnel, it is still the largest in the world. The US military, which is spread around the globe, has only 1.38 million personnel. Russia has nearly twice our territory, but only 1.1 million military personnel, and the United States and Russia both plan to further streamline their military forces. Should we further reduce the size of our military? Can we do so? I believe that the army is still too large and can be cut further. We mainly need to cut administrative departments and noncombat units and personnel; these are areas where there is still plenty of room for downsizing. We need to make up our minds to further reduce personnel and apply the savings to modernizing the army. Naturally, this reduction needs to be appropriate. Our country has a vast territory, long sea and land borders, and a complex neighboring environment and, in particular, relatively backward weapons and equipment; therefore, the army must be maintained on a certain scale. We cannot simply compare our active troops to those of the United States and Russia. We must also consider the state of their other military capabilities and civilian personnel. When researching the size of our active service personnel, we must fully consider the structure and development of all our military capabilities, including reserves and armed police forces.

In our past efforts to streamline and reorganize the army, we concentrated more on downsizing. Although we undertook some work to adjust its structure, it was insufficient. Structural problems, such as relations being disproportionate in some important areas, have become a major hindrance to efforts to improve the army's overall combat capability. All branches of the army must optimize their internal personnel structure, formulate reasonable classifications of the various types of personnel, and scientifically determine their composition. They each need to reduce the number of ordinary troops using outdated weapons and technology and develop new high-tech troops. We must pay particular attention to maintaining enough combat troops. Another problem with the structure of the army is that the proportion of administrative departments is too high. This gives the army the appearance of a heavy head, light feet and a long tail. There are too many noncombat and administrative departments, which results in a disproportionate ratio of cadres to ordinary soldiers and an enormous total number of cadres, so we must resolve to reduce their numbers. In short, the focus of the adjustments and reforms is to improve the military structure, achieve a balanced ratio in important areas, and develop a scientific and rational internal structure. An important indicator of whether or not we succeed in these adjustment and reform efforts should be how well we optimize the structure, redress imbalances, reduce numbers and improve quality.

Instituting unified combat command is an extremely important issue that must be resolved in the adjustment and reform of the organization and staffing of the army. This is a complex issue requiring thorough and meticulous research. We need to study and learn from the successful experiences of foreign militaries, but we cannot ignore the realities of our country and army.

Problems concerning organization and staffing of our army are closely related to the fact that for a long time the three branches of the army had separate logistics support systems and the army provided all the logistics support it needed entirely on its own. Increasingly, modern warfare depends on logistics support of various kinds, and the army increasingly relies on society and the market for logistics support. On the one hand, integrating and unifying the composition, command, and combat operations of the three branches of the army requires reliable, rapid, efficient, and comprehensive logistics support. On the other hand, due to social and economic progress and the increasingly complex nature of weapons and equipment, the supply and maintenance of huge quantities of weapons and equipment and the production and supply of large quantities of goods and materials can be guaranteed only by relying on society. Therefore, the basic trend is toward combining and integrating logistics support for the three branches of the army, as well as integrating military and civilian logistics support. We must continue to implement reform of logistics systems and methods and strive to improve the effectiveness of logistics support.

D. Improving the quality of science and technology in the army

If we are to keep up with the pace of the new world revolution in military affairs, implementing a strategy for strengthening the army through science and technology and relying on advances in science and technology to accelerate modernization of the army and improve its combat capability are the most fundamental requirements. All comrades in the army, especially leading cadres at all levels, need to increase their sense of urgency concerning strengthening the army through science and technology, diligently study, develop and apply science and technology, and constantly increase scientific and technological content in every aspect of army building.

Developments in world military affairs have not changed and will never change the decisive role of people in war. While continuing to improve weapons and equipment, we must also concentrate on the strategic project of developing talent to provide strong human and knowledge support for modernizing the army and improving military preparedness.

An obvious characteristic of informationized warfare is a high concentration of knowledge and technology. We must set targets for training scientific personnel to produce large numbers of a new type of highly competent military personnel in accordance with the requirements of future wars. Military personnel of this new type must be revolutionaries with a strong foundation in modern scientific and general knowledge; without it there is no way for them to achieve high competence. This issue becomes more prominent with each new generation of weapons and equipment. Therefore, we must emphasize ideological and political education and training in the proper code of conduct during combat for officers and enlisted personnel, and work to raise the level of their modern scientific and general knowledge and modern military skills. Within one or two decades, we must strive to produce a contingent of commanding officers who have strategic insight and a solid grasp of development trends in world military affairs, and understand how to command informationized warfare and build an informationized army. At the same time, we need to develop a team of staff officers who are well versed in scientific and general knowledge, possess a full range of military skills, and have good ideas for army building and combat. We need to cultivate a contingent of scientists who work at the cutting edge of science, as well as organize and plan innovative developments in weapons and equipment and key technological projects. In addition, we need to create a corps of technical personnel who have a good command of the properties of new- and high-technology weapons and equipment, and can quickly overcome all types of obstacles and solve complex and difficult problems. Finally, we need to develop a body of noncommissioned officers who have a solid professional and technical foundation and are proficient in the use of weapons and equipment.

We must rely on the national education system to improve the overall competence of officers and enlisted personnel, particularly their scientific and general knowledge. An innovation we have made in recent years in the training of personnel is to rely more on regular institutions of higher learning to produce cadres for the army. We need to continue down this path, take even greater strides in this direction, look even farther afield and recruit more personnel from across the country who are university-educated, are both morally and ideologically qualified, and have both character and academic credentials. Other qualified personnel can help army building efforts in other ways. Our country currently has nearly 6 million engineering and technical personnel, of whom over 140,000 are experts receiving special government grants, over 5000 are young and middle-aged experts who have made outstanding contributions, and over 7000 are post-doctoral graduates. Taking advantage of these human resources will provide a strong supporting force for strengthening the army through science and technology.

Military schools are the main channel for training the new kind of military personnel. We need to study effective methods of military education in other countries as well as the experiences of local schools in implementing reforms, and deepen adjustments and reforms in the organization and staffing of military schools. Concerning the direction of development, the army can recruit professionals with general skills from local schools, while degree education and some continuing specialized education for commanding officers should also be completed at local schools, enabling us to reduce the number of military schools. In the remaining military schools, we need to strengthen centralized and unified leadership, strengthen logistics support, develop them to a considerable scale, intensify school operations and optimize the allocation of resources for military education. We need to vigorously promote innovation in education, adjust training tasks, systems and methods, reform the content of education and constantly raise its quality. We also need to carry out adjustments and reforms in training and research organizations.

Experience is the best classroom for learning science and technology and the workplace is the basic platform for raising people's scientific and technological level. We need to do more to include science and technology education in military training and carefully organize on-the-job education for officers and enlisted personnel in the basics of high technology and train them in the use of new- and high-technology weapons and equipment. We need to further improve the mechanism for transferring cadres between administrative departments, army units and military schools; gradually transfer cadres between different branches of the army and between military, political, logistics and armament positions; and strive to produce leading and command personnel with a combination of skills.

Cadres at all levels and of all types should foster the habit of lifetime study in order to keep up with the times.

We must spend what it takes to train large numbers of a new kind of highly competent military personnel. The focus of military spending should be expanded to include personnel development. It will be difficult to develop personnel without a certain level of investment. The country is developing a socialist market economy and competition for personnel is fierce in all areas of society, making it difficult for the military to attract and retain needed personnel. The army needs more professional and technical personnel of all types; however, after going to great lengths to train them, it is often difficult to retain them. We need to further strengthen our ideological and political work to increase the sense of responsibility and mission among officers and enlisted personnel to contribute to the modernization of the army. In addition, we need to constantly increase the benefits for officers and enlisted personnel as the economy develops. We need to improve policies and systems and establish a sound mechanism for attracting and retaining personnel in order to attract outstanding talent who will make outstanding contributions to army building. We must truly respect labor, knowledge, talent and innovation and create an atmosphere in which talent can develop and serve the army.

Strive to Seize the Technological Initiative in the Microelectronics, Software, and Computer Industries*

December 10, 2006

I invited you experts in the fields of microelectronics, software, and computers to participate in this symposium, and over the last two days we have exchanged views on issues concerning the development of these fields. All of your remarks have been excellent, and you have made a number of original suggestions and comments that have given me profound inspiration. Some of your suggestions have not only stirred my memory, but also stimulated me to think about these fields in a new way. I would like to take this opportunity to present some ideas and discuss them with you.

I. FOCUS ON THE POSITION AND ROLE OF THE MICROELECTRONICS INDUSTRY

I worked at the Ministry of Electronics Industry just as the world microelectronics industry was rapidly developing. I realized that microelectronics is the foundation of the electronics industry and that without microelectronics producing electronics was like cooking a meal without rice. I took the position that our country needed its own microelectronics industry; otherwise, our electronics industry could not develop. Microelectronics has progressed from integrated circuits to integrated systems, such as microchips. It is difficult to accomplish anything without the use of microelectronics. In fact, it can be said that microelectronics is ubiquitous, and that the microelectronics industry is now the foundation not only of the electronics industry, but also of the whole national economy. After I began working at the Central

---

*Excerpt from a speech at a symposium of academicians and experts in the fields of microelectronics, software and computers from the Chinese Academy of Sciences and the Chinese Academy of Engineering.

Committee in 1989, I determined to launch the 908 Project.[1] It took a great deal of determination to do so at that time. Later, the Central Committee decided to carry out the 909 Project.[2] These two projects laid the foundation for the development of our country's microelectronics industry.

At the beginning of the new century, the government introduced a series of preferential policies for developing the microelectronics industry. At the same time, due to large multinational corporations and Taiwan companies in the industry shifting their operations here, the overall scale of our country's microelectronics industry grew significantly, but the core technology remained under the control of others. The industry has now made breakthroughs in the areas of design, techniques, materials, and production equipment, and constantly breaks boundaries in the areas of systems, equipment, and components. Forecasts suggest that by 2020, leading international microelectronic technology will reach a scale of 14 nm (0.014 μm). How far will we be able to develop in that time? We need to undertake sound research, set targets and adopt policies to reach them. We need to clearly understand that core technology is not for sale and that we must rely on ourselves. We will never attain world advanced levels by importing production capabilities one generation after another. Our researchers need to redouble their efforts; otherwise, developed countries will have a stranglehold over our access to core technology.

II. CREATE OUR OWN SOFTWARE AND COMPUTER TECHNOLOGY SYSTEMS

After more than 50 years of struggle, our software and computer industries have developed considerably. However, we have not yet created complete software and computer technology systems. For the sake of our long-term development, our country should have its own complete, controllable software and computer technology systems. Without them, it will be difficult to ensure information security in a number of key areas. I will not be at peace as long as this problem goes unresolved. China is a great

---

[1]The 908 Project is the project to build integrated circuits in the 1990s during the implementation of the Eighth Five-Year Plan for National Economic and Social Development.
[2]The 909 Project is the project to build very-large-scale integrated circuits in the 1990s during the implementation of the Ninth Five-Year Plan for National Economic and Social Development.

country, and we cannot let multinational corporations monopolize our markets.

Looking back over the last century, we can see that when we built the atomic and hydrogen bombs in the 1960s and launched a satellite in the 1970s, our international standing rose greatly and we won the right to speak on the world stage. In the 21st century, software and computers provide the technological foundation for building an information society, as well as an important material foundation for modern economies. Modern warfare is informationized warfare. While the nuclear threat is undoubtedly very important, creating an information deterrent has already found its place on the agenda. In order to develop the economy and strengthen national defense, our country needs its own software and computer technology systems.

With regard to software development, when I worked at the Ministry of Electronics Industry, I noted that the software industry is knowledge intensive and its producers are not ordinary manual laborers; rather, they are intellectuals, and software engineers are the heart and foundation of software development. Software not only draws upon science and technology, but also has a cultural aspect and thus a bearing on the spread of Chinese culture. This is something we need to always keep in mind. In developing the software industry in an environment of economic globalization and informationization, we need to remain grounded on strategic economic restructuring in order to create a new kind of industrial system. More importantly, we need to promote technological innovation, train high-quality personnel and put them to use in order to achieve world-class status.

III. STRENGTHEN NATIONAL STRATEGIC GUIDANCE

Accelerating development of the microelectronics, software and computer industries, creating an independent, controllable technology system, and strengthening our core technological capabilities are matters of national strategic importance, and our national strategy needs to spur these endeavors. China's Eleventh Five-Year Plan and the National Program for Long- and Medium-Term Scientific and Technological Development have already given high priority to the development of core microelectronics, software and computer technologies. We need to adopt strong organizational measures, formulate effective support policies, and concentrate on achieving breakthroughs in core technologies in the areas of design, techniques, materials and equipment. We need to be sure to abide by the objective laws of technological development, make good use of our ability to concentrate resources to accomplish large undertakings, prevent people from going their own way and diffusing our energies, and strive to progressively seize the technological initiative within a short period of time.

INDEX

Note: Page numbers followed by "f" indicate figures "t" indicate tables "b" indicate boxes.

Printed and bound by CPI Group (UK) Ltd, Croydon, CR0 4YY

08/05/2025

01864869-0001